AF860342

Themis BAR REVIEW

Themis Bar Review
Simulated Multistate Bar Exam

THE MBE

MULTISTATE BAR EXAMINATION

ncbe

ISBN 978-1-935445-59-3
1-935445-59-6

MULTISTATE BAR EXAMINATION

Time—6 hours

This book contains a simulated Multistate Bar Exam (MBE) comprised of simulated exam questions, and presented in the same format that the MBE will appear when you take it. We recommend that you take this exam under actual exam conditions. That is, you should schedule two consecutive **uninterrupted** 3-hour blocks of time (with an hour-long break in between) in which to complete this exam.

During the actual exam, your score will be based on the number of questions you answer correctly. It is therefore to your advantage to try to answer as many questions as you can. Use your time effectively. Do not hurry, but work steadily and as quickly as you can without sacrificing your accuracy. If a question seems too difficult, go on to the next one. Give only one answer to each question; multiple answers will not be counted.

After you have completed this simulated exam, you may grade your work using the answer key provided. In order to fully understand each question and answer, we recommend that you review the explanatory answers at the back of this book in conjunction with the Simulated MBE Analysis lectures in your myThemis™ Learning Portal.

Please do not take this exam until your myTo-Do List has prompted you to do so. (Flex study students: Be sure you have completed all MBE lectures and practice sessions, as well as the first two Milestone Exams, before beginning this exam.)

SIMULATED MBE: AM

Name: ______________________ Date: ______________

Start Time: ______________ End Time: ______________

1 A B C D	26 A B C D	51 A B C D	76 A B C D
2 A B C D	27 A B C D	52 A B C D	77 A B C D
3 A B C D	28 A B C D	53 A B C D	78 A B C D
4 A B C D	29 A B C D	54 A B C D	79 A B C D
5 A B C D	30 A B C D	55 A B C D	80 A B C D
6 A B C D	31 A B C D	56 A B C D	81 A B C D
7 A B C D	32 A B C D	57 A B C D	82 A B C D
8 A B C D	33 A B C D	58 A B C D	83 A B C D
9 A B C D	34 A B C D	59 A B C D	84 A B C D
10 A B C D	35 A B C D	60 A B C D	85 A B C D
11 A B C D	36 A B C D	61 A B C D	86 A B C D
12 A B C D	37 A B C D	62 A B C D	87 A B C D
13 A B C D	38 A B C D	63 A B C D	88 A B C D
14 A B C D	39 A B C D	64 A B C D	89 A B C D
15 A B C D	40 A B C D	65 A B C D	90 A B C D
16 A B C D	41 A B C D	66 A B C D	91 A B C D
17 A B C D	42 A B C D	67 A B C D	92 A B C D
18 A B C D	43 A B C D	68 A B C D	93 A B C D
19 A B C D	44 A B C D	69 A B C D	94 A B C D
20 A B C D	45 A B C D	70 A B C D	95 A B C D
21 A B C D	46 A B C D	71 A B C D	96 A B C D
22 A B C D	47 A B C D	72 A B C D	97 A B C D
23 A B C D	48 A B C D	73 A B C D	98 A B C D
24 A B C D	49 A B C D	74 A B C D	99 A B C D
25 A B C D	50 A B C D	75 A B C D	100 A B C D

Themis BAR REVIEW

SCORE

RESCORE

SIMULATED MBE: PM

Name: ______________________________ Date: ____________________

Start Time: ________________ End Time: ________________

101 ⊏A⊐ ⊏B⊐ ⊏C⊐ ⊏D⊐	126 ⊏A⊐ ⊏B⊐ ⊏C⊐ ⊏D⊐	151 ⊏A⊐ ⊏B⊐ ⊏C⊐ ⊏D⊐	176 ⊏A⊐ ⊏B⊐ ⊏C⊐ ⊏D⊐
102 ⊏A⊐ ⊏B⊐ ⊏C⊐ ⊏D⊐	127 ⊏A⊐ ⊏B⊐ ⊏C⊐ ⊏D⊐	152 ⊏A⊐ ⊏B⊐ ⊏C⊐ ⊏D⊐	177 ⊏A⊐ ⊏B⊐ ⊏C⊐ ⊏D⊐
103 ⊏A⊐ ⊏B⊐ ⊏C⊐ ⊏D⊐	128 ⊏A⊐ ⊏B⊐ ⊏C⊐ ⊏D⊐	153 ⊏A⊐ ⊏B⊐ ⊏C⊐ ⊏D⊐	178 ⊏A⊐ ⊏B⊐ ⊏C⊐ ⊏D⊐
104 ⊏A⊐ ⊏B⊐ ⊏C⊐ ⊏D⊐	129 ⊏A⊐ ⊏B⊐ ⊏C⊐ ⊏D⊐	154 ⊏A⊐ ⊏B⊐ ⊏C⊐ ⊏D⊐	179 ⊏A⊐ ⊏B⊐ ⊏C⊐ ⊏D⊐
105 ⊏A⊐ ⊏B⊐ ⊏C⊐ ⊏D⊐	130 ⊏A⊐ ⊏B⊐ ⊏C⊐ ⊏D⊐	155 ⊏A⊐ ⊏B⊐ ⊏C⊐ ⊏D⊐	180 ⊏A⊐ ⊏B⊐ ⊏C⊐ ⊏D⊐
106 ⊏A⊐ ⊏B⊐ ⊏C⊐ ⊏D⊐	131 ⊏A⊐ ⊏B⊐ ⊏C⊐ ⊏D⊐	156 ⊏A⊐ ⊏B⊐ ⊏C⊐ ⊏D⊐	181 ⊏A⊐ ⊏B⊐ ⊏C⊐ ⊏D⊐
107 ⊏A⊐ ⊏B⊐ ⊏C⊐ ⊏D⊐	132 ⊏A⊐ ⊏B⊐ ⊏C⊐ ⊏D⊐	157 ⊏A⊐ ⊏B⊐ ⊏C⊐ ⊏D⊐	182 ⊏A⊐ ⊏B⊐ ⊏C⊐ ⊏D⊐
108 ⊏A⊐ ⊏B⊐ ⊏C⊐ ⊏D⊐	133 ⊏A⊐ ⊏B⊐ ⊏C⊐ ⊏D⊐	158 ⊏A⊐ ⊏B⊐ ⊏C⊐ ⊏D⊐	183 ⊏A⊐ ⊏B⊐ ⊏C⊐ ⊏D⊐
109 ⊏A⊐ ⊏B⊐ ⊏C⊐ ⊏D⊐	134 ⊏A⊐ ⊏B⊐ ⊏C⊐ ⊏D⊐	159 ⊏A⊐ ⊏B⊐ ⊏C⊐ ⊏D⊐	184 ⊏A⊐ ⊏B⊐ ⊏C⊐ ⊏D⊐
110 ⊏A⊐ ⊏B⊐ ⊏C⊐ ⊏D⊐	135 ⊏A⊐ ⊏B⊐ ⊏C⊐ ⊏D⊐	160 ⊏A⊐ ⊏B⊐ ⊏C⊐ ⊏D⊐	185 ⊏A⊐ ⊏B⊐ ⊏C⊐ ⊏D⊐
111 ⊏A⊐ ⊏B⊐ ⊏C⊐ ⊏D⊐	136 ⊏A⊐ ⊏B⊐ ⊏C⊐ ⊏D⊐	161 ⊏A⊐ ⊏B⊐ ⊏C⊐ ⊏D⊐	186 ⊏A⊐ ⊏B⊐ ⊏C⊐ ⊏D⊐
112 ⊏A⊐ ⊏B⊐ ⊏C⊐ ⊏D⊐	137 ⊏A⊐ ⊏B⊐ ⊏C⊐ ⊏D⊐	162 ⊏A⊐ ⊏B⊐ ⊏C⊐ ⊏D⊐	187 ⊏A⊐ ⊏B⊐ ⊏C⊐ ⊏D⊐
113 ⊏A⊐ ⊏B⊐ ⊏C⊐ ⊏D⊐	138 ⊏A⊐ ⊏B⊐ ⊏C⊐ ⊏D⊐	163 ⊏A⊐ ⊏B⊐ ⊏C⊐ ⊏D⊐	188 ⊏A⊐ ⊏B⊐ ⊏C⊐ ⊏D⊐
114 ⊏A⊐ ⊏B⊐ ⊏C⊐ ⊏D⊐	139 ⊏A⊐ ⊏B⊐ ⊏C⊐ ⊏D⊐	164 ⊏A⊐ ⊏B⊐ ⊏C⊐ ⊏D⊐	189 ⊏A⊐ ⊏B⊐ ⊏C⊐ ⊏D⊐
115 ⊏A⊐ ⊏B⊐ ⊏C⊐ ⊏D⊐	140 ⊏A⊐ ⊏B⊐ ⊏C⊐ ⊏D⊐	165 ⊏A⊐ ⊏B⊐ ⊏C⊐ ⊏D⊐	190 ⊏A⊐ ⊏B⊐ ⊏C⊐ ⊏D⊐
116 ⊏A⊐ ⊏B⊐ ⊏C⊐ ⊏D⊐	141 ⊏A⊐ ⊏B⊐ ⊏C⊐ ⊏D⊐	166 ⊏A⊐ ⊏B⊐ ⊏C⊐ ⊏D⊐	191 ⊏A⊐ ⊏B⊐ ⊏C⊐ ⊏D⊐
117 ⊏A⊐ ⊏B⊐ ⊏C⊐ ⊏D⊐	142 ⊏A⊐ ⊏B⊐ ⊏C⊐ ⊏D⊐	167 ⊏A⊐ ⊏B⊐ ⊏C⊐ ⊏D⊐	192 ⊏A⊐ ⊏B⊐ ⊏C⊐ ⊏D⊐
118 ⊏A⊐ ⊏B⊐ ⊏C⊐ ⊏D⊐	143 ⊏A⊐ ⊏B⊐ ⊏C⊐ ⊏D⊐	168 ⊏A⊐ ⊏B⊐ ⊏C⊐ ⊏D⊐	193 ⊏A⊐ ⊏B⊐ ⊏C⊐ ⊏D⊐
119 ⊏A⊐ ⊏B⊐ ⊏C⊐ ⊏D⊐	144 ⊏A⊐ ⊏B⊐ ⊏C⊐ ⊏D⊐	169 ⊏A⊐ ⊏B⊐ ⊏C⊐ ⊏D⊐	194 ⊏A⊐ ⊏B⊐ ⊏C⊐ ⊏D⊐
120 ⊏A⊐ ⊏B⊐ ⊏C⊐ ⊏D⊐	145 ⊏A⊐ ⊏B⊐ ⊏C⊐ ⊏D⊐	170 ⊏A⊐ ⊏B⊐ ⊏C⊐ ⊏D⊐	195 ⊏A⊐ ⊏B⊐ ⊏C⊐ ⊏D⊐
121 ⊏A⊐ ⊏B⊐ ⊏C⊐ ⊏D⊐	146 ⊏A⊐ ⊏B⊐ ⊏C⊐ ⊏D⊐	171 ⊏A⊐ ⊏B⊐ ⊏C⊐ ⊏D⊐	196 ⊏A⊐ ⊏B⊐ ⊏C⊐ ⊏D⊐
122 ⊏A⊐ ⊏B⊐ ⊏C⊐ ⊏D⊐	147 ⊏A⊐ ⊏B⊐ ⊏C⊐ ⊏D⊐	172 ⊏A⊐ ⊏B⊐ ⊏C⊐ ⊏D⊐	197 ⊏A⊐ ⊏B⊐ ⊏C⊐ ⊏D⊐
123 ⊏A⊐ ⊏B⊐ ⊏C⊐ ⊏D⊐	148 ⊏A⊐ ⊏B⊐ ⊏C⊐ ⊏D⊐	173 ⊏A⊐ ⊏B⊐ ⊏C⊐ ⊏D⊐	198 ⊏A⊐ ⊏B⊐ ⊏C⊐ ⊏D⊐
124 ⊏A⊐ ⊏B⊐ ⊏C⊐ ⊏D⊐	149 ⊏A⊐ ⊏B⊐ ⊏C⊐ ⊏D⊐	174 ⊏A⊐ ⊏B⊐ ⊏C⊐ ⊏D⊐	199 ⊏A⊐ ⊏B⊐ ⊏C⊐ ⊏D⊐
125 ⊏A⊐ ⊏B⊐ ⊏C⊐ ⊏D⊐	150 ⊏A⊐ ⊏B⊐ ⊏C⊐ ⊏D⊐	175 ⊏A⊐ ⊏B⊐ ⊏C⊐ ⊏D⊐	200 ⊏A⊐ ⊏B⊐ ⊏C⊐ ⊏D⊐

Themis BAR REVIEW

SCORE

RESCORE

AM Session

Time—3 hours

Directions: Each of the questions or incomplete statements below is followed by four suggested answers or completions. You are to choose the best of the stated alternatives. Answer all questions according to the generally accepted view, except where otherwise noted.

For the purposes of this test, you are to assume that Articles 1 and 2 of the Uniform Commercial Code have been adopted. You are also to assume relevant application of Article 9 of the UCC concerning fixtures. The Federal Rules of Evidence are deemed to control. The terms "Constitution," "constitutional," and "unconstitutional" refer to the federal Constitution unless indicated to the contrary. You are to assume that there is no applicable statute unless otherwise specified; however, survival actions and claims for wrongful death should be assumed to be available where applicable. You should assume that joint and several liability, with pure comparative negligence, is the relevant rule unless otherwise indicated.

1. A collector owned a painting that needed professional restoration. The collector brought the painting to a restorer and after examining the painting, the restorer quoted the collector a price for the restoration. The restorer told the collector that, since she was going on a vacation and would be unreachable, the collector had a month to make his decision. Two days later, the collector mailed a letter to the restorer accepting the restorer's price. Through no fault of the collector, this letter was lost in the mail and never delivered. The next day, the collector learned of another person who would do the restoration more cheaply and would begin immediately. The collector mailed a second letter to the restorer that stated that he did not require her services. On arriving home from her vacation, the restorer received the collector's second letter. As a consequence, she contacted another art owner and began restoration work for that owner. In the meantime, the collector became dissatisfied with the work of the second restorer. He contacted the original restorer and demanded that she begin the restoration work on his painting, which she refused to do. The collector is suing the restorer for breach of contract in a jurisdiction that follows the mailbox rule.

Will the collector prevail?

(A) No, because the restorer relied on the collector's revocation.

(B) No, because the restorer never received the collector's acceptance.

(C) Yes, because the collector had timely accepted the restorer's offer.

(D) Yes, because the "mailbox rule" does not apply when both a revocation and an acceptance are sent.

2. The defendant's attorney in a fraud case called a witness to testify as to the defendant's character. On cross-examination, the prosecutor asked the witness whether he had ever been arrested for writing bad checks. In fact, the witness had been arrested two years ago for writing bad checks, but charges had been dropped due to a total lack of evidence that the witness had committed the crime. The defendant's attorney objects to the question.

Should the prosecutor be allowed to ask the question?

(A) No, because a witness who is not the defendant may not be cross-examined with prior bad acts.

(B) No, because the witness was never charged with the crime.

(C) Yes, because writing bad checks is probative of the witness's untruthfulness.

(D) Yes, because the arrest occurred only two years ago.

3. A company owned and operated a private golf course. One of the fairways on the course ran parallel to a navigable body of water. As the company was aware, golfers frequently but unintentionally hit golf balls into the water when playing that hole, since there were no natural or artificial barriers to prevent the balls from going into the water. A 12-year-old child, while sailing on the water, was struck by one such ball and suffered a serious physical injury.

The injured boater's parent has filed a public nuisance action against the company, on behalf of his child, to recover for his injuries.

Is the plaintiff precluded from recovering?

(A) No, because the boater was seriously injured while on navigable water due to the company's negligence.

(B) No, because of the attractive nuisance doctrine.

(C) Yes, because the boater did not have an ownership interest in land.

(D) Yes, because the golfer's action was unintentional.

4. The president of a closely-held corporation personally purchased an inn from a seller. In addition to a small down payment, the president executed a note for the remainder of the purchase price. The note was secured by a mortgage on the property. The mortgage and related deed were timely and properly recorded. The note contained a due-on-sale clause, which required the president to obtain the seller's consent in order to transfer the inn. The president transferred the inn to her corporation without the seller's permission or knowledge.

For several years, the president continued to make timely payments on the note from her personal bank account in order to conceal the transfer from the seller, until shortly before the president filed for personal bankruptcy, at which time the seller learned of the transfer. In the bankruptcy proceeding, the note is subject to discharge unless the seller's failure to exercise his rights under the due-on-sale clause is due to intentional misrepresentation by the president. The current value of the inn is less than the outstanding balance owed on the note.

Does the president's conduct constitute intentional misrepresentation?

(A) No, because the president's statement was not in writing.

(B) No, because the recorded deed gave the seller constructive knowledge of the transfer.

(C) Yes, because the president, who was under a duty to disclose the transfer, failed to do so and the seller justifiably relied on that failure to his detriment.

(D) Yes, because transaction involved the sale of land rather than goods.

5. Under his will, a bachelor devises his farm to his brother. The language of the devise makes no mention of the need of the brother to survive the testator. The will contains a residuary clause that leaves all property not otherwise devised by the will to the bachelor's sister. The bachelor's brother dies more than a year before the bachelor, but the brother has two children, both of whom survive the bachelor.

There is an anti-lapse statute that applies to a devise by a testator to a relative who is a descendant of the testator, the testator's parents, or the testator's grandparents.

Are the brother's children entitled to their uncle's farm?

(A) No, because their father did not survive his brother.

(B) No, because the will contained a residuary clause.

(C) Yes, because the language of the will did not require the brother to survive the testator.

(D) Yes, because the anti-lapse statute operates to save the lapsed devise.

6. During a trial for injuries a plaintiff sustained in a car accident with the defendant, the plaintiff's attorney called a witness to the stand to testify that the witness, a 25-year-old woman, saw the defendant run a stop sign and crash into the plaintiff's car. The witness was not associated with the defendant in any way. The plaintiff's attorney questioned the witness in an attempt to get her to testify that she saw the defendant run the stop sign, but she would not do so, and seemed to be deliberately avoiding the topic. Finally, the plaintiff's attorney asked that the witness be treated as hostile, and asked her, "Did you see the defendant run the stop sign on the day in question?" The defendant's attorney objected to the form of the question.

How is the court likely to rule on the defendant's objection?

(A) Overrule it, because a party may generally ask leading questions of his own witnesses.

(B) Overrule it, because a leading question was necessary to develop the witness's testimony.

(C) Sustain it, because a party may not treat his own witness as hostile.

(D) Sustain it, because leading questions are not appropriate for this witness.

7. A man and his girlfriend spent the afternoon at the beach; each of them had consumed a significant quantity of alcohol. The man saw one of the town's wealthiest residents arrive at the beach, spread out a beach towel, put down a large cloth bag on the towel, drop what looked like a wallet into the bag, and run into the ocean. The man told his girlfriend what he had seen the wealthy man do. She didn't respond, but walked over to the bag and opened it. The bag did not contain the man's wallet, but it did contain an expensive ring. She took the ring, and closed the bag. The wealthy man's companion, who was just coming onto the beach, observed the girlfriend's actions. The girlfriend was arrested. Soon thereafter, the man was arrested as well.

The man is charged, among other crimes, with conspiracy to commit larceny. The applicable jurisdiction has adopted a conspiracy statute based on the Model Penal Code. Which of the following is the weakest argument that the man can advance in defense of the charge?

(A) The man's conversation with his girlfriend was inadequate to form a conspiracy agreement.

(B) The theft of the ring was beyond the scope of the conspiracy.

(C) The man did not perform an overt act to advance the conspiracy.

(D) The man's intoxicated state prevented him from forming the intent necessary to commit the crime.

8. A state feared abuse of its statute providing for welfare benefits, which was administered by its department of public assistance. The department believed that an individual who had been receiving welfare payments for the past year was not eligible for them because the individual had adequate means of support. The department informed the individual in writing of its decision to terminate his welfare benefits. The department also informed the individual that he could schedule an administrative hearing, which would be held in approximately one month, to contest that decision and to present any evidence on his own behalf.

If the individual challenges this termination on constitutional grounds, will he likely be successful?

(A) Yes, because welfare benefit recipient had a Due Process right to a notice and hearing before his welfare benefits were terminated.

(B) Yes, because the department of public assistance has impaired the obligations of its contract with the welfare recipient in violation of the Contracts Clause.

(C) No, because the department has provided him with notice and a hearing sufficient to satisfy the Due Process Clause.

(D) No, because a state can establish the procedures for terminating an interest that the state itself has created, as distinguished from a purely private interest.

9. A retail furniture store ordered 10 sofas from a manufacturer at $1,000 each, plus shipping, to be delivered and paid for in five equal monthly installments. With the first shipment of two sofas, the manufacturer sent an invoice to the retailer, billing the retailer $2,000 plus shipping. The invoice also noted that the manufacturer retained a security interest in all sofas shipped until the purchase price for all sofas ordered was paid in full.

Not happy with the security interest term, the retailer immediately notified the manufacturer that this term was unacceptable. After sending payment for the first two sofas, the retailer told the manufacturer not to send any more sofas. The manufacturer sued the retailer for breach of contract.

In the breach of contract action by the manufacturer against the retailer, what will be the result?

(A) The manufacturer will prevail, because both parties are merchants.

(B) The manufacturer will prevail, but can only enforce the terms of the original offer.

(C) The retailer will prevail, because the knock-out rule voids the contract.

(D) The retailer will prevail, because the additional terms materially affected the bargain.

10. A developer purchased a 60-acre parcel of wooded land and divided the parcel into 20 three-acre lots. The developer advertized the rustic character of the lots and the intent to sell the lots for development as single-family residences. This was in conformity with the zoning restrictions on the land, which required that the land be used for residential purposes and that the size of each lot not be less than two acres. Over a period of several years, the developer sold 15 of the lots.

The deed for each of these lots contained the following provision:

> This deed is subject to the condition that the property may only be used for residential purposes and may not be subdivided but must be sold in its entirety. This condition shall be a covenant running with the land and shall be binding on all owners, their heirs, devisees, successors, and assignees.

The deed for each lot was promptly and properly recorded.

The developer, facing financial difficulty, sold the remaining five lots to a land speculator. The deeds to these lots did not contain the character and size provision that the developer had inserted into the other deeds, nor did the speculator have actual knowledge of the developer's advertizing related to the character and size of the lots. The land speculator, acting in response to a zoning change that reduced the minimum permissible size of a lot to only one acre, has obtained governmental approval to divide each of the five remaining lots in thirds and is now offering the 15 lots for sale.

An owner of one of the three-acre lots has brought suit against the speculator seeking an injunction to prevent him from selling the lots in less than three-acre parcels. Can the speculator successfully defend against this lawsuit?

(A) Yes, because the speculator's deeds did not contain the character and size provision.

(B) Yes, because the speculator has obtain governmental approval to subdivide the lots.

(C) No, because the lots purchased by the speculator are subject to an implied servitude.

(D) No, because the speculator purchased the lots for commercial rather than residential purposes.

11. A couple sought to purchase a house in large part because they believed, based on their research, that a certain historical figure had lived in it. The owner, having not previously heard about this association, neither confirmed nor denied their belief, merely shrugging his shoulders in response to their inquiries about it. The owner did not investigate the matter. The couple purchased the house from the owner. Later, the couple found out that the historical figure had not in fact lived in the house.

If the couple sues to void the contract, will they prevail?

(A) Yes, because the owner's failure to investigate the historical figure's connection with the house constituted a breach of the duty of good faith.

(B) Yes, because the couple's purpose in entering into the contract was frustrated by the mistake.

(C) No, because the risk of this unilateral mistake was borne by the couple.

(D) No, because the fact that the historical figure did not live there did not materially affect the bargain.

12. Congress passed the Equality in Employment Act ("EEA"), which was co-sponsored by both senators from a particular state and enjoyed the support of all of that state's federal representatives. Section 1 of the EEA required every state, within 18 months of passage, to enact legislation prohibiting employment discrimination based on sexual orientation. Section 2 of the EEA provided that any state which enacted such legislation before the deadline would receive $20 million in federal funding for programs designed to eliminate employment discrimination against gays and lesbians. Two years after passage of the act, the state had not enacted a statute prohibiting such discrimination.

If the United States sues the state for violating this act, what would be the most likely decision by the Supreme Court with regard to these two sections?

(A) Strike down Section 1 as exceeding Congress's power under the Commerce Clause, but uphold Section 2 as a proper exercise of the Spending Power

(B) Strike down Section 1 as a "commandeering" of state legislatures to enact laws, but uphold Section 2 as a proper exercise of the Spending Power

(C) Uphold Section 1 as a proper exercise of Congress's power under the Commerce Clause, but strike down Section 2 as an improper exercise of the Spending Power

(D) Uphold Sections 1 and 2 against any federalism-based challenge because the state's own congressional delegation supported the EEA and thus consented to any possible infringement on the state's sovereignty

13. A witness to an armed robbery identified a suspect in a proper police lineup that was not attended by the suspect's attorney. Charges were brought against the suspect, but the witness, a tourist from out of the country, had returned to her home country before the trial began. At trial, the prosecutor seeks to introduce the witness's prior statement of identification into evidence. The defendant objects to the introduction of the evidence.

Should the court allow the prior statement of identification into evidence?

(A) Yes, it should be admissible as nonhearsay.

(B) Yes, because the witness is unavailable, the statement of identification falls under a hearsay exception.

(C) No, because the defendant's attorney was not present at the identification.

(D) No, because the witness is unavailable.

14. A witness who was not a defendant invoked his Fifth Amendment right to remain silent during a federal criminal trial for insider trading. After being given derivative-use immunity, the witness testified. Several weeks later, the witness was a defendant in a state-law civil fraud proceeding based on his previous testimony in the federal trial. He moved to dismiss the case on the grounds that the previous grant of immunity protected him against a future action against him.

Will the defendant's motion be granted?

(A) Yes, because a grant of immunity can be given to a witness who is not a defendant.

(B) Yes, because the defendant was given derivative-use immunity.

(C) No, because the defendant's immunity was limited to federal prosecution.

(D) No, because the defendant's immunity does not extend to a subsequent civil trial.

15. A law makes it a crime to "knowingly sell, distribute, or barter a sexually explicit film featuring actors younger than the age of majority." A woman owned an adult video store, where she sold explicit videos featuring 18-year-old actors. She took reasonable steps to ensure that no videos featuring younger actors were sold in her store. She incorrectly believed that the age of majority in the jurisdiction was 18; in fact, the age of majority was 19 years old.

The woman was arrested and charged with violating the statute in a jurisdiction that has adopted the Model Penal Code. The prosecution does not contest that the woman's error was made honestly. Should she nonetheless be convicted?

(A) Yes, because the woman's error was a mistake of law, which is not a valid defense.

(B) Yes, because the woman knowingly sold the illegal videos.

(C) No, because the woman's error negated the requisite *mens rea*.

(D) No, because the woman's conscious objective was not to engage in selling the illicit videos.

16. In a phone conversation with a longtime friend, the owner of a ranch granted the friend a 90-day option to purchase the ranch for $10 million. As per the terms of their option agreement, the friend gave the owner $1,000 cash the following day. Later that same day, the owner was stricken with an illness that has left the owner unable to manage her own affairs. As a consequence, a guardian for the owner's property has been appointed. The friend proposed to the guardian that he would purchase the ranch immediately for $9.5 million. The guardian rejected this offer. Subsequently, but prior to the expiration of the 90-day period, the friend presented the guardian with a valid check for $10 million, which the guardian refused to accept.

In an action brought by the friend to compel the guardian to sell the ranch, if the court rules for the guardian, what is the reason?

(A) The option was not in writing.

(B) The option terminated at the time that the owner became incapacitated.

(C) The option was revoked by the friend's counteroffer.

(D) The option constituted a restraint on alienation of the ranch.

17. The maker of a prescription drug provides physicians who prescribe the drug with detailed instructions regarding its use. The instructions include a warning about the possibility of an allergic reaction that could result in serious physical harm if the drug is taken with a common over-the-counter medication. However, the allergic reaction is only likely to occur in a very small portion of the population and so the drug maker does not provide this warning to consumers of the drug.

A physician who had received the detailed instructions from the drug maker prescribed the drug for a patient. The physician did not warn the patient about the possible allergic reaction. The patient experienced an allergic reaction from taking the drug in combination with the over-the-counter medication and suffered a debilitating injury.

The patient brought a strict products liability action against the drug maker based on its failure to warn the patient of the possibility of an allergic reaction. Who will prevail?

(A) The patient, because the drug maker failed to warn the patient of the allergic reaction.

(B) The patient, because the drug maker, as a commercial supplier, is liable for harm done by the drug.

(C) The drug maker, because it warned the prescribing physician of the allergic reaction.

(D) The drug maker, because the number of persons at risk was very limited.

18. An individual, invoking her status as an American citizen and taxpayer, filed suit in an appropriate federal court seeking an order to remove the President from office. The individual asserted that the President was not born in the United States and was therefore ineligible to serve as President, because the Constitution provides that the President must have been born in the United States. Which doctrine would the court likely rely upon to dismiss this suit?

(A) Standing

(B) Ripeness

(C) The political question doctrine

(D) Abstention

19. The owner of a chain of retail stores built a warehouse that was financed by a loan from a bank. In exchange for the loan, the bank took a mortgage on the warehouse.

Several years later a thief broke into the warehouse by cutting a hole in the roof. The owner hired a contractor to repair the roof but, due to the contractor's shoddy work, the roof leaks whenever it rains, making a large portion of the warehouse unusable. Due to a contraction in the owner's business, the remaining usable space of the warehouse is sufficient for the owner's needs, but the unusable space impairs the bank's security interest.

Learning of the condition of the warehouse, the bank requested that the owner repair the warehouse roof. The owner refused. The bank brought an action to compel the owner to properly repair the roof.

The mortgage provides that it was made with recourse to the personal liability of the owner. Neither the mortgage nor the deed contain a covenant requiring the owner to maintain or repair the premises. The owner is not in default with respect to the required mortgage payments. The applicable jurisdiction follows a lien theory with regard to ownership of a mortgage and does not have an anti-deficiency statute.

Will the bank succeed?

(A) No, because the owner is not liable for waste.

(B) No, because the owner is not in default with respect to the required mortgage payments.

(C) Yes, because the mortgaged property is not residential.

(D) Yes, because the condition of the roof impairs the bank's security interest.

20. A large clothing retailer contracted with a firm that specialized in custom printing to print the logo of a major sporting event onto 5,000 jerseys. The logo was coupled with an identifying landmark of the city in which the event was to take place. The retailer planned to sell the jerseys as souvenirs at the event. As called for in the contract, the retailer supplied the firm with the jerseys and paid half the contract price. Shortly before the event and before any shirts had been printed, the stadium where the game was to be held was damaged by an earthquake. As a consequence, the event was moved to another city.

The retailer demanded the return of its payment and the jerseys. The supplier, claiming that it was entitled to the benefit of its bargain, kept its anticipated profit of $2,000 but returned the jerseys and the remainder of the payment to the retailer. The retailer filed a lawsuit seeking rescission of the contract and return of the $2,000.

What is the retailer's best argument in support of its suit?

(A) Performance of the contract has become impracticable because the relocation of the sporting event was an unforeseeable occurrence.

(B) The relocation of the sporting event has made enforcement of the contract on its original terms unconscionable.

(C) The contract is void due to mutual mistake, as both parties were mistaken as to an essential element of the contract.

(D) The retailer's contractual duties are discharged because the game's relocation frustrated the purpose of the contract.

21. On a winter day, a youth, seeking refuge from the cold, entered a small neighborhood grocery store without the knowledge of the store's owner, who was standing at the cash register. Shortly thereafter, the only other person in the store approached the register and requested an item located on a shelf behind the owner. As the owner turned to retrieve the requested item, the individual drew a gun and commanded the owner to give him the money in the register. As the owner turned back toward the customer, the customer fired the gun at her and missed. The owner grappled with the customer and succeeded in knocking the gun out of the customer's hand. As the customer retrieved his gun, the owner grabbed her own gun, for which she had a valid license. They fired at each other, each missing the other. Although the owner's actions did not create an unreasonable risk of harm to the youth, the bullet from the owner's gun nevertheless struck and killed the youth.

The estate of the youth filed a wrongful death action against store owner. Who will prevail?

(A) The store owner, because the owner acted in self-defense.

(B) The store owner, because the owner's shooting of the youth was not negligent.

(C) The estate of the youth, because youth was an invitee.

(D) The estate of the youth, because the youth was not a co-conspirator with the robber.

22. An organization against drunk driving sought permission from the owner of a mall to pass out leaflets in favor of tougher drunk driving laws in front of a liquor store. The mall owner denied the organization permission. The organization, filing an action in an appropriate court, sought an injunction permitting the organization to pass out its leaflets in accord with its free speech rights.

The state's highest court, interpreting the state constitution, permits the exercise of free speech rights on private property that is regularly held open to the public. Of the following reasons, which is the best argument for granting the injunction?

(A) Leafleting is a form of speech that is protected by the First Amendment of the United States Constitution.

(B) The reason for leafleting was related to the place where the organization sought to leaflet.

(C) The leafleting was permitted by the state constitution.

(D) By admitting members of the general public, the mall constituted a limited public forum.

23. The defendant was convicted of first-degree murder. He sought out and stabbed his victim multiple times after a dispute over a soccer match. The prosecution sought the death penalty. The statute in effect states that the death penalty is reserved for only those crimes that are "especially heinous or brutal." The defendant was sentenced to death. He is now appealing his sentence.

Should the appellate court vacate his sentence?

(A) Yes, because the requirement that death penalty crimes be "especially heinous or brutal" is unconstitutionally vague.

(B) Yes, because the only permissible statutory criteria for determining whether the death penalty should be applied is whether the murder was premeditated.

(C) No, because the "especially heinous or brutal" requirement does not describe a characteristic that applies to every murder defendant.

(D) No, because a reasonable jury could determine that the murder was in fact especially heinous or brutal.

24. In a criminal trial for arson, a prosecution witness testifies under oath that she saw the defendant set fire to the victim's home. The defendant's attorney does not cross-examine the witness, but seeks to admit testimony that the witness gave at a deposition several months before the trial. At the deposition, the witness testified under oath that she did not see the defendant set fire to the victim's home.

Should the court admit the deposition testimony?

(A) The court should admit the witness's testimony given at the deposition for impeachment purposes, but not as substantive evidence.

(B) The court should admit the witness's testimony given at the deposition for impeachment purposes and as substantive evidence.

(C) The court should not admit the witness's testimony given at the deposition because the defendant's attorney did not allow the witness the chance to explain her inconsistent testimony.

(D) The court should not admit the witness's testimony given at the deposition because it is hearsay.

25. A man whose terminally ill aunt had promised to devise an undeveloped parcel of land to him sold the parcel to a friend. The friend purchased the property based on the nephew's false assertion that he owned the parcel; the friend was unaware of the aunt's ownership of the parcel. The friend did not perform a title search and did not record the deed, which was a general warranty deed.

Subsequently, the aunt died. As promised, she devised the parcel to her nephew. The personal representative of the estate executed and recorded a deed transferring title to the parcel to the nephew. After the aunt's death, no one paid the property taxes on the parcel. Eventually, the state seized the parcel and sold it through a tax sale. Before expiration of the redemption period that is statutorily permitted to the owner of the real property, the friend learned of the sale of the parcel for delinquent taxes. Claiming ownership of the parcel, the friend sought to pay the delinquent taxes and other costs and fees associated with the sale and thereby redeem the parcel. The buyer of the parcel at the tax sale, who had no prior knowledge of the friend's claim with respect to the parcel, objected.

In an action to determine ownership of the parcel, if the court finds for the friend, what is the likely reason?

(A) The friend was record owner of the parcel.

(B) The friend purchased the parcel for value and without notice.

(C) Under the doctrine of equitable conversion, the friend is owner of the parcel.

(D) Title to the parcel vested in the friend upon the nephew's acquisition of the parcel.

26. The owner of an electronics store brought a civil suit for the value of stolen electronics against one of his former employees, who had previously been convicted in a criminal court for the theft of the same goods. During the civil trial, the plaintiff-owner called a witness whom he hoped would testify that she saw the defendant in possession of the stolen goods the day after the electronics store was robbed. The witness, however, testified that she did not see the defendant in possession of the goods, and that she was actually out of town the day after the robbery. The plaintiff seeks to introduce the witness's testimony in the criminal case, in which she testified that she saw the defendant in possession of the goods the next day. The defendant objects to the introduction of the statement.

Should the court allow the testimony into evidence?

(A) Yes, for impeachment only

(B) Yes, as substantive evidence only

(C) Yes, for both impeachment and as substantive evidence

(D) No, not for any reason

27. In a bicycle race with a $5,000 prize for the winner, a cyclist was leading by a significant margin. A spectator at the race was married to the second place rider. Sensing that her husband would not win unless she took action, the spectator drove to a point two miles ahead on the course, scattered several nails in the middle of course, and then left the area. Soon thereafter, the cyclist approached the area and noticed the nails. He attempted to swerve around the obstruction but a nail punctured his tire. He fell off his bike, suffered significant physical injuries, and was unable to complete the race.

If the cyclist sues the spectator, under what theory is the cyclist least likely to recover maximum punitive damages?

(A) Assault

(B) Intentional infliction of emotional distress

(C) Trespass to chattels

(D) Battery

28. An artist who had designed a sculpture to be made out of steel went to the website of a merchant that sold specialized tools. Using the chat feature, the artist explained to an employee of the merchant that the artist wanted to purchase a tool that could cut through steel. The employee suggested that the artist purchase a particular saw. The employee, pointing out that the website's description of the saw indicated that it could cut through most metals, added that the saw "should cut through steel with no problem." The artist purchased the saw from the merchant's website for a total cost of $450. Conspicuously appearing on the page where the artist had to indicate his consent in order to purchase the saw was the following: "There are no implied warranties provided with this product other than the general warranty of merchantability." The tool failed to cut through the steel that the artist intended to use for his sculpture. The artist sued the merchant for damages attributable to breach of the implied warranty of fitness for a particular purpose.

Which party is likely to prevail?

(A) The merchant, because the merchant disclaimed the warranty of fitness for a particular purpose.

(B) The merchant, because warranties do not apply to goods valued under $500.

(C) The artist, because the merchant's employee knew that the artist wanted a saw that would cut steel and relied on his judgment that the saw would do so.

(D) The artist, because the implied warranty of fitness for a particular purpose cannot be disclaimed by a merchant.

29. A 15-year-old male was being tried in state court as an adult for murder. At voir dire, the prosecutor exercised all of his peremptory challenges to exclude persons under the age of 30 from the jury. The defendant's attorney timely raised the issue as to whether the prosecutor had utilized his peremptory challenges in an unconstitutional manner. In response to questioning by the court, the prosecutor stated that it was his intent to exclude persons who, because of their age, would be sympathetic to the defendant. The judge found that the prosecutor's reason was genuine and not pretextual.

Should the judge sustain the defendant's objection?

(A) Yes, because the prosecutor's use of his peremptory challenges violates the defendant's Sixth Amendment right to trial by an impartial jury.

(B) Yes, because the defendant was a member of the affected class.

(C) No, because the prosecutor is permitted to exercise his peremptory challenges for any rational reason.

(D) No, because the prosecutor's use of his peremptory challenges does not violate the Equal Protection Clause.

30. Concerned with protecting the use of federal funds from the deleterious effects of bribery, Congress enacted a statute criminalizing the acceptance of a bribe by a state or local official where the state or local government received at least $10,000 in federal funds.

A county government, in exchange for its agreement to permit the housing of federal prisoners in the county's jail, received a payment of federal funds for each prisoner. The total amount received by the county government for housing federal prisoners exceeded $100,000 annually. A federal prisoner housed in the county jail agreed to transfer title to a pickup truck to a prison guard in exchange for the guard permitting the prisoner to receive illegal conjugal visits. The prison guard was charged with violating the statute. Is the application of the statute to the guard's taking title to the prisoner's truck constitutional?

(A) No, because the bribe did not directly relate to the federal funds.

(B) No, because a federal statute that criminalizes noneconomic behavior must have a significant impact on interstate commerce.

(C) Yes, because the statute was a valid congressional exercise, pursuant to the Necessary and Proper Clause, of ensuring that its power to appropriate money for the general welfare was not thwarted.

(D) Yes, because the statute was a valid congressional exercise of its inherent police powers.

31. A farmer was diagnosed by his doctor with a terminal illness. Upon arriving home immediately after having received the news, the farmer wrote the following, "I, farmer, now transfer my farm, Blackacre, to my son." The farmer, who owned Blackacre in fee simple absolute, then signed and dated the document. The farmer neither discussed the document nor its contents with anyone else, but simply placed it with his personal papers.

Soon thereafter, the farmer died. Among the farmer's personal papers, in addition to the document, was a will. The farmer had executed the will in compliance with the required formalities 10 years prior to his death. Under the terms of the will, the farm was devised to the farmer's daughter. The daughter and son were the farmer's only heirs.

After learning of the document and the will, the son and daughter each claimed ownership of Blackacre outright.

In an appropriate action to determine ownership of the farm filed by the personal representative of the farmer's estate after admission of the will to probate, who is entitled to ownership of farm?

(A) The daughter, because the unwitnessed document is not a valid deed and therefore the farm passed to her by the terms of the will.

(B) The daughter, because the document, which was never delivered to nor accepted by the son prior to the farmer's death, was not a valid deed and therefore the farm passed to her by the terms of the will.

(C) The son, because the document was a deed that took effect during the farmer's lifetime.

(D) The son, because the document was executed after the will and therefore superseded the will.

32. Engrossed in a cell phone conversation, a pedestrian in a rural area fails to look out for traffic while crossing a road. The driver of an oncoming car notices the pedestrian and begins to brake, which causes a cake sitting on the front passenger seat to slide off the seat and onto the floor of the car. Distracted by the cake, the driver, who is 17 years old and properly licensed to operate the car without supervision, momentarily forgets about the pedestrian. When the driver's attention returns to the road, the driver does not have sufficient time to avoid striking the pedestrian who suffers serious physical injuries.

The applicable jurisdiction has adopted a modified comparative negligence statute.

The pedestrian brings a negligence action against the driver for damages stemming from the pedestrian's physical injuries, which total $200,000. The jury determines that the driver was 80% at fault and the pedestrian was 20% at fault.

How much will the pedestrian be permitted to recover?

(A) Nothing, because the pedestrian was negligent.

(B) $160,000, because the pedestrian's damages are reduced by the percentage that the pedestrian was at fault.

(C) $200,000, because the driver had the last clear chance to avoid the accident.

(D) $200,000, because the driver was engaged in an adult activity.

33. A testator's will contained a devise of the testator's residence to the testator's daughter and bequeathed $100,000 to the testator's son. At the time of the testator's death, the testator owned the residence in fee simple absolute. The residence was not subject to any encumbrances. The testator's only other asset at the time of her death was a bank account that had a balance of $5,000. The personal representative of the testator's estate applied the money in the bank account to the satisfaction of the testator's outstanding debts and transferred title of the testator's residence to the daughter.

The son filed an action in probate court challenging the personal representative's distribution of the testator's residence to the daughter. The son asserted that the personal representative should have sold the residence and divided the proceeds between the two children.

Which of the following legal concepts provides the best support for personal representative's action?

(A) Abatement

(B) Ademption

(C) Exoneration

(D) Lapse

34. A city council passed an ordinance prohibiting all police officers from working a second job. The council wanted to have its officers available in case of an emergency, such as a blizzard, or for certain major events, such as professional football games. Other city employees, including members of the city council, had no such restriction on secondary employment.

A veteran and well-respected city police officer was upset because she would have to give up her well-paying second job as an exotic dancer at a local club. The club complies with all of the city's entertainment and liquor licensing regulations and employs the officer on an at-will basis.

The officer challenged the constitutionality of the ordinance in the appropriate federal court. Is she likely to prevail?

A) Yes, because the ordinance restricts the officer's First Amendment right to freedom of expression.

B) Yes, because the ordinance unreasonably discriminates against police officers in violation of the Equal Protection Clause.

C) No, because the ordinance is rationally related to the city's legitimate interest in public safety and social welfare.

D) No, because the ordinance does not amount to an unconstitutional taking.

35. A man decided to master the art of throwing knives. He practiced for several years, until he had the perfected his skills and was able to hit a spot no larger than a dime with confidence. After demonstrating his prowess to a friend, the man convinced the friend to stand against a wall while the man threw knives at her. The man threw three knives extremely close to the friend, but the fourth knife struck the friend, injuring her slightly. Although the friend's injury was minor, unbeknownst to the man, she had a rare blood disorder that caused her to bleed to death.

The crimes below are listed in ascending order of seriousness. What is the most serious common law crime for which the man can be convicted?

(A) Battery

(B) Involuntary manslaughter

(C) Voluntary manslaughter

(D) Murder

36. A pregnant mother and a soccer coach of the mother's young child were involved in a serious verbal altercation. The argument continued escalating until the coach suddenly punched the mother in the face and pushed her to the ground. The coach immediately fled the area. The mother did not suffer serious physical injury. Nonetheless, the incident greatly traumatized her. In the weeks following the attack, she had many sleepless nights and suffered several panic attacks.

The mother brought suit against the coach for intentional infliction of emotional distress. The coach filed a motion for summary judgment. How should the court rule on the motion?

(A) Grant the motion, because the coach did not intend to cause severe emotional distress.

(B) Grant the motion, because the mother did not suffer a significant physical injury.

(C) Deny the motion, because a jury could find that the coach was reckless as to the risk of causing emotional distress.

(D) Deny the motion, because the doctrine of transferred intent applies.

37. A plaintiff sued the owner of a small clothing store for injuries she sustained when she slipped and fell while shopping in the defendant's store. The defendant wants to introduce into evidence a written record of the event made by one of his employees. The record detailed the fact that the plaintiff slipped on her own drink that she had spilled without reporting to anyone. It also included the plaintiff's threat to sue the store, and the store owner's instructions to the employee to immediately write a report, so that there was a record of what happened in the event that the plaintiff sued. The employee is unavailable to testify. The plaintiff objects to the introduction of the document.

Should the court sustain the plaintiff's objection to the introduction of the document?

(A) Yes, because the document violates the best evidence rule.

(B) Yes, because the document is hearsay not within any exception.

(C) No, because the document is a business record.

(D) No, because the employee is unavailable to authenticate the record.

38. A college student enters the back yard of a zoology professor, to attend a social gathering for students to be held there. The professor is cleaning out the cage of a pet porcupine. The professor has carelessly allowed the porcupine to roam free. The porcupine, well camouflaged in a pile of leaves, is sunning itself. The student doesn't see the porcupine, trips over it, and breaks his hand.

The applicable jurisdiction permits the keeping of a porcupine as a pet.

In a strict liability action by the student against the professor, who will prevail?

(A) The student, because the professor possessed a wild animal.

(B) The student, because the professor, aware that students were coming to a social gathering, failed to act with reasonable care.

(C) The professor, because the student was only a licensee, not an invitee.

(D) The professor, because the student was not injured as a consequence of a dangerous propensity of the animal.

39. A man who suffered from a mental illness shot and killed his neighbor after making plans to do so. The man was arrested and charged with murder. At trial, the man admitted that he intended to kill the neighbor, and that he appreciated that what he was doing was illegal. However, he also testified that he performed the killing under orders from his pet goldfish, who was possessed by a demonic spirit, and that he was unable to resist the goldfish's constant urging to kill the neighbor.

The Model Penal Code test of criminal responsibility applies in the applicable jurisdiction.

If the man timely and properly pleads that he was not criminally responsible, can the man be found not guilty of murder but criminally responsible by reason of insanity?

(A) Yes, because the man was unable to resist the goldfish's constant urging.

(B) Yes, because the man suffered from a mental illness.

(C) No, because the man understood that killing his neighbor was illegal.

(D) No, because the man planned to kill his neighbor.

40. A publishing company entered into a contract to purchase a newspaper company. The contract specified that "it shall be a condition precedent to buyer's obligation to pay that the newspaper shall have 200,000 subscribers by December 31 of this year." In anticipation of the purchase, the publishing company purchased $200,000 of new equipment to be used in printing the newspaper; the newspaper was aware of the investment.

At the end of the business day on December 31, the newspaper had only 199,750 subscribers, and had no justification for the shortfall. The publishing company immediately redirected $100,000 of the new equipment to print one of its magazines, but the other $100,000 of equipment was custom-made for the newspaper and could not be used elsewhere. The publishing company then sued the newspaper company for $100,000. Is it likely to prevail?

(A) Yes, because the newspaper company did not comply with the condition precedent.

(B) Yes, because the publishing company mitigated its damages to the maximum extent reasonably possible.

(C) No, because the newspaper company substantially complied with the condition precedent.

(D) No, because failure of a condition precedent does not give rise to damages.

41. An attorney represents a corporation in a federal securities case. As the attorney reviewed her files before court, she discovered that—despite her diligence—a memo marked "PRIVILEGED AND CONFIDENTIAL" had inadvertently been included in a folder containing public financial documents. The attorney knew that she had copied this folder and produced it in its entirety to opposing counsel during discovery. However, the memo is detrimental to her client's case. The attorney immediately contacted opposing counsel and requested that the memo be returned to her, that all copies be destroyed, and that the information within the memo not be used at trial; she included the judge on this correspondence. Opposing counsel refused to return the memo, and informed the attorney that they did plan to use it at trial. The memo in question was from the corporation's chief executive officer to the attorney, and contained the chief financial officer's thoughts and questions regarding the attorney's trial strategy.

Should the court allow the defendant to introduce the memo into evidence at trial?

(A) Yes, because the attorney waived the privilege when she disclosed the memo to opposing counsel.

(B) Yes, because the memo was not privileged to begin with.

(C) No, because the attorney did not waive the privilege.

(D) No, because all documents from clients to attorneys are privileged.

42. A buyer purchased a newly constructed house from a builder for use as a residence. The buyer did not perform an inspection of the house prior to purchase. Neither the contract nor the deed contained any warranties as to the condition of the house.

Six months later, during a heavy downpour, the basement flooded. Since that time, whenever there has been a substantial rain, there has been water in the basement. The source of the problem has been identified as several cracks in the foundation wall that surrounds the basement. An expert hired by the buyer has opined that the cracks formed due to settling after the home was built and could have been prevented by adherence to proper construction methods. The builder has repeatedly refused to address the problem.

Just before the first anniversary of the purchase, the buyer filed suit against the builder for the defective foundation wall and the resulting damages. There are no applicable state statutes that address the issue.

Who will prevail?

(A) The builder, because the builder did not give the buyer a written warranty as to the condition of the house.

(B) The builder, because the buyer failed to conduct a home inspection.

(C) The buyer, because the builder of a residence is liable for any material defects in the house.

(D) The buyer, because the builder breached the warranty of fitness or suitability.

43. Two individuals who were homosexual had been in a monogamous relationship for ten years. They applied for a marriage license. State officials denied their request because the state code defined marriage as "a voluntary union between an adult man and woman." The state had always adhered to this definition of marriage. The state justified its law based on this historical tradition and the need to encourage heterosexual marriage as society's most basic institution. If the two individuals bring a suit claiming that the state law is unconstitutional, which of the following is the state's best argument for upholding the law?

(A) The law does not unconstitutionally discriminate against gays and lesbians, but merely prevents them from obtaining special rights and benefits under state law.

(B) The Supreme Court has not recognized either a fundamental liberty interest or an equality right to marry a member of the same sex, and the state has a rational basis for this civil law.

(C) The state can protect the First Amendment right of association of heterosexual married couples.

(D) The federal courts should not interfere because matters of family law are political rather than judicial questions that have always been committed to the state political process.

44. During a severe storm, a horse came onto a rancher's property. The rancher discovered the horse the next morning, and saw a serious wound on one of its legs. The rancher paid a veterinarian to examine and treat the horse, and the rancher then provided the horse with food and shelter.

Two weeks later, the horse's owner arrived at the rancher's home and asked for the return of his horse. The rancher returned the horse to its owner, and asked the owner for reimbursement for the veterinary visit and for the expenses incurred in feeding and sheltering the horse. The horse's owner refused to pay.

The rancher sued the horse's owner for the costs of veterinary care, food, and shelter. Is he likely to prevail?

(A) Yes, because the rancher's conduct created an implied-in-fact contract.

(B) Yes, because the horse's owner would be unjustly enriched if he is not forced to pay the rancher's expenses.

(C) No, because a valid contract was never formed between the rancher and the horse's owner.

(D) No, because the horse's owner never engaged in any conduct to signify that he assented to the rancher's expenditures.

45. A plaintiff sued a defendant for injuries sustained when the defendant ran a red light and struck the plaintiff as she crossed the street. The defendant denies that he ran the red light. The intersection where the accident took place features a camera that automatically captures a series of images of vehicles passing through the intersection when the light is red. During discovery, the plaintiff's attorney subpoenaed the city for copies of the photographs. The city printed two sets of the requested photographs directly from the camera, and sent one set to the plaintiff's counsel and the other set to the defendant's counsel. After laying a proper foundation, the plaintiff's attorney plans to introduce her set of the pictures into evidence. The defense attorney objects.

Is the plaintiff's set of photographs taken by the camera admissible?

(A) Yes, because the set of photographs is relevant and not excluded by a specific rule or law.

(B) Yes, because photographic evidence is always admissible.

(C) No, because of the best evidence rule.

(D) No, because there is no photographer to testify.

46. The United States Supreme Court, overruling *Roe v. Wade* and *Planned Parenthood v. Casey*, held that women do not have a constitutional right to abortion. Pursuant to the Commerce Clause of Article I, Section 8, and the Fourteenth Amendment, Congress responded by passing the Abortion Rights Restoration Act (ARRA). This Act restored the essential holdings of *Roe* and *Casey* by prohibiting any government from unduly burdening a woman's exercise of the constitutional right to abortion. The preamble to the Act stated that an abortion is a commercial activity that, considered in the aggregate, substantially affects interstate commerce, but no facts were presented to support this conclusion.

In a constitutional challenge to the validity of ARRA, will the federal court probably strike down the act?

(A) No, because Congress stated that an abortion is a commercial activity that, considered in the aggregate, substantially affects interstate commerce.

(B) No, because Congress is defining constitutional rights more expansively than the Supreme Court, not restricting them.

(C) Yes, because Congress is not remedying the violation of a judicially recognized constitutional right, but rather is attempting to create a new constitutional right.

(D) Yes, because it violates the constitutional principle of federalism.

47. Police officers have a reasonable suspicion, but not probable cause, that a suspect committed a robbery. The police officers, acting without a warrant, went to the suspect's home and requested that the suspect come to the stationhouse for fingerprinting. The suspect refused until the police officers threatened him with arrest. The suspect, reasonably believing that he was not free to deny the officers' request, accompanied the police officers to the stationhouse, where he was fingerprinted. His fingerprints matched those taken from the scene of the crime. Consequently, the suspect was arrested and charged with the robbery. At his trial, the defendant moved to suppress the fingerprint evidence. Should the judge grant this motion?

(A) Yes, because the police officers' action constituted an unlawful seizure and evidence seized as a consequence must be excluded.

(B) Yes, because the procedure violated the defendant's Fifth Amendment privilege against self-incrimination.

(C) No, because fingerprinting is a reliable form of scientific evidence that would assist the trier of fact.

(D) No, because the police officers' reasonable suspicions justified the suspect's warrantless detention for the purpose of fingerprinting.

48. A buyer purchased a residence from an individual seller. Within the buyer's deed, which was not recorded, was a provision that the buyer, his heirs, assignees, and successors promised to adhere to the community association guidelines and to recognize the association's right to enforce those guidelines. Among the guidelines issued by the community association was the following: "No fence greater than six feet in height shall be installed or maintained by homeowner." The community association has rigorously enforced this guideline.

The buyer subsequently died and devised the residence to her husband for life and then to her son. The husband, without actual knowledge of the guidelines or their contents, installed an eight-foot-high fence. The local zoning ordinance permits fences no greater than eight feet in height to be constructed in the residential neighborhood.

The community association has sought an injunction against the husband to compel him to remove the fence. Who will prevail?

(A) The community association, because the provision in the buyer's deed creates an equitable servitude.

(B) The community association, because the fence constitutes waste.

(C) The husband, because he only possesses a life estate.

(D) The husband, because neither he nor his wife acquired the residence from the community association.

49. A middle-aged farmer who lived by himself in a rural area had surgery to correct an orthopedic problem. Since his recovery would take about a year, he contacted a retired nurse about serving as his caretaker. While the farmer was still in the hospital, the two reached an agreement, the terms of which were specified in two letters. The letter written by the nurse identified the farmer by name and stated, "I agree to take care of your medical needs for a period of one year, starting when you leave the hospital." The letter written by the man identified the nurse by name and stated, "I agree to pay you $10,000 per month." Each letter was signed by its drafter. Before his discharge from the hospital, the man found out that the hospital had a less expensive program for home care, and cancelled the contract.

Unable to find other employment, the nurse brought a breach of contract action against the man. Based solely on the letters, will the nurse be able to establish the existence of a contract?

(A) Yes, because this agreement can be performed within one year.

(B) Yes, because the writings, taken together, sufficiently state the essential terms of the agreement.

(C) No, because the Statute of Frauds precludes enforcement.

(D) No, because the writings do not evidence a valid offer and acceptance.

50. A small restaurant utilized the same beverage supplier for many years. The owner of the restaurant had developed a very strong working relationship with the supplier's employees. The contract between the supplier and the restaurant only obligated the supplier to provide beverages, but the supplier's employees frequently performed repairs on the restaurant's soda dispensers, and were available to fill emergency orders even late at night and on weekends. Furthermore, the restaurant received a commission for each beverage sold at its restaurants, which the beverage supplier, unlike many other suppliers, paid in cash. The restaurant received lucrative offers to switch to other distributors, but repeatedly chose to stay with its supplier because of the personalized service.

The beverage supplier decided that it would be advantageous to concentrate its business solely on larger accounts. Without obtaining approval from the restaurant, the supplier "assigned all rights and delegated all duties" arising under its contract with the restaurant to a second beverage distributor. The second distributor did not pay any consideration for this transfer. While there was no anti-assignment clause its contract with the original supplier, the restaurant was not pleased with the assignment, and refused service from the new distributor.

The new distributor filed suit against the restaurant, claiming breach of contract. What is the restaurant's strongest argument in defense?

(A) While rights under a contract may normally be assigned, delegations of contractual duties are generally not permitted.

(B) The new distributor's failure to pay any consideration to the original supplier makes the assignment unenforceable.

(C) The failure to seek the restaurant's approval of the transfer of contractual rights and duties means that the restaurant is not bound by the transfer.

(D) The restaurant has a substantial interest in having the original beverage supplier perform the contract.

51. An employee at a toy store intervenes in a dispute between two unrelated customers, a mother and a grandfather, over who is entitled to a particular hard-to-come-by doll, which is the only remaining one at the store. The employee arbitrarily determines that the mother had possession of the doll first and awards her the right to purchase the doll. When the grandfather protests the employee's decision, the mother threatens to inflict physical harm on the grandfather and raises her arm to strike him. Fearful that the mother will do so, the grandfather looks to the employee for help. The employee, who because of his size could easily have forestalled the mother's attack, simply shrugs his shoulders. Before the mother makes contact with the grandfather, he crumples to floor, the victim of a stroke caused by the mother's threat.

The grandfather initiates a lawsuit against the mother, the employee, and the owner of the store on the grounds of assault for damages attributable to his stroke. The owner of the store moves to dismiss the complaint against herself for failure to state a cause of action. How should the court rule?

(A) Deny the motion, because the grandfather was reasonably apprehensive of an immediate battery.

(B) Deny the motion, because the employee failed to act to protect the grandfather.

(C) Grant the motion, because the owner is not vicariously liable for assault by one customer upon another.

(D) Grant the motion, because *respondeat superior* does not apply to an employee's intentional torts.

52. A man's wife wanted to remarry. Though her husband had not been seen for five years, there was no evidence that he had died. The wife wanted the court to declare that her husband was deceased. An applicable statute provided that there is a rebuttable presumption that a person who had not been seen or heard from in five years, after a diligent search for that person, was presumed to have died. One of the husband's family members did not want the court to declare him dead, and she sought to introduce the testimony of a witness who claimed to have seen the husband alive at a gas station. The witness believed that the man had a similar build to the husband. Additionally, she heard him speak to the gas station attendant in an accent similar to the husband's, and she saw him get into a car with license plates from the husband's home state. However, as the witness did not see the man's face or speak to him herself, she could not be sure.

The wife opposes the introduction of the witness's testimony. Is the witness's testimony admissible?

(A) No, because the matter is governed by a presumption that the husband, who has not been heard from in five years, is dead.

(B) No, because the witness is not certain that the man she saw is actually the husband.

(C) Yes, because the Dead Man's Statute expressly permits this type of testimony.

(D) Yes, because it is relevant and not otherwise prohibited.

53. A city often required persons seeking building permits to agree to aesthetic and environmental conditions in order to obtain such permits.

A company applied for a permit to construct a 300,000 square foot warehouse on its land in the city. The city conditioned the permit on the company's agreement to plant 45 trees on the property and to limit the building's height to 70 feet. The city had imposed similar conditions on other property owners. The effect of these conditions was to reduce the value of the company's property by three percent, but they did not prevent the construction of a warehouse on the land.

The company sued, claiming that the imposition of these conditions violated his constitutional rights. Would a court be likely to strike down these conditions?

(A) Yes, because they constitute an unconstitutional taking of private property for public use.

(B) Yes, because they are not substantially related to an important governmental interest.

(C) No, because, under the Takings Clause, they advance a legitimate government interest and do not deny the company the economically viable use of its land.

(D) No, because, under the Takings Clause, they are valid restrictions, but the court should require the city to compensate the company for the three percent reduction in its property value.

54. A customer at a restaurant ordered a dessert from the menu, which stated that the desserts were made by an independent third party. The restaurant had priced the dessert below its cost in order to attract customers to the restaurant. The dessert contained small slivers of glass. The glass was not detected by the restaurant, even though the restaurant conducted a reasonable inspection of the dessert and otherwise had no reason to suspect that the dessert contained the glass. The customer ate the dessert and incurred serious injuries from the glass slivers.

If the customer brings suit against the restaurant based on strict products liability for injuries suffered from eating the dessert, who will prevail?

(A) The customer, because the restaurant was a commercial supplier of the dessert.

(B) The customer, because the restaurant failed to warn him of the presence of the glass in the dessert.

(C) The restaurant, because the dessert was not produced by the restaurant.

(D) The restaurant, because the restaurant did not make a profit from the sale of the dessert.

55. An individual acquired a newly constructed house with a purchase money mortgage. Although the deed was recorded, through an oversight by the mortgagee, the mortgage was not.

Several years later, the individual sold the house at its fair market value to a couple who obtained a purchase money mortgage through another mortgagee. Both the deed and the mortgage were recorded. Neither the couple nor the second mortgagee were aware of the prior mortgage.

Shortly thereafter, the couple was killed in an accident, survived by their two young children. The couple did not leave a will. Under the law of intestate succession, the young children are the rightful heirs of their parents. The children's financial guardian, having been contacted by both mortgagees, has filed an appropriate action to determine ownership of the house.

The jurisdiction is a lien state with regard to mortgages. In addition, the applicable recording act reads, "No conveyance or mortgage of real property shall be good against subsequent purchasers for value and without notice unless the same be recorded according to law."

Who is entitled to priority with respect to the house?

(A) First mortgagee, second mortgagee, children

(B) Second mortgagee, first mortgagee, children

(C) Second mortgagee, children, first mortgagee

(D) First mortgagee, children, second mortgagee

56. To remedy past discrimination against women in college athletics, Congress required state colleges and universities to achieve "gender equity" in funding athletics. The percentage that each school must allocate to women's athletics was based on a formula that took into account the average percentage of athletic department funds allocated to men's and women's programs over a five-year period. Depending on the school's past record, this allocation could be greater than the percentage of women enrolled in the school. A state with any schools out of compliance forfeited a percentage of its federal educational funding.

A state military college first admitted women five years ago. Only 10% of its student body is currently female. To comply with the federal funding formula, the college must allocate 25% of its athletic budget to women's sports.

A male student, whose wrestling program is being discontinued because of the budget allocation, filed suit in an appropriate federal court challenging the federal law's constitutionality. Will he probably prevail?

(A) Yes, because the government will be unable to prove that the law's discriminatory funding requirements are necessary to achieve a compelling government interest.

(B) Yes, because principles of federalism prohibit the federal government from dictating the budget allocations of state educational institutions.

(C) No, because the government will be able to prove that the law's funding requirements are substantially related to the important government objective of remedying past discrimination.

(D) No, because remedying past discrimination is a legitimate government interest, and the law's funding requirements are rationally related to that interest.

57. A prosecutor called a witness to testify in a battery trial. The witness, a friend of the defendant, behaved in a hostile manner to the prosecutor, refusing to testify that the defendant was the initial aggressor in the altercation at issue, as the prosecutor believed he would. The prosecutor decided to call a second witness to minimize any damage done by the first witness's testimony. This second witness, who was the first witness's sister, testified that because the first witness (her brother) had been in a fight similar to the one in question, it was her opinion that her brother was not a good witness. The defendant's attorney objects to the sister's testimony.

Should the prosecutor be allowed to ask the witness about the fight?

(A) Yes, because the credibility of a witness may be attacked by reputation or opinion evidence.

(B) Yes, because the witness put his character at issue by testifying on the witness stand.

(C) No, because a party cannot impeach her own witness.

(D) No, because the altercations have no bearing on the witness's character for untruthfulness.

58. Seeking to protect its small wine industry, a state law prohibited a large, out-of-state corporation that engaged in the wine business in the state from entering into any new business deals within the state. The corporation sues in an appropriate federal court to enjoin state officials from enforcing this law.

On which of the following grounds would the court hold that state's law is unconstitutional?

(A) The Dormant Commerce Clause of Article I, Section 8

(B) The Privileges and Immunities Clause of Article IV, Section 2

(C) The Privileges or Immunities Clause of the Fourteenth Amendment

(D) The Contracts Clause of Article I, Section 10

59. One summer night, a man attended a party at one of the most lavish homes in town. Midway through the party, the man asked the party host if he could use the restroom, and the host directed him to a restroom on the second floor of the house. After using the restroom, the man became curious about the other rooms upstairs, and wondered if they were as beautiful as the rest of the house. His curiosity got the best of him, and he turned the handle and opened a door, which turned out to be the master bedroom. He stepped inside the room and immediately saw a large pearl necklace on the vanity table. He walked over to the table, grabbed the pearls, put them in his pocket, left the room, and went downstairs. Later in the evening, the party host saw the pearls slip out of the man's pocket. She immediately confronted the man and called the police.

If the man is later charged with common-law burglary, what is the man's best defense to the charge?

(A) The man did not break and enter the home.

(B) The man did not intend to steal anything when he entered the room.

(C) The man did not use any force to enter the bedroom.

(D) The man did not leave the premises with the pearls.

60. A paving company entered into a contract with a real estate developer to repave a large parking lot in the developer's shopping center. Since the paving company wanted to establish a good reputation in the market, it discounted its price. The paving company expected to make $20,000 in profit on the contract.

Midway through the project, the developer notified the paving company to cease work; the paving company immediately complied. At the time of the notice, the paving company had incurred costs of $200,000. The cost of hiring another contractor to perform the same work would have been $225,000. The paving work performed had increased the value of the shopping center by $100,000. The paving company filed a lawsuit against the developer. The factfinder determined that the developer's repudiation of the contract was without justification. What is the maximum amount of damages the paving company can be awarded?

(A) $100,000, the amount by which the value of the shopping center was increased.

(B) $200,000, the costs incurred by the paving company.

(C) $220,000, the developer's expectancy damages.

(D) $225,000, the amount that the developer would have had to pay for the portion of the paving job that was completed.

61. A defendant was charged with fraud in a state-law civil proceeding. During cross-examination, he was asked to state whether a note being entered into evidence was in his handwriting. Since the note contained a material false statement on which the plaintiff had relied, the defendant invoked his Fifth Amendment privilege against self-incrimination to avoid answering the question. The judge upheld the defendant's assertion of the privilege.

Was the judge correct in permitting the defendant to invoke his Fifth Amendment privilege against self-incrimination?

(A) Yes, because the handwriting evidence is always testimonial in nature.

(B) Yes, because the defendant's answer is testimonial evidence.

(C) No, because the defendant may not invoke his Fifth Amendment privilege in a civil proceeding.

(D) No, because the Fifth Amendment privilege against self-incrimination is not applicable in state-law proceedings.

62. Two defendants were on trial for conspiracy to commit robbery. The prosecution would like to introduce the testimony of a security guard at the store that was to be robbed. The security guard caught one of the defendants trying to sneak in a back entrance of the store the day before the robbery was to take place, hoping to "scope out" the store. In a panic, the defendant had said, "we haven't even done anything wrong yet! We weren't even going to do anything until tomorrow!" The prosecutor would like to introduce this statement against both defendants, as evidence of their intent to rob the store the next day. The defendants object.

Against which defendant should the statement be admitted?

(A) Against both defendants.

(B) Against the declarant-defendant only.

(C) Against the non-declarant defendant only.

(D) Against neither defendant.

63. The owner of a ring advertized its sale over the internet. A buyer purchased the ring from the owner, paying by check. The check was dishonored by the bank upon its presentment by the owner. The buyer sold the ring to a third party who purchased the ring in good faith for cash. The owner, unable to recover damages from the buyer due to the buyer's insolvency, learned of the third party's possession of the ring.

The owner sought its return from the third party. When the third party refused, the owner filed an action to recover the ring from the third party. None of the parties was a merchant with respect to the ring. Will the owner prevail?

(A) Yes, because the buyer did not give value for the ring since the check was dishonored by the bank.

(B) Yes, because the buyer was not a merchant to whom the owner had entrusted the ring.

(C) No, because the third party was a good faith purchaser of the ring.

(D) No, because the third party was not a merchant.

64. A prosecutor called a child who witnessed a murder to testify at trial. The child was having trouble remembering all of the events surrounding the murder. Shortly after the child had witnessed the murder, a child psychologist, who helped the child cope with the experience, asked the child to draw a series of pictures depicting what he had seen. To help the child with his testimony, the prosecutor handed the child the pictures. After looking at them, the child was able to recollect the details of the murder scene, and was able to testify to them. The defendant's attorney had previously seen the pictures, and objected to their use.

How should the court rule on the defense's objection?

(A) Sustain it, because the pictures are covered by the psychotherapist-patient privilege.

(B) Sustain it, because the pictures are inadmissible.

(C) Overrule it, because a child witness may be afforded assistance that other witnesses are not.

(D) Overrule it, because the pictures refreshed the witness's recollection of events.

65. A landowner subdivided his land into two parcels, retaining the parcel on which his residence was located and selling the other parcel to a stranger. In the deed, the landowner retained the right to use a path that accessed a river running through the parcel sold to the stranger. The stranger recorded the deed. After the sale, the landowner regularly made use of the path and maintained it as a path.

Several years later, the landowner's daughter, over her father's objections, purchased the parcel from the stranger. Upon the landowner's death shortly thereafter, the parcel retained by the landowner passed by will to his daughter. Within a year, she gave this parcel to her son and sold the other parcel to a third party. The deeds conveying the parcels were recorded but made no reference to the right of access.

After the father's death, no one made use of the path for four years. Recently, the son, remembering hikes to the river with his grandfather, cleared and began using the path again. Upon learning of the son's actions, the third party objected to the son's use of the path.

The son has consulted a lawyer as to his use of the path. Should the lawyer advise the son that he has the right to use the path?

(A) No, because the right of access had been abandoned.

(B) No, because the right of access had been lost through merger.

(C) Yes, because the right of access was an express easement.

(D) Yes, because right of access was an implied easement.

66. A manufacturer of hot water heaters contacted a supplier of plastic resin about using the resin in the manufacturing of a heater. The supplier gave the manufacturer technical advice about how to mold the resin into a hot water tank. The supplier told the manufacturer that, in order to withstand the temperatures specified by the manufacturer, the resin would need to be at least one inch thick. The manufacturer ordered the resin from the supplier. The manufacturer designed and made the tank for its hot water heaters three-quarters of an inch thick using the supplier's resin.

A homeowner purchased a hot water heater made by the manufacturer from a local plumbing supply store. Due solely to the walls of the tank being too thin, the tank melted when used by the homeowner. The homeowner did not suffer physical injury, but experienced substantial property damage as a consequence of the melted tank.

The homeowner initiated a strict products liability action against the plastic supplier for damages suffered as a consequence of the melted hot water tank. Who will prevail?

(A) The homeowner, because the supplier was a commercial seller of the plastic resin.

(B) The homeowner, because the melting of the material provided by the supplier caused the homeowner's harm.

(C) The supplier, because the homeowner did not suffer a physical injury.

(D) The supplier, because the defect in the hot water heater was not attributable to the supplier.

67. A series of burglaries was committed while the inhabitants were away from their homes. A police officer, relying in good faith on a valid search warrant for evidence related to these burglaries, knocked on the door of the residence specified in the warrant but did not identify himself as a police officer. Without waiting for the door to be opened by the inhabitants, the officer pried it open with a crowbar, even though the officer had no specific reason to believe that the evidence would be destroyed or that he personally was in danger. The officer did not find any evidence related to the burglaries, but did find a cache of illegal drugs in plain view.

The applicable statute provides that an officer can break into a house "if, after notice of his authority and purpose, he is refused admittance."

Prior to the trial of the homeowner for possession of the illegal drugs found during the search, the homeowner moved to exclude the drugs as evidence. Should the court grant this motion?

(A) No, because the officer relied in good faith on the search warrant.

(B) No, because the officer had a valid search warrant and the drugs were in plain view.

(C) Yes, because the drugs were not covered by the search warrant.

(D) Yes, because the search was illegal.

68. A manufacturer entered into a contract with a forklift supplier to purchase 10 new forklifts for use in the manufacturer's warehouse. The contract specified that the forklifts were to be delivered within 45 days of the execution of the contract.

The day after entering into the contract, the supplier was told by a reliable source that the manufacturer was in a precarious financial position. That day the supplier, reasonably relying on the information, which was in error, sent a written notice to the manufacturer demanding assurance of the manufacturer's ability to pay.

Thirty-five days after receiving the notice, the manufacturer sent the supplier its most recent financial statements, which adequately demonstrated that the manufacturer was not in a precarious financial position and had the wherewithal to pay for the forklifts, along with a statement of its willingness to receive the shipment of the forklifts. Immediately upon receiving the manufacturer's correspondence the following day, the supplier called the manufacturer's CEO and demanded his personal guarantee of payment for the forklifts before the supplier would deliver the forklifts. When the manufacturer's CEO declined, the supplier refused to deliver the forklifts. The manufacturer then purchased forklifts from another distributor at a higher price.

The manufacturer sued the forklift distributor for breach of contract. Should the manufacturer prevail?

(A) Yes, because the supplier breached the contract by failing to deliver the forklifts.

(B) Yes, because the supplier's information regarding the manufacturer's financial position was in error.

(C) No, because the manufacturer failed to provide adequate assurances in a timely manner.

(D) No, because the manufacturer's CEO refused to guarantee payment of the forklifts.

69. A widower owned a residence in fee simple absolute. He contracted to sell it to a couple. The couple did not record the contract. The contract did not require either party to acquire or maintain casualty insurance on the premises, and neither party did so.

After the parties entered into the contract, the widower continued to occupy the residence. A week before closing, the residence was completely destroyed by the fire caused by a lightning strike.

On whom does the risk of loss fall?

(A) The couple, because they failed to record the contract.

(B) The couple, because of the doctrine of equitable conversion.

(C) The widower, because he, as possessor of the residence, had a duty to insure it.

(D) The widower, because he retained possession of the residence.

70. A 14-year-old girl suffered from pelvic pain, but did not want to go to a gynecologist. Her 19-year-old boyfriend, who reasonably believed that the girl was 16 years old, told her that having sexual intercourse with him would cure the problem. The boyfriend knew that his statement was false. Relying on his statement, the girl gave her consent, and the two had sexual intercourse. Later, the girl learned that intercourse could not and did not cure her problem, and notified the police.

Rape is defined by statute as "sexual intercourse with a person against that person's will or with a person under the age of 14 years old." Rape is a second degree felony unless (i) in the course thereof the actor inflicts serious bodily injury upon anyone, (ii) the victim is under the age of 14, or (iii) the victim is 14 or 15 years old and the actor is at least four years older, in which cases the offense is a first degree felony.

The boyfriend was convicted of first degree rape of the girl. The boyfriend has appealed the conviction, contending that he is not guilty of the crime of rape. Should the appellate court overturn the conviction?

(A) Yes, because the intercourse was not against the girl's will and she was 14 years old.

(B) Yes, because the boyfriend was at least four years older than the girl.

(C) No, because the boyfriend obtained the girl's consent through fraudulent means.

(D) No, because lack of knowledge as to the age of the victim is not a defense.

71. A man and his neighbor were involved in an increasingly serious dispute. One afternoon, the man backed his car out of his driveway, and headed down the street past the neighbor's house. Suddenly, the man heard two "pop" sounds coming from his right. Looking in that direction, the man saw his neighbor standing on his porch, tossing a gun into the bushes. The man drove away as quickly as possible. Once he was a safe distance away, he got out of his car and surveyed the damage. He immediately noticed a bullet hole in the front right fender. Later, he repaired his vehicle, at a substantial cost.

Based on the foregoing facts, which intentional tort claim by the man is most likely to result in the greatest monetary recovery?

(A) Intentional infliction of emotional distress

(B) Conversion

(C) Assault

(D) Trespass to chattels

72. A man played in a recreational ice hockey league that had a well-known reputation for aggressive play. The games often became quite physical, and injuries were common. In one game, the man scored the winning goal as time expired in the game. After the referee had blown his whistle ending play, the man launched into a particularly exuberant celebration. An opposing player, angered by the celebration, but without intending to harm the man, hit him on the forearm with a hockey stick. The man collapsed in pain; tests later revealed that he suffered a severe forearm fracture as a result of the incident.

If the man sues the opposing player for battery, will he prevail?

(A) Yes, because the opposing player's conduct was willful and wanton.

(B) Yes, because the opposing player intentionally used force beyond the man's implied consent.

(C) No, because the man impliedly consented to rough play.

(D) No, because the opposing player did not intend to cause injury.

73. An appropriate representative of a resident in a state mental health facility sued an official of the facility in federal court. The resident, who remained a citizen of another state, sought an injunction to compel the official to comply with state law regarding the use of the least restrictive environment approach for the care of the mentally ill.

The official moved to dismiss the action as unconstitutional under the Eleventh Amendment. Should the court grant the official's motion?

(A) No, because an injunction, not damages was sought as a remedy.

(B) No, because the action was brought against a state official rather than the state.

(C) Yes, because a fundamental right is not involved.

(D) Yes, because the action sought the enforcement of state law rather than federal law.

74. An auto collector hired a restorer to refurbish a classic car she had purchased at an auction. The written restoration agreement was signed by the collector and the restorer, and contained only an identification of the vehicle, an enumerated list of the work that was to be done, and the price for the job. The agreement specified that the car's engine was to be replaced. When the collector was shown the restored car, she was upset that the engine that was in the car when it was purchased had not been rebuilt, since the complete replacement of the car's engine lowered the value of the car as a classic. The collector refused to pay the agreed-upon price for the restoration, and instead filed suit against the restorer for breach of contract.

At trial, the collector seeks to introduce a note in her handwriting that she had shown to the restorer prior to the execution of the agreement that contained the phrase "rebuild engine." Is this note admissible?

(A) Yes, because the agreement was only partially integrated.

(B) Yes, because the parol evidence rule only applies to oral communications.

(C) No, because of the parol evidence rule.

(D) No, because the Uniform Commercial Code does not apply this transaction.

75. In order to finance the purchase of a property, the buyer received a loan and in return gave the lender a promissory note secured by a mortgage on the property. Subsequently, the buyer divided the property into two parcels, retaining one of the parcels and selling the other to a friend. The friend took the parcel subject to the mortgage. The buyer and the friend agreed that each will be liable for one-half of the outstanding mortgage. One year later the buyer disappeared. Since the buyer is no longer paying one-half of the mortgage obligation, the lender threatens to foreclose on the property. The friend pays off the outstanding balance of the loan.

The applicable jurisdiction recognizes the lien theory of mortgages.

Can the friend bring a foreclosure action against the buyer's parcel?

(A) Yes, because the friend is subrogated to the lender's rights in the parcel.

(B) Yes, because the friend obtained ownership rights in his own parcel by purchase.

(C) No, because the friend does not have an ownership interest in the parcel since the jurisdiction adheres to the lien theory of mortgages.

(D) No, because the friend was not under a legal duty to pay the buyer's portion of the mortgage.

76. A car was parked in front of a man's house for a week without being moved. The man honestly but unreasonably believed that the car had been abandoned. He found a spare key attached to the underside of the car and, using that key, drove the car into his driveway, intending to make it his own. Several days later, the car's owner returned. Seeing his car in the man's driveway, the owner notified the police. The man was charged with larceny. Taking abandoned property is not a crime under the laws of the jurisdiction.

Should the man be convicted of larceny?

(A) No, because taking abandoned property is not a crime.

(B) No, because the man's mistake was honestly made.

(C) Yes, because an honest mistake of law does not negate the man's *mens rea*.

(D) Yes, because the man's mistake was unreasonable.

77. In a civil trial regarding a store owner's negligence in clearing ice from his front walkway, the defendant store owner testified on direct examination that he had cleared the ice from his front walkway on the morning of the plaintiff's injury. On cross-examination, the plaintiff's attorney asked the store owner if he was sure that he cleared all of the ice off of the walkway, without missing any, and the defendant replied that he had. The plaintiff's attorney then sought permission to ask the defendant about two prior incidents in the last three winters where the defendant's customers claim to have fallen on patches of ice that the defendant failed to clear. The defendant's attorney objected to the introduction of this evidence.

Should the court allow the plaintiff's attorney to question the defendant about the prior incidents?

(A) Yes, because the two prior incidents serve as evidence that the defendant has a habit of failing to clear ice from his front walkway.

(B) Yes, because the two prior incidents bear on the defendant's credibility, since he claims to have cleared all the ice in this case.

(C) No, because failing to clear ice on the two prior incidents does not bear on the defendant's credibility and does not contradict his testimony in this case.

(D) No, because there is no evidence here as to the outcome of the prior claims.

78. A defendant was convicted of murder. During the trial, his lawyer made a strategic judgment call to refrain from introducing certain mitigating evidence. The defendant was convicted and sentenced to a long prison term. The lawyer's decision with respect to that evidence and her overall performance did not fall below an objective standard of competence for attorneys in a similar situation.

After the trial, the defendant's lawyer apologized to the defendant for not introducing the evidence, saying that in hindsight she was wrong not to have done so. The defendant now seeks to reverse his conviction on the grounds that he received ineffective assistance of counsel.

Will the defendant succeed?

(A) No, because decisions regarding trial strategy rest solely with the lawyer.

(B) No, because the defendant's lawyer's performance met the objective standard of care.

(C) Yes, because the lawyer's performance fell below the lawyer's subjective standard, and the defendant was actually prejudiced by the result.

(D) Yes, because the defendant was actually prejudiced by the result of his lawyer's performance.

79. To preserve the environment and enhance the quality of life, a city located on an ocean had restrictive property regulations. The city limited non-residential buildings to its major thoroughfare. In residential areas, single-family dwellings were strongly preferred. People can apply for "special use" permits in residential areas, but they are denied 99% of the time.

An organization that operated day-care centers for mentally retarded children applied for a special-use permit to build and operate, in a residential area, a 7,000 square foot day care center for 15 children. The city denied the application, based primarily upon the increased traffic and noise the center would generate, which would disturb the tranquil quality of life and the environment of the residential neighborhood. The city routinely denied special-use permits to a variety of other groups on similar grounds.

On behalf of the retarded children, the organization brought an action against the city based on a constitutional claim in an appropriate federal court. Will this organization prevail?

(A) Yes, because the city's stated reasons for denying the permit do not constitute a compelling interest sufficient to justify an action that discriminated against the mentally retarded.

(B) Yes, because the city's reasons for denying the permit do not constitute an important government interest sufficient to justify an action that discriminated against the mentally retarded.

(C) No, because the city has a compelling interest in preserving the environment and enhancing the quality of life by protecting the tranquility of residential neighborhoods.

(D) No, because the mentally retarded are not members of a suspect classification, and the city had a rational basis for denying the special-use permit.

80. A telephone company was removing wooden utility poles on a residential street and replacing them with new steel poles. The old poles were approximately 25 feet tall, and weighed several tons each. One morning, telephone company employees were removing an old pole. As a 10-year-old boy walked past the construction site, the old utility pole fell and crushed him to death. When the news was conveyed to the boy's mother, who was at work several miles away, she immediately fainted. For the next 48 hours, the mother was unable to function due to shock over the event. In the following months, the mother had difficulty sleeping due to nightmares as a result of the incident.

The mother sued the telephone company for negligent infliction of emotional distress stemming from her son's death. She produced evidence at trial conclusively establishing that the telephone company was negligent in allowing the old utility pole to fall. The applicable jurisdiction has abandoned the zone of danger requirement for this type of action. Which party is likely to prevail?

(A) The mother, because she was closely related to the boy.

(B) The mother, because she suffered severe emotional distress.

(C) The telephone company, because the mother was not present at the scene of the accident.

(D) The telephone company, because its actions were not extreme and outrageous.

81. During a personal injury trial, a plaintiff calls an eyewitness to testify. On cross-examination, the defense attorney asked the witness about a previous conviction. Seven years ago, when the witness was 16 years old, she was convicted of check fraud. The plaintiff objects to the introduction of this conviction, but the defense attorney maintains that he can introduce it for impeachment purposes.

Is evidence of the witness's conviction admissible?

(A) No, because the witness is testifying in a civil trial.

(B) No, because the conviction constitutes a prior bad act.

(C) Yes, because it was a conviction of a crime involving fraud or deceit.

(D) Yes, because the conviction is less than 10 years old.

82. A homeowner hired a contractor to finish her basement. They agreed on a price of $20,000 for the job. During the final stages of the remodeling, the contractor discovered that there was mold in the basement, the existence of which was unknown to either party. The contractor refused to complete the job unless the homeowner paid an additional $2,000 to the contractor for removal of the mold. The homeowner reluctantly agreed, and the contractor is finished the basement in accord with the modified contract. The homeowner paid the contractor $20,000.

In a breach of contract action to recover the $2,000, will the contractor prevail?

(A) No, because a contractual modification is not enforceable without consideration.

(B) No, because the unforeseen circumstances did not rise to the level of impracticability.

(C) Yes, because the homeowner agreed to the price increase.

(D) Yes, because the modification was based on a mutual mistake.

83. At a fundraising dinner for a homeless shelter, a wealthy philanthropist told the shelter's director that he would give $50,000 to the shelter at the end of the year. The shelter did not provide consideration for the philanthropist's promise and there is no evidence that the shelter relied on the philanthropist's promise. After a falling out with the director, the philanthropist refused to make the promised payment to the shelter.

In an action for breach of contract to recover the $50,000, will the shelter be successful?

(A) No, because a promise to make a gift is unenforceable without consideration.

(B) No, because an oral promise to make a gift does not create an enforceable contract.

(C) Yes, because the philanthropist's promise is enforceable as a charity subscription.

(D) Yes, because a charity need not establish that it has relied on philanthropist's promise in order to enforce that promise.

84. In a particular state in the United States, a mortgagee routinely required the mortgagor to convey title to the secured land to the mortgagee via a deed absolute; the mortgagee would reconvey title only upon complete repayment of the loan. The deed absolute transaction also allowed the mortgagee to dispose of the land immediately upon the mortgagor's default, thereby avoiding the cost and delay of foreclosure proceedings.

A new election in this state brought into power a majority of pro-consumer legislators. The legislature enacted a statute that immediately outlawed use of the deed absolute and declared that all such deeds would be considered mere liens against the secured property. The statute applied not only to future loans, but also to loans already in existence—even though many of those outstanding loans never would have been made without the extra security provided by the deed absolute.

Mortgagees who had loaned money secured through deeds absolute challenged the constitutionality of the new statute. What is their best argument?

(A) As applied to loans made after the statute was enacted, the law substantially and unreasonably impairs the mortgagees' contract rights in violation of the Contracts Clause.

(B) As applied to loans outstanding at the time the statute was enacted, the law substantially and unreasonably impairs the mortgagees' contract rights in violation of the Contracts Clause.

(C) The statute violates the freedom of contract protected by the Fourteenth Amendment Due Process Clause.

(D) The statute violates the Fourteenth Amendment's Equal Protection Clause by discriminating against mortgagees.

85. The owner of a small commercial building contracted to sell the building and the lot on which it is located to a buyer for five million dollars. The owner constructed the building after purchasing the lot from a widow. The widow had taken title to the lot under the terms of her husband's will that devised the lot to her in fee simple absolute. Prior to selling the lot, the widow had executed a will in which the lot was devised to her nephews. Neither of the nephews were parties to the contract to sell the lot to the owner nor did they execute a deed to the owner.

The contract between the buyer and the owner does not contain a warranty of marketable title. The building is subject to a mortgage with an outstanding balance of three million dollars. The buyer will not be assuming or taking the property subject to that mortgage.

If the buyer no longer wishes to purchase the property, can the buyer rescind the contract?

(A) Yes, because the property is subject to a mortgage.

(B) Yes, because the widow's nephews did not join in the contract to sell the property to the owner.

(C) No, because a marketable title clause is only implied in a residential land sale contract.

(D) No, because title to the property is marketable.

86. An avid runner was diagnosed with a serious heart condition. The runner's doctor advised her to avoid strenuous physical activity, including running, as such activity would create a substantial risk of cardiac arrest. The runner refrained from such activity for a month, but in that time she gained 15 pounds and felt very unhealthy. Deciding that the health benefits of running outweighed the risk involved, one morning she set out on her normal running path—the shoulder of a flat rural road. Five miles into the run, the runner suffered a heart attack, collapsed, and lapsed into a coma.

Two minutes later, the runner's feet and legs—which were partially sticking out into the travel lane—were run over by a car. The driver of the car, who had been traveling at a reasonable speed, was aware of the runner but was unable to avoid her due to a locking up of the car's brakes that the driver had negligently failed to have repaired.

The runner survived, but suffered serious injuries to both of her legs. The runner sued the driver for those injuries in a jurisdiction that applies traditional contributory negligence rules. Is the runner likely to prevail?

(A) No, because the runner was contributorily negligent.

(B) No, because the driver was aware of the runner's predicament before the accident occurred.

(C) Yes, because of the runner's helpless peril at the time of the accident.

(D) Yes, because the driver was negligent in driving the car with brakes in need of repair.

87. A mother made a gift of unimproved real property to her son. The son promptly and properly recorded the deed, but did not inspect the property nor otherwise make use of it by building structures or making other improvements. The son, however, did pay the real estate taxes imposed on the property.

Subsequently, the mother, forgetting about her conveyance of the property, sold it at its fair market value to a buyer. The buyer promptly and properly recorded the deed. The buyer, who was not aware of the son's ownership of the property, began to construct a house on the property. Upon learning about the buyer's construction activities, the son, unaware of his mother's transaction with the buyer, brought an appropriate legal action to halt the buyer's activities and declare title to the property.

Will the buyer be successful in defending against the son's lawsuit?

(A) Yes, because the recording act does not protect a donee of real property.

(B) Yes, because the son did not make productive use of the real property.

(C) No, because the son recorded his deed before his mother made the subsequent conveyance to the buyer.

(D) No, because the son paid the real estate taxes on the property.

88. A father and son are charged with burglary. Prior to the trial, the prosecutor approaches the son and asks him if he would be willing to testify against his father in exchange for a reduced sentence. After discussing the son's role in the burglary and some negotiation, the prosecutor and the son's defense attorney reach a settlement agreement. The son pleads guilty, and is called to testify against his father. On cross-examination of the son, the father's attorney brings up the fact that the son was also originally charged with the burglary, and asks whether it is true that he received a lesser sentence for agreeing to testify against his father. The prosecutor objected to this line of questioning.

How should the court rule on the prosecutor's objection?

(A) The objection should be sustained, because the response calls for hearsay.

(B) The objection should be sustained, because it is against public policy to introduce evidence of a plea agreement.

(C) The objection should be overruled, because the question concerns bias.

(D) The objection should be overruled, because the son's own sentence is irrelevant to the guilt of the father.

89. A state maintained its departments, including its fish and game department, through tax revenues collected primarily from its residents. The department required all recreational deer hunters (i.e., those who hunt purely for sport) to obtain a deer hunting license. The license fee was $25 a year for state residents and $150 a year for out-of-state residents. An out-of-state resident wanted to go deer hunting for sport. He objected to paying a license fee that was six times the fee paid by in-state residents. He sued in an appropriate federal court.

Will the court hold that the licensing fee scheme for recreational deer hunting is unconstitutional?

(A) Yes, because the scheme violates the Equal Protection Clause by discriminating against out-of-state hunters.

(B) Yes, because the scheme violates Article IV's Privileges and Immunities Clause by failing to accord out-of-state residents the same rights as state residents.

(C) No, because the scheme is constitutionally valid under the Dormant Commerce Clause because the subject of the fees, deer hunting, is a recreational activity, not a commercial one.

(D) No, because the scheme is constitutionally valid under Article IV's Privileges and Immunities Clause because recreational deer hunting is not a fundamental right, and a state may charge its residents a lower fee because their taxes support the Fish & Game Department.

90. The owner of a lakefront home in a retirement community that greatly restricts access by nonresidents was aware that her dock needed repair, but was unable to afford the considerable expense to do so. The owner placed a large heavy chair at the entrance to the dock with a sign that read, "Please do not enter. Dock in need of repair."

Two children, a six-year boy and a ten-year old girl, entered the property without permission from, or knowledge of the owner. The children quickly discovered the dock. The girl read the sign out loud to the boy and advised him, "You shouldn't go out on the dock." The boy, responding "But it's not dangerous," climbed over the chair and walked out onto the dock. As the boy ran to the end of the dock, a rotten plank on which the boy stepped gave way, and he fell into the lake and drowned.

As permitted by the applicable jurisdiction, the boy's parents sued the owner in a wrongful death action alleging that her negligence with respect to the dock caused the boy's death. At trial, the boy's parents argued that the dock constituted an attractive nuisance.

Which of the following may protect the owner from liability that otherwise would arise under this doctrine?

(A) The owner lives in retirement community that greatly restricts access by nonresidents.

(B) The boy was not attracted to property by the presence of the dock.

(C) The boy was a trespasser.

(D) The boy was aware of the owner's warning.

91. A uniformed police officer learned about a possible burglary of a home, and went to investigate. When the officer arrived, she attempted to get into the home through the front door, but found it locked. Going to the back of the home, the officer found a door slightly open. Drawing her gun, she entered the home and announced that she was a police officer. The homeowner, honestly but unreasonably fearing that the officer was the person who had broken into the home earlier, shot and killed the officer.

The homeowner was charged with murder of the police officer. The jurisdiction recognizes "imperfect" self-defense. Can the homeowner be convicted of this crime?

(A) Yes, because homeowner killed the police officer.

(B) Yes, because the homeowner's use of deadly force was unreasonable.

(C) No, because the homeowner had no duty to retreat before using deadly force.

(D) No, because the homeowner honestly believed that the police officer threatened him with death or serious bodily injury.

92. A defendant in a federal securities case introduced the testimony of a witness who had claimed on direct examination that the defendant had no prior knowledge of a change within a corporation's executive board; the defendant's knowledge of this fact is a central issue in the case. The prosecutor did not cross-examine the witness. On rebuttal, the prosecutor called a witness who claimed to have been with both the defendant's witness and the defendant when the defendant learned of the change in question, and had heard the defendant's witness say, on more than one occasion, that the defendant knew of the change. Further, the prosecutor introduced a properly authenticated email that the defendant's witness had sent to the witness containing the same information. The defendant's attorney objects that the testimony of the prosecutor's witness and the email are inadmissible.

Should the court admit the testimony of the prosecutor's witness and the email?

(A) Yes, because the defendant's witness may be properly impeached with them.

(B) Yes as to the testimony, but no as to the email, because the prosecutor did not present the email to the defendant's witness on her cross-examination of him.

(C) No, because the defendant's witness was not given an opportunity to explain the evidence before introduction of the prosecutor's witness.

(D) No, because the testimony and email are immaterial.

93. A retail store that specializes in glass objects entered into a written contract to purchase 100 hand-blown glass ornaments from an artisan. Because of the artisan's popularity, the store paid in full for the ornaments at the time that the contract was executed. The contract specified that the store would pick up the ornaments after notification that they were ready. The contract contained no other terms related to delivery of the ornaments and did not allocate the risk of loss. When the ornaments were ready, the artisan notified the store. The parties made arrangements for the store to pick up the packaged ornaments no later than 2:00 pm the next day. The employee assigned by the store to make the pickup did not arrive until 6:00 pm. In the late afternoon just before the store employee arrived, a short but intense storm caused a large, healthy tree on the artisan's property to fall over and destroy all the ornaments. Neither party had insured the ornaments against such a loss.

Who bears the risk of the lost with respect to the ornaments?

(A) The store, because the artisan had tendered delivery of the ornaments to the store prior to the loss.

(B) The store, because the artisan's insurance did not cover the loss.

(C) The artisan, because the store had not taken possession of the ornaments.

(D) The artisan, because the store was a merchant.

94. After a man suffered a major epileptic seizure, he reported the seizure to his state's Motor Vehicle Administration, in compliance with the following statute:

> Drivers' license holders diagnosed with epilepsy shall be required to report their epilepsy and seizures to the State Motor Vehicle Administration (SMVA). The SMVA shall refer their license applications to the Medical Advisory Board for review. The Board may, in its discretion, suspend or revoke a person's driver's license or refuse to renew a license, for longer than 90 days if the person's driving may be adversely affected by a seizure.

Pursuant to its authority, the Medical Advisory Board revoked the man's driver's license. Nonetheless, the man kept driving his car to work, and one morning, he hit a pedestrian with his car. The pedestrian was crossing the street in a crosswalk.

There is no evidence that the man was suffering an epileptic seizure at the time of the incident. The pedestrian sued the man, and during trial, argued that the man's actions constituted negligence *per se*. Will the pedestrian's argument be successful?

(A) No, because the man was not suffering a seizure at the time of the accident.

(B) No, because the harm suffered by the pedestrian was not of the type contemplated by the statute.

(C) Yes, because the man was driving in violation of the Medical Advisory Board's order.

(D) Yes, because the pedestrian is in the class of persons intended to be protected by the statute.

95. In a murder trial, the prosecutor plans to call an eyewitness to the stand to testify that he saw the defendant kill the victim. However, the witness recently suffered a severe head injury that seriously affected his memory. The witness can no longer remember witnessing the murder. Prior to the witness's injury, he testified to what he saw before the grand jury. The prosecutor would like to introduce the witness's grand jury testimony as substantive evidence that the defendant committed the murder. The defendant objects to the introduction of the evidence.

Should the court admit the witness's grand jury testimony into evidence?

(A) Yes, because the witness is unavailable to testify.

(B) Yes, if used to refresh the witness's recollection.

(C) No, because the witness does not meet the "unavailability" standard.

(D) No, because the former testimony exception does not apply to these facts.

96. In the Labor Management Relations Act, Congress expressly authorized the President to seize plants to avert a labor shutdown if the President determined that a shutdown would threaten national security.

In response to a threatened national strike by America's steel workers, the President ordered the government to seize and operate steel mills to ensure steel production that the President deemed vital to the War on Terrorism and hence to national security. Subsequent to the order, Congress did not explicitly approve or disapprove of the President's action.

One of the companies affected by the President's order filed a suit in an appropriate federal court claiming that the order violated the Constitution. What is the most likely ruling?

(A) Congress unconstitutionally delegated its legislative power to the President because the statutory standard—that a shutdown would "threaten national security"—does not provide a specific, intelligible standard.

(B) The President lacked power as Commander-in-Chief to take this action because it involved domestic affairs, not military decisions in the foreign theater of war.

(C) The President had Article II power to take this action.

(D) The President's action would be lawful only if Congress explicitly approved it.

97. The owner of a rural, wooded property devised one-half of the property to his daughter and the other half to his son. At the time of the devise, there was a cabin on the daughter's property, which continues to be maintained and used by her. A private road that ran through the property of a third party and that was built with the permission of the third party connected the daughter's property to the only public road in the area. Subsequently, the son built a cabin on his own property and constructed another road across the property of the third party with the third party's permission in order to connect with the public road.

Several years later, the third party dammed a stream on its property, creating a large lake. The lake flooded the land in such a way that the daughter's road is now underwater, but the son's road is unaffected. Due to the size and location of the lake, it would not be possible for the daughter to build another road across the third party's property. Having no other way to reach the public road, the daughter sought permission from the son to build a road on the son's property to link up with his road that runs through the third party's property to the public road, but the son refused.

In an action by the daughter to compel the son to permit her access across his land to the public road, who will prevail?

(A) The daughter, because access across the son's property is strictly necessary.

(B) The daughter, because she sought permission from the son before filing her court action.

(C) The son, because the son never owned the entire wooded property.

(D) The son, because there has been no prior use of his property in the manner that the daughter proposes.

98. A recidivism statute calls for a mandatory life sentence for a defendant who is convicted of three felonies. The defendant was convicted of felony theft three separate times and was sentenced to life in prison after his conviction for the third theft. In each case, the defendant stole the items from stores when nobody was watching. He did not use any weapons, nor was he violent. The defendant challenges the sentence on constitutional grounds.

Will the defendant succeed?

(A) Yes, because the sentence violates the Eighth Amendment prohibition on cruel and unusual punishment because the defendant's crimes were non-violent.

(B) Yes, because the sentence violates the Double Jeopardy Clause.

(C) No, because the Eighth Amendment prohibition on cruel and unusual punishment only applies to degrading or painful sentences involving the use of force.

(D) No, because the recidivism statute is constitutional even when applied to non-violent offenders.

99. A homeowner hired a contractor to paint the homeowner's residence. The written contract stated that it was the parties' final and complete agreement and that all prior agreements between the parties merged into the written document. Prior to executing the contract, the contractor noted debris in the gutters of the residence. The contractor stated that to prevent such debris from adversely affecting the painting, the gutters should be cleaned. The contractor offered to do this prior to undertaking the painting for $600. The homeowner orally agreed. The homeowner and the contractor then signed the written contract which did not mention cleaning the gutters. The contractor performed all of the work called for in the written contract as well as cleaning the gutters. The homeowner paid the amount specified in the written contract, but refused to pay an additional $600 for the cleaning of the gutters.

In a breach of contract action by the contractor against the homeowner to recover the $600 payment, which of the following is the strongest argument that the homeowner can make to prevent the contractor from recovering?

(A) The agreement regarding cleaning the gutters only serves to supplement the terms of the written contract.

(B) Since the amount sought for cleaning the gutters was more than $500, it can only be evidenced by a writing.

(C) The contract was a complete integration of the agreement between the contractor and the homeowner.

(D) The parol evidence rule bars evidence about an oral agreement between the parties to a written contract.

100. The fee simple owner of land devised it to a private educational institution "for so long as the land herein conveyed is used for educational purposes; if the land is not so used, then to my daughter and her heirs." At the time of the owner's death, the owner's spouse was deceased and the owner's only two children, a son and a daughter, were alive. The owner devised all of his other real property interests to his son. The daughter died shortly after her father, devising her real property's interests to her only child, who was alive at the time of her death.

Immediately after the owner's death, the institution constructed a classroom building on the land and has held classes in the building each year thereafter.

Thirty years after the owner's death, the educational institution seeks to sell the land to a developer who intends to construct single family homes on the land. Both the son and daughter's child, who are the owner's only living heirs, are alive.

The applicable jurisdiction has adopted the following statute: "A nonvested property interest is invalid unless when the interest is created, it is certain to vest or terminate no later than 21 years after the death of an individual then alive, or the interest either vests or terminates within 90 years after its creation."

The applicable jurisdiction does not impose time limitations on the exercise of interests that follow a defeasible fee property interest.

In order to convey marketable title to the developer, who must the institution convince to agree to the transfer?

(A) No one, because the institution owns the land in fee simple.

(B) The daughter's child, because she holds an executory interest in the land.

(C) The son, because he holds a possibility of reverter in the land.

(D) The son and the daughter's children, because they are the owner's living heirs.

STOP.

IF YOU FINISH BEFORE TIME IS CALLED, CHECK YOUR WORK ON THIS TEST.

PM Session

Time—3 hours

Directions: Each of the questions or incomplete statements below is followed by four suggested answers or completions. You are to choose the best of the stated alternatives. Answer all questions according to the generally accepted view, except where otherwise noted.

For the purposes of this test, you are to assume that Articles 1 and 2 of the Uniform Commercial Code have been adopted. You are also to assume relevant application of Article 9 of the UCC concerning fixtures. The Federal Rules of Evidence are deemed to control. The terms "Constitution," "constitutional," and "unconstitutional" refer to the federal Constitution unless indicated to the contrary. You are to assume that there is no applicable statute unless otherwise specified; however, survival actions and claims for wrongful death should be assumed to be available where applicable. You should assume that joint and several liability, with pure comparative negligence, is the relevant rule unless otherwise indicated.

101. At trial, a criminal defense attorney seeks to introduce evidence that his client told several people that he believed he was the President of the United States, in an effort to prove that the defendant suffers from a mental defect. The prosecutor contends that the evidence is inadmissible.

Is evidence of the defendant's statement admissible?

(A) No, because the statement constitutes hearsay.

(B) No, because the statement does not meet the requirements of the "state of mind" exception to the hearsay rule.

(C) Yes, because the statement is being offered as circumstantial evidence of the defendant's state of mind.

(D) Yes, because the statement is being introduced by a defense attorney in a criminal trial.

102. An indigent defendant was indicted for driving under the influence of alcohol, a misdemeanor. Although a lawyer was appointed to represent the defendant, the lawyer suffered a fatal heart attack on his way to the courthouse on the day scheduled for the trial. In discussing the absence of the defendant's lawyer with the defendant, the trial judge learned from the defendant that he intended to plead guilty. The judge indicated that, in exchange for the defendant's guilty plea, the defendant would not serve time in prison. The defendant agreed and was sentenced to two months in prison, with the sentence suspended.

The defendant appealed his conviction, contending that he was denied his Sixth Amendment right to counsel at trial.

Should the judge reverse the defendant's conviction?

(A) No, because the defendant was convicted of a misdemeanor.

(B) No, because the defendant's prison sentence was suspended.

(C) Yes, because the defendant was convicted of a crime for which a sentence of incarceration was imposed.

(D) Yes, because the defendant was convicted of a crime that was punishable by imprisonment.

103. An auto dealership sold a limited-production luxury vehicle as part of its business. It typically sold very few of the vehicles per year, but continued the business because it earned $25,000 in profit on each sale. The vehicles sold at retail for $150,000. A car buyer entered into a contact with the dealership to purchase one of these vehicles with the color scheme and options she desired, which the dealership ordered from the manufacturer. She signed a written order form and put down a $50,000 deposit on the vehicle. The form specified that, in the event that the buyer failed to purchase the vehicle, the deposit was non-refundable, representing liquidated damages that did not constitute a penalty.

Later, the car buyer found a better price on an identical vehicle at another dealership, and purchased that vehicle. She demanded the return of her deposit, but the dealership refused. The dealership had difficulty selling the car, and eventually had to sell it at the discounted price of $100,000.

The car buyer filed a lawsuit seeking to void the non-refundable deposit provision of the order form and seeking the return of her deposit. Is she likely to prevail?

(A) Yes, because the amount of the deposit was not reasonable in relation to the damages that could have been anticipated at the time the order form was signed.

(B) Yes, because the vehicle was not a unique good.

(C) No, because the woman signed the order form, which clearly stipulated that the deposit was not to be interpreted as a penalty.

(D) No, because the deposit is reasonable in relation to the actual damages the dealership suffered.

104. A corporation entered into an agreement with an accountant to audit the corporation's books pending a sale of all of the company's assets. The agreement specified that the accountant would perform "all services relating to the sale of assets of the corporation." The agreement was fully integrated, but did not contain a merger clause. The day after the agreement was executed, the corporation and the accountant amended the agreement to include the evaluation of prospective buyers, for $2,000 per buyer. The accountant evaluated two corporations who were potential buyers. The corporation refused to pay the additional $4,000.

In a breach of contract action, will evidence of the evaluation agreement be excluded?

(A) No, because the agreement regarding the evaluation of prospective buyers was entered into after the execution of the writing.

(B) No, because the amendment was supported by new consideration.

(C) Yes, because the agreement was fully integrated.

(D) Yes, because the second agreement dealt with the same subject matter as the first agreement.

105. The president of the United States received reliable information from federal law enforcement authorities that (1) a known terrorist group was planning a terrorist attack on America which would occur within the next two weeks, (2) the terrorists, all of whom were fluent in a particular dialect, were already in America, and (3) the terrorist group's leaders would provide to these terrorists certain details regarding the attack through coded messages contained in a newspaper published in the particular dialect in the United States. There were four such newspapers—in New York, Washington, Los Angeles, and Detroit. The president immediately ordered all four newspapers to shut down for two weeks and notified the newspapers that they were to be fully compensated for any losses they incurred because of the closure order. The newspapers immediately challenged the order as unconstitutional. Which of the following is the president's best argument is that the order should be upheld?

(A) It is not a prior restraint on speech or the press.

(B) The federal government can always suppress subversive speech as long as it pays just compensation to the person whose expression has been suppressed.

(C) The words that would be published constitute a clear and present danger to national security.

(D) Where national security is at issue, the burden is on the newspapers to establish the right to publish the information.

106. In order to purchase undeveloped land, the buyer sought a 10-year loan from a third-party lender. The buyer executed a promissory note and mortgage on the property. The lender promptly and properly recorded the mortgage. As part of the transaction, the lender also required the buyer to execute a quitclaim deed to the property to the lender, which the buyer was to give to an independent escrow agent. Under the terms of the escrow arrangement, the agent was to record the quitclaim deed to the lender upon notification that the buyer had defaulted on the loan. The escrow agreement also provided that, upon recording, the buyer's rights in the property would cease.

The buyer made installment payments on the loan, as required by its terms, for two years, but subsequently was unable to make the required loan payments. The lender notified the escrow agent of the buyer's default and the escrow agent recorded the quitclaim deed. The lender, choosing not to foreclose on the mortgage, has advertized the property for sale at an amount significantly higher than the outstanding balance in the mortgage.

Shortly thereafter, the buyer, receiving a sizeable inheritance, offered to pay the lender the full amount of the outstanding mortgage debt, which was more than 85% of the original mortgage loan. The lender refused to accept the buyer's payment. The buyer has filed an action to compel the lender to accept the payment, release the mortgage, and to void the quitclaim deed.

The applicable jurisdiction has the following statute: "No conveyance or mortgage of real property shall be good against subsequent purchasers for value and *without notice* unless the same be recorded according to law."

Who should prevail?

(A) Buyer, because the lender had notice of the previously recorded mortgage.

(B) Buyer, because the escrow arrangement has clogged the buyer's equity of redemption.

(C) Lender, because, as owner of the property pursuant to the quitclaim deed, the lender is free to sell the property.

(D) Lender, because the buyer had not paid at least half of the original mortgage loan.

107. A man, shopping in a department store, found a suit that he liked but could not afford. He noticed that the store had a system for identifying sale merchandise: all merchandise with a sticky red label on the tag was 50% off the original price. The man then went to an office supply store and purchased a set of identical labels. He returned to the department store with one of the labels, and placed the label on the suit's price tag. The man then took the suit to the register, paid the reduced price for the suit, and took the suit home.

Of which one of the following crimes should the man be convicted?

(A) Forgery

(B) Embezzlement

(C) Larceny by trick

(D) False pretenses

108. In December, a contractor was hired by a power utility company to perform repair work on a large transformer. The contractor performed the work negligently, and severely damaged one of the conducting coils in the transformer. The damage resulted in a two-day power outage in a town with a large industrial park. An electronics manufacturer was a tenant in the industrial park, and the power outage crippled its ability to meet the strong demand for its products during the critical holiday buying season. While none of the electronic manufacturer's machines were damaged, it can prove with certainty that the power outage directly caused it to lose $750,000 in business.

The electronics manufacturer sued the power utility company and the contractor for negligently causing its sales losses. If, at the end of the plaintiff's case, both defendants move for summary judgment, and all the foregoing facts are undisputed, how should the court rule on the motions?

(A) Deny both motions, because both parties were substantial factors in the electronics manufacturer's loss.

(B) Deny both motions, because the burden of proof has shifted to both defendants to exonerate themselves.

(C) Grant the motion as to the contractor, but deny the motion as to the power utility company, because liability is assigned to the principal under the *respondeat superior* doctrine.

(D) Grant both motions, because the electronics manufacturer suffered no tangible injury to its equipment or employees.

109. A federal statute provides that "all persons within the United States shall have the same right in every state to make and enforce contracts as is enjoyed by white persons." The Supreme Court interpreted this statute as applying to all contracts, including private contracts.

A black citizen of a state in the United States claims that an appliance store in her state violated this statute by refusing to enter into a sales contract with her because of her race. The appliance store defended on the ground that the statute is unconstitutional.

A federal court would be most likely to uphold this statute by relying upon which provision of the Constitution?

(A) The Thirteenth Amendment

(B) The Contracts Clause

(C) The General Welfare Clause

(D) The Equal Protection Clause of the Fourteenth Amendment

110. During a criminal trial for a federal racketeering charge, the prosecution would like to call the wife of one of the defendant's co-conspirators to the stand. The wife has knowledge of the defendant's and her husband's criminal activities, having discovered some incriminating paperwork in her husband's office. The wife's husband is on trial for the same charges, though the trials have been severed. The wife is willing to testify against the defendant and her husband in the defendant's trial. The husband is unwilling to waive the marital privilege, and the defendant objects to the wife's testifying.

Should the prosecutor be allowed to put the wife on the stand?

(A) Yes, because the wife will testify in the trial of the defendant, not of her husband.

(B) Yes, because the wife is willing to testify.

(C) No, because the husband refuses to waive the privilege.

(D) No, because the husband and wife are still married.

111. The owner of an undeveloped lot agrees to sell the lot to a buyer. The written agreement sets forth the parties, describes the property in sufficient detail, specifies the price to be paid, and spells out the payment terms. The agreement is signed by the owner. In accord with the agreement, the buyer pays the required down payment to the owner. Subsequently, the buyer constructs a garage on the lot as the first step towards building a three-story residence, but, due to a financial reversal, abandons his construction efforts.

May the seller bring an action to compel the buyer to complete the purchase?

(A) No, because of the Statute of Frauds.

(B) No, because the owner's remedy at law is adequate.

(C) Yes, because of the doctrine of part performance.

(D) Yes, because of the doctrine of detrimental reliance.

112. A fisherman, who lived next to a lake, owned a large sport-utility vehicle equipped with a trailer hitch. He used the vehicle primarily to tow his large fishing boat. One afternoon, a neighbor asked if she could borrow the fisherman's vehicle for a short time in order to tow her boat back from the dock since her car was currently at the repair shop. The fisherman agreed to let the neighbor use the vehicle to tow her boat, but asked her to return the vehicle immediately afterward. The neighbor drove the vehicle to the dock and towed her boat back without incident.

Before returning the vehicle, the neighbor decided to buy a gift for the fisherman as a token of appreciation. While the neighbor was driving the vehicle to the store to buy the gift, she was involved in a serious accident. The neighbor was not seriously hurt, but the vehicle was a total loss.

If the fisherman sues his neighbor for conversion, will he prevail?

(A) Yes, because the neighbor exceeded the scope of her consent.

(B) Yes, because the neighbor's use of the vehicle constituted a frolic rather than a mere detour.

(C) No, because the neighbor was acting for the fisherman's benefit.

(D) No, because the fisherman had consented to the activity, and the damage was accidental.

113. A man carried a handgun for protection, but failed to register it. In the applicable jurisdiction, possession of an unregistered handgun is a felony. The man had little experience with firearms, and negligently carried the gun in a holster designed to fit a different handgun model. While the man was shopping for groceries one day, the gun slipped out of the holster and accidentally discharged when it fell on the floor. The bullet struck a fellow shopper in the chest. The fellow shopper died as a result of the incident.

The crimes below are listed in descending order of seriousness. What is the most serious listed homicide crime for which the man can be convicted?

(A) Felony murder

(B) Voluntary manslaughter

(C) Involuntary manslaughter

(D) No crime

114. Congress enacted the Health Care Act (HCA) "to ensure all Americans' access to health care at a reasonable cost." Congress delegated to an executive agency, the Department of Health & Human Services (HHS), responsibility for promulgating regulations to implement the HCA. The HCA further provided that a joint House/Senate committee can repeal or revise the HHS regulations if the committee determines that they inadequately fulfill the HCA's purpose. Would a court probably hold that the HCA is unconstitutional?

(A) Yes, because it delegates legislative power to an executive agency.

(B) Yes, because it contains a legislative veto provision.

(C) No, because Congress is reasonably trying to vindicate its Article I legislative power by ensuring the accountability of executive agencies that make law.

(D) No, because the joint committee action to repeal or revise an HHS regulation would not constitute the exercise of executive power.

115. A man became intoxicated after drinking at a neighborhood bar for several hours. He left the bar and went to a party at a friend's house, where he struck up a conversation with a woman at the party. After a few minutes, the man grabbed the woman's arm, pulled her into an empty room, and attempted to have intercourse with her. The woman struggled with the man, and, before intercourse occurred, was able to break free and exit the room. The man was arrested and charged with attempted rape. At trial, the man testified that, at the time of the incident, he believed that the woman consented to sexual intercourse with him.

If the jury believes the man's testimony, should he be convicted?

(A) No, because the man's intoxication prevented him from understanding the wrongfulness of his act.

(B) No, because the man believed that the woman consented to intercourse.

(C) Yes, because the man's intoxication was voluntary, and not involuntary.

(D) Yes, because rape is a crime of malice, and intoxication is not a defense to malice crimes.

116. A famous jazz pianist and a nightclub owner executed a contract. The contract called for the pianist to perform five times per week for six months at the nightclub. The contract also prohibited the pianist from giving public performances during the contract period at any other venue located within a specified distance of the nightclub.

Three months into the contract term, the pianist received a more lucrative offer to play a series of shows at a restaurant located within the contractually prohibited area. The pianist accepted the offer. Upon learning about the arrangement between the restaurant and the pianist, the nightclub owner filed a suit seeking an injunction to prevent the pianist from performing at the restaurant. The owner has made no attempt to hire another performer to replace the pianist. The judge determines that the contract restriction on the pianist is reasonable. Is the judge likely to grant the injunction?

(A) No, because the pianist's contractual duties are in the nature of a personal service, and hence enforcement would constitute unconstitutional involuntary servitude.

(B) No, because the nightclub owner has failed to seek a replacement entertainer.

(C) Yes, because the restriction is a valid non-compete clause.

(D) Yes, because an injunction may generally be sought as an alternative to damages in a breach of contract action.

117. A defendant on trial for forging checks took the stand in his own defense. On direct examination, the defendant denied having forged any checks; he stated that before he graduated from college the year before, he worked in his university's academic records office, indicating that he was "a trustworthy person." On cross-examination, the prosecutor asked the defendant if he had falsified records while working in the academic records office. The defendant denied that he had done so. The prosecutor then wanted to call to the stand his former supervisor from the university to testify that she had to investigate the defendant after allegations of misconduct, and that when questioned, he had admitted to her that he had falsified records. The defendant was removed from his position, but no formal charges had been brought against him.

Should the prosecutor be allowed to call the defendant's former supervisor to the stand to testify as to the falsified records?

(A) Yes, in order to impeach the defendant and to present propensity evidence.

(B) Yes, but only to impeach the defendant.

(C) No, because the testimony would contain hearsay.

(D) No, because the testimony would be extrinsic.

118. An automotive enthusiast owned a sports car that was the fastest production car available in the United States. The enthusiast was friendly with a neighbor, who was 25 years old and had a clean driving record. The neighbor wanted to borrow the sports car to drive to a social event and impress some clients. The enthusiast allowed the neighbor to borrow the sports car, but told him very clearly and sternly that he was to drive very carefully, that he was not to exceed the speed limit, and that he was to bring the sports car back as soon as the event concluded.

After the event concluded, the neighbor drove the car around for an additional two hours, often at very high speeds. Finally, he slammed into another car while driving over 100 miles per hour. The driver of the other car survived, but sustained serious injuries in the accident.

The driver of the other car sued the enthusiast in a jurisdiction without a permissive use statute, claiming that the enthusiast negligently entrusted his neighbor with the vehicle. The foregoing facts are undisputed. If the enthusiast files a motion for a directed verdict, which party is likely to prevail?

(A) The enthusiast, because his specific instructions regarding use of the car were ignored.

(B) The enthusiast, because the neighbor had no history of negligent behavior.

(C) The other driver, because the jurisdiction does not have a permissive use statute.

(D) The other driver, because the neighbor's negligent behavior is imputed to the enthusiast.

119. In order to purchase her residence, a homeowner gave a lender a promissory note in exchange for a loan. The note was secured by a mortgage on the residence. Five years later, the homeowner gave a second lender a promissory note in exchange for a loan, in order to add another room to the residence. This note was also secured by a mortgage on the residence. Three years later, the homeowner gave a third lender a promissory note in exchange for a loan in order to construct a deck on the residence. This note was also secured by a mortgage on the residence. Each mortgage was properly recorded promptly after execution.

Recently, the homeowner has failed to make timely payments with regard to the first mortgage. The first lender has declared the homeowner in default and, in accord with the terms of the mortgage, accelerated the obligation. The first lender forecloses on the mortgage. At the foreclosure sale, the third lender purchases the residence.

To which of the following mortgages is the residence now subject?

(A) Only the first mortgage.

(B) Only the second mortgage.

(C) Both the first and the second mortgages.

(D) Neither the first nor the second mortgages.

120. A city fire department required all firefighter applicants to pass a demanding physical fitness test. The test was designed to ensure that firefighters could handle the physical rigors of the job, such as lifting heavy equipment, carrying injured people, and withstanding intense heat. Asian American applicants failed this physical fitness test at twice the rate of white applicants. Moreover, in the city, people of Asian descent were historically the victims of many forms of discrimination.

An Asian American firefighter applicant applied to be a firefighter but was rejected because the applicant failed the physical fitness test. He sued the fire department based on a constitutional claim of discrimination. Will he prevail?

(A) Yes, because the fire department's physical fitness test had a negative disparate effect on Asian American applicants.

(B) Yes, because the unusually high current failure rate of Asian Americans on this test most likely has resulted from past intentional governmental discrimination.

(C) No, because the plaintiff failed to establish that he had any property interest in potential employment with the fire department that has been denied because of the test.

(D) No, because there is no evidence that the fire department used the test to intentionally discriminate against Asian Americans.

121. A patron at a resort ranch took part in a supervised horseback trail ride. Prior to the ride, the patron executed a valid release that enumerated the inherent risks of horseback riding and, by its terms, relieved the resort from liability from any loss, damage or injury to the guest's person or property suffered during the ride attributable to the negligence of the ranch or its employees. The patron was injured by a fall from the horse. The horse reared in response to negligent behavior of another rider who was also a patron at the ranch.

The patron filed suit against the ranch and the other rider for damages resulting from his injuries that totaled $400,000. At trial, it was determined that the ranch was 75% at fault for the patron's injuries due to its selection and training of the horse, and that the other rider was 25% at fault.

The applicable jurisdiction recognizes the validity of such releases and has enacted both a modified comparative negligence statute and a pure several liability statute.

How much can the patron recover from the ranch?

(A) Nothing

(B) $100,000

(C) $300,000

(D) $400,000

122. During a trial for insurance fraud, the prosecution would like to introduce the testimony of an insurance claims processor. The claims processor received an insurance claim that he knew contained a forgery of a doctor's signature, because he was familiar with the doctor's signature and handwriting, having processed many claims from the doctor's office before. The prosecutor wants to call the claims processor at the alleged forger's trial to testify that the signature was forged.

Is the claims processor's testimony admissible?

(A) Yes, because an insurance claims processor is an expert on handwriting by occupation.

(B) Yes, because it is based on the processor's own perception and is helpful to the jury.

(C) No, because the claims processor is not a certified expert on handwriting and cannot give an opinion based on specialized knowledge.

(D) No, because the jury itself must compare the alleged forgery to a genuine signature and assess any differences.

123. A homeowner who sought to sell his home entered into an agreement with a real estate agent to market the home. The agreement specified that the agent was entitled to a commission if the agent procured a buyer who was "ready, willing, and able" to purchase the home in accord with the contract terms.

The agent found a buyer who agreed to pay the seller's asking price for the home and who pre-qualified for a loan to enable to the buyer to finance the purchase. The buyer and seller entered into a contract of sale. Among the provisions in the contract was a home inspection clause, which permitted the buyer to enter the property and conduct an inspection of the home. After conducting the inspection, during which the buyer learned of the antiquated nature of the electrical system that did not satisfy the electrical code for newly constructed homes, the buyer, in accord with the inspection clause, presented the seller with a request to upgrade the electrical wiring. Because of the cost of such an upgrade, the seller refused. Under the terms of the inspection clause, the inability of the buyer and seller to agree resulted in the voiding of the contract.

Is the agent entitled to a commission to be paid by the homeowner?

(A) No, because the contract was subject to a condition precedent that was not satisfied.

(B) No, because the buyer who demanded the seller upgrade the electrical wiring was responsible for the termination of the contract.

(C) Yes, because the buyer entered into a contract to purchase the home.

(D) Yes, because the seller, by refusing to upgrade the wiring for economic reasons, was responsible for the termination of the contract.

124. A concert violinist received an offer by mail to play a concerto with a local symphony orchestra. She checked her schedule, and thinking that she had the date free, mailed a letter to the symphony orchestra accepting the offer. Later that day, when she was checking her calendar about another matter, she realized that she had a rehearsal for another performance on that date. The violinist called the orchestra manager and declined the offer to play the concerto.

In a breach of contract action by the orchestra against the violinist, will the orchestra prevail?

(A) Yes, because the acceptance was sent before the rejection phone call was made.

(B) Yes, because the phone call was not a proper means of rejecting a written offer under the "mirror image" rule.

(C) No, because the agreement constitutes an unenforceable personal service contract.

(D) No, because the "mailbox rule" does not apply to a rejection.

125. A defendant was convicted of bank robbery in federal court. With regard to the same event, the defendant has now been indicted in the state where the bank is located for the crimes of robbery and conspiracy to commit robbery. The defendant moves to dismiss the state prosecution of these offenses on double jeopardy grounds.

Should the defendant's motion be granted?

(A) Yes, as to both offenses.

(B) Yes, as to the robbery offense only.

(C) Yes, as to the conspiracy offense only.

(D) No, as to either offense.

126. On trial for second degree murder, the defendant pled not guilty, asserting that he acted in self-defense.

The statute in the jurisdiction defines second-degree murder as "the intentional killing of another human being with malice and without provocation." The jurisdiction also has a statute stating that "all affirmative defenses are to be proved by the defense, and the burden of persuasion shall be by a preponderance of the evidence."

The judge instructed the jury that the self-defense evidence presented by the defendant should not be considered by the jury for any purpose unless the jury first determined that this evidence satisfied the "preponderance of the evidence" standard. The jury found the defendant guilty of second degree murder.

The defendant appealed his conviction, contending that the state statute and the jury instructions violated his constitutional rights. How should the appellate court rule on this appeal?

(A) Both the statute and jury instructions violate the Due Process Clause of the Fourteenth Amendment.

(B) The statute violates the Due Process Clause of the Fourteenth Amendment, but the jury instructions do not.

(C) The jury instructions violate the Due Process Clause of the Fourteenth Amendment, but the statute does not.

(D) Neither the statute and jury instructions violate the Due Process Clause of the Fourteenth Amendment.

127. Article I, § 4 of the Constitution provides: "The times, places and manner of holding elections for Senators and Representatives shall be prescribed by each state legislature, but Congress may . . . make or alter such regulations." Congress enacted a statute requiring every state to allow voters to register to vote in federal elections either by mail or at a state motor vehicle department. If a state refuses to comply with the statute and issued by the federal government, will the state likely prevail?

(A) Yes, because Congress cannot "commandeer" state legislatures to enact statutes.

(B) Yes, because Congress cannot "commandeer" state executive officials to carry out federal programs.

(C) No, because Article I, § 4 permits Congress to require states to change their laws regarding federal elections.

(D) No, because the statute, which applies to federal elections only, does not interfere with a traditional government function.

128. During a trial for attempted murder, the prosecutor seeks to introduce into evidence the victim's properly-authenticated emergency room report. The report describes the victim's stab wounds and treatment. The report also includes a statement that the victim made to his doctor during a check-up the following day, naming the defendant as his assailant. The prosecutor wants to introduce the record to prove the extent of the victim's injuries, and as evidence that the defendant was responsible for the victim's harm.

Is the victim's emergency room report admissible?

(A) The report is admissible under the business records exception, but the victim's statement within it is not.

(B) The report is admissible as a whole, because it falls under the business records exception.

(C) The report is admissible under the business records exception, and the statement within is admissible as a statement made for the purpose of medical treatment.

(D) Neither the report nor the statement is admissible, because the victim is alive and available to testify.

129. A buyer who was not a merchant entered into a written contract to purchase a new car from a dealer at a cost of $35,000. Since the buyer desired a particular combination of features on the car and the dealer did not have a car with such features in its inventory, the dealer ordered the car from the manufacturer. When the car arrived, the dealer discovered that the manufacturer had increased the dealer's price for the car by five percent. Acting in good faith, the dealer sought to increase the buyer's price of the new car by a similar percentage. Reluctantly, the buyer orally agreed to the price increase, then had a change of heart and refused to complete the purchase. The car dealer eventually sold the car to another customer for $35,000. The dealer sued the buyer to recover damages for breach of contract. Will the dealer be entitled to damages?

(A) No, because the dealer had a preexisting duty to sell the car for the original contract price.

(B) No, because the price increase was not in writing.

(C) Yes, because the dealer sought the price increase in good faith.

(D) Yes, because the car was specially manufactured for the buyer.

130. A buyer purchased a motor home from a private seller. After taking possession of the motor home, the buyer discovered that the bedroom of the motor home was infested with bed bugs, and pest control treatments were unsuccessful in eradicating the problem. The buyer honestly claims that he would not have purchased the motor home had he known of the infestation.

At the time of the sale, the seller knew of the infestation but did not disclose the condition to the buyer. When the buyer commented to the seller at the time of the sale that the buyer assumed that the motor home did not have bed bugs, the seller simply did not respond. The buyer was justified in relying on the seller's silence as an assertion that the mobile home did not contain bed bugs. The seller's actions violated her duty of good faith and fair dealing, but did not constitute fraudulent conduct. What is the best description of the status of the contract between the buyer and the seller?

(A) The contract is voidable by only the buyer.

(B) The contract is voidable by either the buyer or the seller.

(C) The contract is voidable by neither the buyer nor the seller.

(D) The contract is void.

131. The owner of a residence devised it to his wife for her life and remainder to his son. The son, after his father's death, regularly stopped by the residence to look after his mother and the residence. On some of the visits, the son would perform routine maintenance on the property, such as changing the air filter for heating and air conditioning unit. When the mother permitted a companion to occupy the residence with her, the son became estranged from his mother and stopped visiting her.

Recently, a neighbor who had visited the mother called the son. The neighbor indicated that mother was in good health, but that the condition of the premises was deplorable. The son contacted his mother. She asked him to come over, which he did, but denied him access to the premises when he arrived.

Can the son gain entry to the residence to inspect the premises?

(A) No, because the right to possess the premises belongs to the mother.

(B) No, because mother has denied him entry to the residence.

(C) Yes, because he has a license coupled with an interest.

(D) Yes, because the mother, by permitting someone else on the premises, is estopped from denying her son permission to enter the premises.

132. A woman took her car to an unscrupulous auto mechanic's garage for a tune-up. The woman's car had a new and expensive set of tires that the mechanic coveted. The woman left her car at the garage overnight. Later that night, after the woman had left the premises, the mechanic took the tires off the woman's car, put them into a back room of his garage, and replaced the tires with a cheap, old set. That same evening, the woman's friend told her about the mechanic's unscrupulous nature, and his habit of stealing tires. The woman went back to the garage the next morning. Noticing that the tires on her vehicle were different, she demanded that the new, expensive tires be put back on the vehicle. The mechanic complied, and the woman left the premises.

The woman reported the mechanic to the police, and the mechanic is charged with larceny. Based on the foregoing facts, should he be convicted of the crime?

(A) Yes, because the mechanic moved the tires from the car to the back room.

(B) Yes, because the mechanic had a present intent to permanently deprive the woman of the tires.

(C) No, because the car was left with the mechanic by consent.

(D) No, because the tires were returned to the woman before she was permanently deprived of them.

133. A man and his friend attended their 10-year high school reunion party. There, the two struck up a conversation with a woman who had been a classmate. Neither the man nor his friend had seen her since high school. At the end of the reunion party, the three decided to walk to a nearby bar. As they were walking to the bar, the friend suggested a shortcut through an alley. In the alley, the friend grabbed the woman and began making unwanted sexual advances towards her. The man, despite the woman's pleas to help her, continued walking on towards the bar. Once there, the man ordered a beer and watched a sporting event on television, while his friend raped the woman in the alley.

The man was charged as an accomplice to rape. Should he be convicted of the crime?

(A) No, because the man did not commit an *actus res* for which he could be criminally liable.

(B) No, because there was no agreement between the man and his friend to rape the woman.

(C) Yes, because the man's actions aided and abetted the friend in committing of the rape.

(D) Yes, because the man was aware that the woman did not consent to his friend's sexual advances.

134. Based on an advertisement in a local newspaper, a state resident bought a cross-country roundtrip ticket on a national airline for $450. The ad did not mention that airline charged $75 for any changes to a ticket. Because of illness, the state resident had to change her return flight, and airline charged her $75. The state resident refused to pay, citing a state law that required any ad for the sale of tickets for any event or trip to clearly disclose any monetary penalties for changing tickets.

The airline sued the state resident in federal court for the unpaid fee, arguing that the state law is invalid, citing a federal statute prohibiting states from enforcing any law "relating to the rates, routes, or services" of any airline. Will the airline prevail?

(A) Yes, because, under the Freedom of Press Clause of the First Amendment, the content of commercial speech may not be regulated.

(B) Yes, because Congress has occupied the field of airline rates, routes, and service and hence has preempted the state law.

(C) No, because the court will apply the presumption against preemption.

(D) No, because the state law does not conflict with the federal statute.

135. Four men were bow-and-arrow hunting in a thickly wooded area. Each man was wearing brightly-colored apparel to minimize the risk of an accident. However, midway through the day, one hunter was struck in the leg by an arrow. The wounded man collapsed in agony, and eventually required several surgical procedures and months of rehabilitation in order to walk again. None of the other three men admitted responsibility for the accident.

The injured man sued the other three hunters, claiming negligence. The injured man (i.e., the plaintiff) introduced evidence tending to show that no other hunting parties were within a five-mile radius at the time of the incident, but he was unable to show conclusively which of the three defendants fired the arrow that caused his injury.

At the conclusion of the plaintiff's case, one of the defendants filed a motion for summary judgment. How should the court rule on the motion?

(A) Deny the motion, because the defendant had not yet exonerated himself from responsibility.

(B) Deny the motion, because *res ipsa loquitur* applies.

(C) Grant the motion, because the plaintiff has failed to meet his burden of proof.

(D) Grant the motion, because only one of the defendants was a substantial factor in plaintiff's injury.

136. A defendant on trial for battery arising from a barroom brawl sought to introduce the testimony of his grandmother, who would testify that the defendant had a reputation in her church community for being a "helpful and trustworthy person." Further, the grandmother would offer her testimony regarding an incident that took place when the defendant was 13 years old; he refused to engage in a schoolyard fight with another of his classmates. The prosecution objects to the grandmother's testimony in its entirety.

Should the court allow the grandmother to testify?

(A) Yes, the grandmother's testimony should be admissible in its entirety, because the defendant is allowed to present evidence of his own good character.

(B) The grandmother should be allowed to testify as to the schoolyard incident, but not as to the defendant's reputation.

(C) The grandmother should be allowed to testify as to the defendant's reputation, but not as to the schoolyard incident.

(D) No, the grandmother should not be allowed to testify as to either of these issues, because the testimony is not relevant.

137. A biotech start up firm secured a loan from a private investor to purchase land and to build a laboratory facility on that land with a mortgage on the land and the facility. Subsequently, the firm sold the developed property to a partnership. The deed stated that the partnership took the property subject to the mortgage. Later, the partnership sold the developed property to a corporation. Each deed was properly recorded promptly after its applicable closing. After closing, the president of the corporation orally promised the partnership that the corporation would assume the mortgage.

For four months, neither the corporation nor the previous owners of the facility made the required monthly payments on the mortgage obligation to the lender. The lender has filed an action against the corporation for the past due amounts.

Is the corporation liable for these amounts?

(A) No, because, since the investor was not personally liable for the obligation, the corporation is protected by the shelter principle from personal liability.

(B) No, because the corporation's assumption agreement was not in writing.

(C) Yes, because the corporation assumed the mortgage.

(D) Yes, because the loan was tied to a purchase money mortgage.

138. A defendant is on trial for cocaine possession. The cocaine was found during a warrantless search of the defendant's car by a police officer. The search occurred immediately after the defendant was arrested for driving a car with an inoperative taillight, a misdemeanor punishable only by a fine. The defendant had been placed in a police car prior to the search. The cocaine was found inside a closed bag on the back seat of the passenger compartment of the defendant's car. The defendant now moves to suppress the cocaine.

Will the defendant's motion be granted?

(A) Yes, because the defendant was in the police car at the time of the search.

(B) Yes, because the arrest was unreasonable and the cocaine seized was a fruit of the poisonous tree.

(C) No, because the police may search a car without a warrant under the automobile exception.

(D) No, because the search was a lawful search incident to arrest.

139. At the defendant's trial on a narcotics charge, the prosecution introduced the former testimony of a co-conspirator who had testified against the defendant at a preliminary hearing; the evidence was sufficiently corroborated. The co-conspirator has since fled the country to a jurisdiction with no extradition treaty with the United States. The defendant's attorney now seeks to impeach the credibility of the co-conspirator.

Which of the following types of evidence is the court most likely to admit?

(A) Testimony by a witness that at the time the co-conspirator testified against the defendant, he was doing so in exchange for a deal with the prosecutor for a lesser sentence.

(B) Evidence that the co-conspirator had misdemeanor convictions for public intoxication, disorderly conduct, and vandalism.

(C) Reputation evidence by a witness that the co-conspirator is a violent person.

(D) Evidence that the co-conspirator was convicted of a narcotics-related felony 11 years ago.

140. An adult woman was vacationing at a friend's house on a lake. One afternoon, the woman watched her friend maneuver his motorized personal watercraft around the lake; the friend took a particularly violent spill that temporarily knocked the wind out of him but otherwise left him unharmed. The next morning, without the friend's knowledge, she decided to take the personal watercraft out on the lake herself. Due to her inability to control the vehicle, it flipped over. As a consequence, the woman suffered serious physical injuries.

The woman brought a lawsuit against the friend to recover damages for her injuries. The applicable jurisdiction has adopted comparative negligence rules.

Prior to the submission of the case to the jury, the friend requested that the court specifically instruct the jury on the assumption of the risk defense. Should the court grant this request?

(A) Yes, because the woman voluntarily assumed the risk of being injured.

(B) Yes, because assumption of the risk is an absolute bar to recovery.

(C) No, because the defendant did not have the requisite knowledge for this defense.

(D) No, because assumption of the risk is not recognized as a separate defense.

141. Concerned about problems caused by overpopulation, a state legislature enacted a statute imposing criminal penalties on any person who is the biological parent of more than two children. The stated purpose of the statute was to preserve the state's natural resources and improve the quality of life for the state's residents.

After the statute took effect, a married couple, who had two children, conceived a third. After the wife gave birth to this child, the couple was arrested and convicted under the statute. Which of the following is strongest argument for voiding their convictions?

(A) The statute is an invalid exercise of the state's police power because there is no rational basis for concluding that the statute would further the government's stated interests.

(B) The statute places an unconstitutional burden on the fundamental privacy and procreative rights of married persons.

(C) The statute grants too much discretion to a prosecutor to determine who will be permitted to bear children.

(D) The statute denies the couple their Equal Protection rights.

142. In January, a garden center contacted a farmer who owns a greenhouse about growing seedlings for sale in the spring. The garden center promised in writing to buy all of the seedlings that the farmer raised in his greenhouse at a fixed price. As a consequence, the farmer purchased containers and seeds and hired a worker to prepare the containers, to plant the seeds, and to tend to the seedlings. Just prior to the delivery of any seedlings, the garden center notified the farmer that it would not purchase any of the seedlings. The farmer sold the seedlings at a price far below the price set by the garden center.

The farmer filed a breach of contract action to recover damages. Will the farmer likely succeed?

(A) Yes, because the farmer accepted garden center's offer by beginning performance.

(B) Yes, because the doctrine of promissory estoppel made the offer irrevocable.

(C) No, because the garden center revoked offer before it was accepted by farmer.

(D) No, because the garden center did not receive consideration for its promise to buy the farmer's output.

143. A homebuyer was discussing the purchase of a house with the seller. Of particular concern to the buyer was whether the house had a termite problem. The seller, aware of the buyer's concern, ordered an inspection from a licensed inspection company. The company issued a report stating that the house was free of termites. In fact, the company's inspector was negligent, and the house's foundation had a modest termite problem. Relying on the report, the seller told the buyer that the house was free of termites.

The buyer is seeking to avoid the contract. Will he prevail?

(A) Yes, because the buyer reasonably relied on the misrepresentation.

(B) Yes, because enforcing the contract would be unconscionable.

(C) No, because the misrepresentation did not rise to the level of a mutual mistake.

(D) No, because the inspector, not the seller, was negligent.

144. Eleven years ago, the owner of a condominium unit located in another state bequeathed the condominium unit to his wife for her life and then to their son. A year after the owner's death, the wife had a stroke that left her incapacitated. The son sought and was granted both personal and financial guardianship over his mother. Six months later the son suddenly died. By will, the son devised his real property to his daughter, who was unaware of the condominium unit and took no action with regard to it. The daughter assumed guardianship over her grandmother who remains alive but unable to care for herself.

Shortly after the owner's death, the wife granted an acquaintance the right to occupy the condominium unit for the following month. At the end of that month, the acquaintance tried unsuccessfully to obtain the wife's permission to remain longer. Deciding to remain despite the lack of permission, the acquaintance, since that time, has resided in the unit, maintaining it as well as paying the annual condominium fees and real estate taxes on it.

The applicable statutory period to acquire title by adverse possession is 10 years.

The acquaintance brings an appropriate action to determine title to the condominium unit. What type of ownership interest in the condominium unit will the acquaintance be found to possess?

(A) Fee simple absolute

(B) A life estate measured by the wife's life

(C) A remainder interest

(D) None

145. On behalf of an elementary school, the school's principal entered into a written contract to purchase shirts for the school's students for a total cost of $5,000. The name of school was to be imprinted on the back of each shirt. After the seller had acquired the shirts but before they had been imprinted, the principal emailed the seller and requested, in good faith, that a picture of the school's mascot be imprinted on the front of the shirts at no additional cost. In a reply email, the seller agreed to the principal's request. When the shirts arrived at the school, only the school's name appeared on the back of each shirt; the school's mascot did not appear on the shirt. The principal rejected the shirts and refused to pay for them. The seller sued the school for breach of contract. Who will prevail?

(A) The seller, because the shirts were specially manufactured goods.

(B) The seller, because the seller did not receive consideration for the modification.

(C) The school, because the school was not a merchant.

(D) The school, because of the perfect tender rule.

146. After consuming too much alcohol, an actor tripped over his own feet and smashed face first into a sidewalk. The actor delayed seeking medical attention for his facial injuries for several days, which aggravated those injuries. When the actor finally sought treatment from a plastic surgeon, the plastic surgeon negligently performed the operation on the actor's face. After surgery, the actor failed to follow the surgeon's post-operative instructions. All of the actor's actions coupled with the surgeon's negligence contributed to the actor's permanent facial scarring.

The actor received a reimbursement for some of his medical expenses from an insurer under a health insurance policy.

The actor sued the plastic surgeon for damages attributable to the surgeon's medical treatment of the actor's facial injuries. The applicable jurisdiction has not modified the common law collateral source rule.

Assuming that the monetary effect of each of the following can be established with reasonable certainty, which can be taken into account to reduce the damages to which the actor would otherwise be entitled due to the surgeon's negligence?

(A) The plaintiff's negligent behavior that initially led to his facial injuries.

(B) The plaintiff's failure to promptly seek medical care.

(C) The plaintiff's failure to follow the surgeon's post-operative instructions.

(D) The reimbursement for medical expenses received by the plaintiff.

147. The defense attorney in a criminal rape case wants to introduce testimony that the alleged victim has a reputation in the community for promiscuity. The testimony will come from one of the victim's past sexual partners. The prosecutor objects to the introduction of the testimony, but the defense maintains that because consent is at issue in the case, the testimony is relevant.

Should the court allow the testimony?

(A) Yes, because reputation testimony is an admissible form of character evidence.

(B) Yes, because the victim's past sexual behavior can be used to prove consent.

(C) No, because evidence of a victim's past sexual behavior is inadmissible.

(D) No, because this evidence of the victim's other sexual behavior is not relevant.

148. A state law provided that, before an abortion may be performed, a woman must (a) have a consultation with a physician, who should try to persuade the woman to have her baby, and (b) wait another 24 hours before seeking an abortion. A woman in the middle of her first trimester of pregnancy challenges the constitutionality of the law.

Would a court be likely to strike down this law?

(A) No, because the state has a rational basis for requiring the consultation and 24 hour waiting period.

(B) No, because the state's purpose is not to hinder women's right to choose abortion, but merely to persuade women to choose birth and to ensure that their decisions are deliberate.

(C) Yes, because the law violates the woman's liberty interest in abortion protected by the Fourteenth Amendment.

(D) Yes, because a state's power to regulate abortions does not include the power to impose waiting periods.

149. A pest control company fumigated one of two buildings in an apartment complex with a toxic gas in order to eliminate unwanted insects. Even though the company exercised reasonable care, the gas escaped into the other building, which adjoined the fumigated building, where the gas caused serious illness to a tenant in that building. The tenant had received a written advance notice about the fumigation that advised the tenant of the need to vacate his apartment during the hours the fumigation was conducted. The tenant chose instead to remain there in order to watch a favorite television program.

The applicable jurisdiction treats fumigation as an ultrahazardous activity.

The injured tenant filed an action against the pest control company. Who will prevail?

(A) The tenant, because the pest control company is strictly liable for the harm that resulted from the fumigation.

(B) The tenant, because the pest control company was negligent in conducting the fumigation.

(C) The pest control company, because the tenant was not a resident of the fumigated building.

(D) The pest control company, because the tenant assumed the risk.

150. A physician enters into a written agreement to purchase land from his aunt. The agreement, which is secured by not only the land itself but also all future improvements, requires the physician to make annual installment payments to the aunt. The deed from the aunt to the physician is recorded, but it makes no mention of this agreement. The agreement itself is not recorded.

The following year, the physician obtains a loan from the local bank to build a house on the land in exchange for a mortgage on the property and any structures built on it. The physician informs the bank about the agreement with his aunt. The bank requires the aunt to sign an agreement subordinating her loan to the bank's loan. The mortgage agreement is recorded, but the agreement between the bank and the aunt is not recorded.

After the house is built, the physician is successfully sued by a patient for malpractice. The judgment is promptly and properly recorded so that it becomes a lien against the residence of the physician. The patient is unaware of the physician's financial dealings with his aunt or the bank.

The physician fails to make timely payments on the mortgage. In accord with the terms of the mortgage, the bank declared the full mortgage obligation due and properly foreclosed on the property. At the time of the foreclosure sale, which was properly conducted, the physician's outstanding balance with regard to the agreement with his aunt was $100,000, and with regard to the mortgage was $500,000. The total amount owed with respect to the judgment was $400,000. After expenses, the sale of the mortgaged property netted only $550,000.

The applicable jurisdiction has the following two statutes:

"No conveyance or mortgage of real property shall be good against subsequent purchasers for value and without notice unless the same be first recorded according to law."

"Any judgment properly filed shall, for twelve years from filing, be a lien on the real property then owned or subsequently acquired by any person against whom the judgment is rendered."

What is the amount due to the aunt from the sale?

(A) $100,000, because the aunt's interest predated the other interests.

(B) $100,000, because the aunt's interest was a seller-financed purchase money security interest.

(C) $50,000, because the aunt's interest has priority over the patient's judgment lien, but not the bank's mortgage.

(D) Nothing, both the patient's judgment lien and the bank's mortgage have priority over the aunt's interest.

151. In a state known for its game fish, there are a number of guide-led fishing expeditions marketed to tourists. The state enacted a statute that required all fishing guides who charge a fee to have a license. The purpose of the statute is to protect the state's game fish from overfishing. The license costs $100 for in-state residents and $300 for out-of-state residents.

If an out-of-state resident challenges the constitutionality of this statute, what is the most likely result?

(A) The statute will be struck down under the Privileges and Immunities Clause of Article IV, Section 2.

(B) The statute will be struck down under the Equal Protection Clause.

(C) The statute will be upheld because engaging in fishing is not a fundamental right.

(D) The statute will be upheld because regulation of fishing is traditionally a state rather than national function.

152. A defendant is on trial for robbery. A witness picked the defendant's picture out of a photo array that was conducted by a police officer at the police station after the defendant's arrest. The photo array was impermissibly suggestive. No counsel was present for the defendant at the photo array. Later, at trial, the witness identified the defendant. Because of the witness's extended opportunity to view the defendant at the time of the crime, this identification was reliable.

The defendant moves to suppress the identification.

Should the court grant this motion?

(A) Yes, because the defendant's right to counsel was violated.

(B) Yes, because the identification procedure was impermissibly suggestive.

(C) No, because the identification was reliable.

(D) No, because the photo array was conducted by a police officer at a police station.

153. In a trial for murder in which the defendant asserted the affirmative defense of self-defense, the defendant's attorney introduced evidence that the victim had a reputation as a violent person. In turn, the prosecutor wanted to introduce the testimony of a witness, the victim's wife, who would testify that in her opinion, the victim was a peaceful person who would not have provoked a fight. Additionally, the prosecutor wanted to introduce evidence that the defendant has a reputation for being violent.

Should the court allow the prosecutor's evidence to be admitted?

(A) Yes, as to both.

(B) No as to the testimony regarding the victim, because the victim's character is not relevant to the defendant's actions, but yes as to the testimony regarding the defendant's reputation.

(C) No, as to the testimony regarding the defendant's reputation, because the defendant did not "open the door" by putting his own character at issue, but yes as to the testimony regarding the victim.

(D) No, as to both.

154. While working on an addition to a residence, a carpenter took an expensive necklace from the owner's bedroom. The owner walked into the bedroom from an adjoining bathroom as the carpenter was slipping the necklace into his pocket. The carpenter exited the bedroom and fled the premises in his truck. As the carpenter drove away, the owner called the police. Notified of the theft by a police dispatcher, a nearby patrolman spotted the carpenter and gave chase. After several miles, the carpenter abandoned his truck and headed into a wooded area. The patrolman called for backup. Sometime later, a police helicopter flew over the area in an attempt to locate the carpenter who, by that time, was several miles away, having coffee at a convenience store. The helicopter developed mechanical problems and crashed, killing the helicopter pilot.

Later, the carpenter was apprehended and charged with felony murder of the helicopter pilot. Which of the following, if established, would not be a defense to the charge?

(A) The helicopter pilot's death was not causally connected with the carpenter's felony.

(B) The helicopter pilot's death did not occur during the commission of the felony.

(C) The carpenter did not commit an inherently dangerous felony.

(D) The carpenter did not act maliciously with regard to the death of the helicopter pilot.

155. The owner of an office building leased space to a physician in general practice for a term of five years. The physician's written lease with the owner restricted use of the space to a doctor's office, but permitted the assignment of the office with the written permission of the owner, which, according to the terms of the lease, could be withheld for any reason.

At the end of second year of the lease, the physician decided to move to another building and rented the space to a lawyer for one year. The lawyer's monthly payments were the same as those called for in the lease between the owner and the physician. The owner's permission was not sought, but the owner accepted rental payments directly from the lawyer.

At the end of the third year of the lease, the physician found a psychiatrist to rent the space for a year. As with the lawyer, the psychiatrist's monthly payments were to be the same as those called for in the lease between the owner and the physician. When contacted by the physician, the owner at first orally agreed, and then, upon learning the identity of the psychiatrist, refused due to personal animosity towards the psychiatrist.

Can the owner be compelled to accept the psychiatrist as a tenant?

(A) Yes, because the lease does not restrict the physician from subletting the office space.

(B) Yes, because the owner has waived the right to object by accepting the physician's previous sublet of the office space.

(C) No, because the physician did not obtain the owner's written permission.

(D) No, because the owner properly exercised his right to reject the psychiatrist as a tenant.

156. A toy company specialized in producing high-end toy racecars. Three months prior to the holiday shopping season, the toy company received an order of 50,000 racecars from a major retailer. The toy company immediately contracted with two of its major suppliers, a metalworking company and a paint company, to provide essential parts and paint for the racecars. The metalworking company and the paint company were both extremely busy with orders from other manufacturers, but agreed to supply needed parts and paint for the racecars.

One month later, the metalworking company, without justification, informed the toy company that it would not be able to perform the contract. The toy company found a replacement metal parts supplier, but the new supplier was only able to provide 25,000 parts. Consequently, the toy company reduced its order with the paint company by 25,000 units.

The paint company then sued the metalworking company, seeking the profits it lost because of the reduced order. The contract between the toy company and the metalworking company was silent on the issue of third-party liability. Is the paint company entitled to such relief?

(A) Yes, because the paint company is a volume seller of paint.

(B) Yes, because the paint company has a vested right to enforce the contract between the toy company and the metalworking company.

(C) No, because the paint company is not an intended beneficiary of the contract between the toy company and the metalworking company.

(D) No, because the contract between the toy company and the metalworking company did not explicitly grant third-party rights in the paint company.

157. An American helicopter manufacturer contracted with a foreign hospital located in a severely war-torn region to sell five helicopters specially outfitted for medical use. The helicopter manufacturer, in turn, contracted with a subcontractor to provide five flight systems for use in the helicopters. The subcontractor was not informed about the contract between the helicopter manufacturer and the foreign hospital, nor the location where the helicopters would be used.

After the two contracts were formed, the country in which the hospital was located descended deeply into civil war. The United Nations imposed an embargo against all shipments to that country. The helicopter manufacturer directed the subcontractor to stop all work on the contract, and to place any completed systems into storage. At that point, the subcontractor had finished three of the five flight systems called for by the subcontract. The systems were custom-built, and could not be used for any other purpose.

The subcontractor sued the helicopter manufacturer for breach of contract. Is the subcontractor likely to prevail?

(A) Yes, because the subcontractor was a vested third-party beneficiary of the contract between the helicopter manufacturer and the foreign hospital.

(B) Yes, because the helicopter manufacturer assumed the risk of the failure of the contact.

(C) No, because the contract was rendered impracticable by the United Nations embargo.

(D) No, because the failure of the contract between the helicopter manufacturer and the foreign hospital frustrated the purpose of the subcontract.

158. A father was an avid golfer who often practiced chipping the ball in his backyard. To facilitate this practice, he always left a golf club, a wedge, and bucket of golf balls inside the house next to the back door. One afternoon, the father's 15-year-old son—an experienced golfer—came home from school, saw the golf club next to the back door, and decided to take some practice swings. On the son's second swing, the golf club slipped out of his hands, flew into the next yard, and struck a neighbor in the head. The neighbor collapsed in pain, and was later diagnosed with a concussion.

If the neighbor sues the father for his son's actions, which party should prevail?

(A) The neighbor, because the son breached his duty of care for a child his age.

(B) The neighbor, because the father is vicariously liable.

(C) The father, because he had no duty to supervise his son.

(D) The father, because his actions were reasonable.

159. During the extensive remodeling of a residence, the owner of the residence granted a local gas and electrical company an easement for underground electrical power lines and natural gas pipes to run through the lot on which the residence was located. The easement was properly recorded by the company.

Two years after the remodeling was completed, the owner gave the property to his child. The owner transferred the lot together with the residence by general warranty deed to the child. Recently, the child sold the property at fair market value to a third party and transferred the lot together with the residence by a special warranty deed to the third party.

Each deed was properly recorded by the grantee shortly after the deed was received by the grantee. Each deed contained a covenant against encumbrances, but neither contained a mention of the easement.

After moving into the residence, the third party contacted a contractor about building a swimming pool on the property. The contractor discovered the existence of the underground electrical lines and gas pipes and informed the third party that the cost of rerouting the underground utilities would more than double the cost of the project.

If the third party sues the child for breach of warranty for the presence of the utility lines and pipes, will the third party prevail?

(A) Yes, because the third party recorded the deed.

(B) Yes, because the third party was bona fide purchaser of the property.

(C) No, because the child's father granted the utility easement.

(D) No, because the child received the property by gift.

160. A state statute makes the possession of all venomous snakes unlawful. The state legislature's purpose in enacting the statute was to address the problem of a rising number of fatal snakebites occurring within the state.

A religious entity, based in the state, teaches that God will protect its members against all harm, and that therefore its members must handle venomous snakes during the entity's religious services to witness their true faith. An ordained minister of the entity, who sincerely believes all of the religious entity's teachings, sued in an appropriate federal court to have the statute declared unconstitutional because it prevents him from exercising his religious beliefs. Will the court probably uphold the statute?

(A) Yes, because it is a neutral law of general applicability.

(B) Yes, because it does not have the primary effect of advancing religion and does not excessively entangle the government in religion.

(C) No, because it is not the least restrictive means of achieving the state's compelling interest in public health and safety.

(D) No, because it interferes with an integral part of the religious entity's worship services.

161. In reporting on the death of a city official whose bullet-ridden body was found in a barren apartment, a newspaper attributed the death to a "drug deal that went sour." The newspaper reporter who filed the report had serious doubts about the official's involvement with drugs. Later, the newspaper determined that the official neither used nor sold illegal drugs, but instead was killed because he had been involved in a graft scheme that went awry.

The executor of the official's estate brought an action for defamation against the newspaper. The executor is unable to establish special damages. Who will prevail?

(A) The executor, because presumed damages are permitted for a libel action.

(B) The executor, because the newspaper acted with malice.

(C) The newspaper, because the city official was dead.

(D) The newspaper, because the statement regarding the person's involvement in criminal activity was substantially true.

162. A local contractor entered into a valid contract with a state to repave a state highway for $3 million. In accord with the terms of the contract, the contractor was paid $500,000 immediately. The remaining amount was to be paid upon completion of the contract. At a time that the contractor had substantially completed the paving project, the governor of the state announced that the state's budget crisis threatened all state projects and services, and decided to delay payments owed by state. With regard to the paving contract, the state, rather than paying the contractor upon completion of the project, will pay the contractor $500,000 each year for the next five years, plus the prevailing interest on the overdue amount.

If the contractor sues the state in an appropriate federal court, what is state's best argument?

(A) Under the Tenth Amendment and federalism, the state has plenary power over all matters pertaining to state road repairs.

(B) The state's action does not violate the Dormant Commerce Clause because the state is acting as a market participant.

(C) The contractor lacks Article III standing.

(D) The state's action does not substantially and unreasonably impair the contractor's contract rights.

163. A borrower owed a substantial sum of money to an unsavory lender. One afternoon, the lender knocked on the borrower's door. When the borrower opened the door, the lender was holding a baseball bat and said, "If you don't get me the money you owe within the next two hours, I'll break your legs." The borrower was extremely frightened, and immediately gave the lender the cash needed to satisfy the debt.

If the borrower later sues the lender for assault, will the borrower prevail?

(A) Yes, because the lender threatened the borrower with harmful or offensive bodily contact.

(B) Yes, because the lender intended to place the borrower in apprehension of harmful or offensive bodily contact.

(C) No, because the lender's words alone cannot give rise to an assault claim.

(D) No, because the lender gave the borrower two hours to deliver the money.

164. A buyer and seller executed a fully-integrated written contract for the sale of a car. The contract specified that the seller would deliver the car to the buyer's home within five days of the execution of the contract. The day after the contract was executed, the buyer emailed the seller suggesting that she pick the car up from the seller the following day, as she would be in the seller's neighborhood. This arrangement was more convenient for the seller, so the seller immediately responded that she agreed. Afterwards, the buyer decided not to go to the seller's neighborhood, and demanded that the seller deliver the car as originally agreed. The seller refused. The buyer threatened to sue the seller for breach of contract, and the seller responded that she would simply produce the email from the buyer in response. The buyer, a first year law student, claims that the parol evidence rule would prohibit the seller from introducing the email at trial.

Would the parol evidence rule prohibit the introduction of the email?

(A) Yes, because the contract was fully integrated.

(B) Yes, because the email contradicts a term in the agreement.

(C) No, because the email was sent after the contract was executed.

(D) No, because there was no fraud or duress on the part of either party.

165. A man asked a friend to burn down the man's residence so the man could collect the fire insurance proceeds. The friend stated that she would be willing to set fire to the residence for $20,000. The man offered $10,000, but the friend refused. Later, the man set fire to an office building that he owned, in order to collect the fire insurance proceeds. The man honestly, but unreasonably and incorrectly, believed that there was no one in the building when he set the fire. There was a person in the office building at the time of the fire who escaped unharmed. The man is charged with solicitation and arson.

The relevant statute defines arson as "the malicious burning of any dwelling or occupied structure."

Can the man be convicted of these crimes?

(A) No, as to both solicitation and arson.

(B) Yes, as to both solicitation and arson.

(C) Yes, as to arson only.

(D) Yes, as to solicitation only.

166. The defendant and his friend rented a house together. Although both signed the lease and each paid half of the monthly rent, each had exclusive control over his own bedroom.

Two police officers, with probable cause that the house contained stolen large-screen televisions, sought permission from the friend to search for them. The friend, certain that there were no such televisions on the premises, voluntarily told the officers that they could search the entire house for the televisions. The officers did not warn the friend that he had the right to refuse to consent to the search. Reasonably relying on the friend's permission, the officers searched the house and found two stolen televisions in defendant's bedroom under his bed.

The defendant was charged with theft and possession of the stolen televisions. The defendant moved to exclude the televisions as evidence.

Will the defendant's motion to suppress be granted?

(A) Yes, because the police failed to warn the friend of his right to refuse to consent to the search.

(B) Yes, because the friend had no authority to grant permission for the search of the defendant's bedroom.

(C) No, because the police reasonably believed that the roommate had the authority to grant permission for the search.

(D) No, because the police had probable cause to search the house.

167. A plaintiff and a defendant are in settlement negotiations to resolve the lawsuit the plaintiff brought to recover for injuries she suffered when she fell off a horse at the defendant's stable. In exchange for the plaintiff's agreeing to drop the case, the defendant offered to pay the plaintiff $5,000, which would cover her medical expenses and leave a little extra for pain and suffering. The plaintiff counter-offered $7,000, which the defendant refused. The case went to trial. The plaintiff prayed for $20,000 in damages, and reiterated during her testimony that that amount is the least amount she can accept to make her whole. The defendant testified that the plaintiff's injuries were not severe enough to warrant a $20,000 judgment, and added, "The plaintiff was willing to settle for $7,000; it's ludicrous that she is now asking for $20,000." The plaintiff's attorney objected to the defendant's statement.

How should the court rule on the plaintiff's objection?

(A) Sustain it, because the testimony contains hearsay not within any exception.

(B) Sustain it, because the testimony discloses communications regarding a settlement offer.

(C) Overrule it, because the testimony contains a prior inconsistent statement.

(D) Overrule it, because the testimony impeaches the plaintiff's credibility.

168. The owner of a parcel of land validly devises the parcel "to my wife for life, but if she remarries, then to my son for his life; then to my son's children who attain the age of 21." At the time of the conveyance the son has one child, a daughter.

Subsequently, the son is killed in an automobile crash. At the time of the crash, the son also has a second daughter. A year after the son's funeral, the owner's wife remarries.

The oldest daughter, who is now 21, contacts a lawyer about ownership of the parcel of land. Her sister is currently 18 years old.

The jurisdiction follows the common law Rule Against Perpetuities and has abolished the common law rule regarding the destructibility of contingent remainders, and follows the rule of convenience with regard to class gifts.

Which of the following should the lawyer advise the oldest daughter that prevents her from owing all of the parcel in fee simple absolute?

(A) The Rule Against Perpetuities.

(B) Her sister's interest in the parcel.

(C) Her father's death and grandmother's remarriage before she turned 21 years old.

(D) Her grandmother is still alive.

169. A widow and widower were engaged to be married. After some discussion as to how to pay for the wedding, the son of the widow and the daughter of the widower each orally agreed to give $50,000 to the other's parent, as a gesture of approval of the upcoming union. The son and daughter shook hands in agreement as to the arrangement, but before either gift had been made, the two became embroiled in a serious disagreement, and both agreed to forego making the gifts. In spite of this, the son of the widow did make a gift of $50,000 to the widower at the time of the wedding.

Soon after the marriage of the widow and widower, the widower died. Subsequently, the widow learned of the arrangement and sued the daughter of widower to compel her to pay $50,000. Is the widow likely to prevail?

(A) Yes, because the widow was an intended beneficiary of the agreement between the children.

(B) Yes, because the agreement between the children was not required to be in writing.

(C) No, because the agreement between the children was unenforceable as promises to make gifts.

(D) No, because the agreement between the children was rescinded before the widow's rights vested.

170. Congress has enacted many laws regulating navigation generally, but not the specific subject of water pollution by ships sailing on navigable bodies of water. A state enacted a law prohibiting any ship from discharging specified pollutants, including oil, into the navigable waterways of the state. Violation of the law was punishable by fines based on the amount of the discharge. The law is necessary to the important state interest of prevent pollution; there are no reasonable alternatives available. In addition, the benefits of the law to the state outweigh the burdens it imposes on interstate commerce.

A ship owner from another state is fined pursuant to this law for discharging oil into a waterway in the state. Will a challenge by the ship owner to the state law as unconstitutional be successful?

(A) Yes, because the law regulates interstate commerce, which may be regulated only by Congress.

(B) Yes, because the fine constitutes an impermissible ad valorem tax.

(C) No, because the law is necessary to the important state interest of prevent pollution and there are no reasonable alternatives available.

(D) No, because the law does not discriminate against interstate commerce and does not impose an undue burden on interstate commerce.

171. In a well-trafficked downtown location, a voyeur concealed a video camera near a sidewalk grate. As the voyeur was aware, a natural spurt of air coming up from the grate would occasionally lift a woman's skirt and reveal her underwear. In reviewing the video taken one day, the voyeur discovered a short sequence involving a prominent female politician who at the time was not wearing underwear. The voyeur contacted the politician and demanded a substantial payment in exchange for not posting the video on an internet site.

The politician sued the voyeur in an invasion of privacy action based on intrusion upon her seclusion. The voyeur moved to dismiss the action for failure to state a cause of action. Should the court grant this motion?

(A) No, because the politician did not consent to the video.

(B) No, because the video intruded into her privacy in a manner highly offensive to a reasonable person.

(C) Yes, because the video was made in a public place.

(D) Yes, because the video was not revealed to a third party.

172. A 16-year-old entered into a written agreement to buy a car from a dealership. He made a small down payment and took out a loan from the dealership for the remainder of the purchase price. The deal was fair in every respect and the same as the car dealership would give any other customer. After the sale was finalized, the salesman's supervisor reviewed the contract, and upon researching the matter further, discovering that the boy was only 16. He told the salesperson to call the boy and cancel the contract, which he did.

In a breach of contract action brought on behalf of the boy, the court held for the boy. What is the reason?

(A) The contract is one for necessities.

(B) The contract cannot be disaffirmed because of the boy's part performance.

(C) The contract is not voidable because the terms were fair.

(D) The dealer did not have the right to void the contract.

173. Two vehicles were involved in an automobile accident. The driver of one car ran to the other car and said, "Ma'am, are you ok? Oh my goodness, I didn't even see that stop sign. I'm calling an ambulance right now." The injured woman sued the other driver. At trial, the other driver testified that the woman was the one who ran the stop sign. The woman's attorney then seeks to introduce the other driver's statement as evidence that he ran a stop sign and caused the accident.

Upon proper objection, should the court admit the statement into evidence?

(A) Yes, both as substantive evidence and for impeachment purposes.

(B) No, because as a prior inconsistent statement, it can only be used to impeach the other driver.

(C) No, because the declarant is available to testify and subject to cross-examination.

(D) No, because the statement is hearsay not within any exception.

174. A state law provided that all police officers must have been born in the United States. The state adopted this law in order to assure that police officers can speak and understand English well enough to avoid miscommunications that can endanger public safety. An individual who was born in a foreign country and became a naturalized United States citizen resides in the state. Because of the law, he was denied a job as a police officer for which he was otherwise qualified. He challenged the constitutionality of this law in an appropriate court. Will his challenge likely be successful?

(A) Yes, because the law discriminates against the plaintiff based on his national origin and is not narrowly tailored to further the state's compelling interest in protecting public safety.

(B) Yes, because the law deprives the plaintiff of his fundamental civil right to pursue his chosen calling in violation of the Fourteenth Amendment's Due Process Clause.

(C) No, because the law prohibits the plaintiff from gaining a job that has a direct effect on basic functions of the state government.

(D) No, because the law deprived the plaintiff of his First Amendment rights by limiting his freedom to speak a language other than English.

175. A landowner devised real property to his three children, a daughter and two sons. The children were given equal, joint interests in the property and, upon the death of any child, that child's interest was to pass automatically to any surviving joint interest holders. Two years later the daughter sold her interest in the property to a cousin. A year after that one of the sons died. Under the terms of his will, his interest in the property passed to a friend.

Who has an interest in the land and what interest does he/she hold?

(A) The cousin and the surviving son each own an equal share as tenants in common.

(B) The cousin and the surviving son each own a share as tenants in common; the cousin owns a one-third share and the surviving son a two-thirds share.

(C) The cousin, friend, and surviving son each own an equal share as tenants in common.

(D) The cousin, friend, and surviving son each own an equal share as joint tenants.

176. A hospital placed an order to purchase scalpel blades from a medical supply company. The hospital specified that the blades were to be shipped immediately. Upon receipt of the order, the supply company, discovering that it did not have the type of blade ordered by the hospital, shipped instead a different type of blade to the hospital along with a note that these blades were not the type ordered by the hospital but were sent as an accommodation. The hospital rejected and returned the shipped blades, then sued the supply company for breach of contract. Will the hospital be successful in its suit?

(A) Yes, because of the perfect tender rule.

(B) Yes, because acceptance of the hospital's order could be made by shipment as well as by a promise.

(C) No, because the hospital order could only be accepted by shipment of the type of scalpel blades ordered.

(D) No, because the medical supply company did not accept the hospital's offer.

177. A large manufacturer, seeking to trim costs, entered into an agreement with an outside contractor to provide its employees with "appropriate and safe workplace tools and equipment," and to maintain that equipment in safe working order. A rotary saw provided by the outside contractor malfunctioned as a result of improper maintenance, and severely injured one of the manufacturer's employees.

The employee sued the manufacturer for negligence. Is the employee likely to succeed?

(A) No, because the manufacturer was relieved of liability when it outsourced its activities to an independent contractor.

(B) No, because the manufacturer is free to subcontract functions which are not inherently dangerous.

(C) Yes, because a principal remains simultaneously liable for the torts of its independent contractor.

(D) Yes, because workplace safety is uniquely the responsibility of the manufacturer.

178. Despite being served with a warrant, the defendant objected to having his blood drawn to determine whether it matched blood found at the scene of a robbery. Nevertheless, the police properly executed the warrant to perform the procedure, and a doctor drew the defendant's blood. The defendant was later charged with robbery, a felony. The blood at the scene matched the sample obtained from the defendant. At his robbery trial, the defendant moved to suppress this evidence. Should the judge grant this motion?

(A) Yes, because obtaining evidence through a forced medical procedure shocks the conscience.

(B) Yes, because the procedure violated the defendant's Fifth Amendment privilege against self-incrimination.

(C) No, because the blood was obtained pursuant to a warrant and drawing blood is reasonable, a minimally invasive medical procedure.

(D) No, because the defendant was charged with a felony.

179. During a burglary trial, the prosecutor plans to put an eyewitness on the stand. The eyewitness is the burglary victim's neighbor, and she saw the defendant climb out of the victim's window on the night of the burglary. At the time of the trial, the eyewitness can no longer recall what the person she saw climbing out of the victim's home looked like. However, she wrote his detailed description in her diary right after she called the police on the night in question. When the eyewitness is on the stand, the prosecutor asks the witness to read the diary entry to herself to see if it refreshes her memory. When the witness admits that it does not, the prosecutor seeks to have the witness read the diary entry containing the description to the jury and to introduce the diary entry as an exhibit. The defendant objects to both.

Should the court allow the witness to read the diary entry to the jury and introduce the diary as an exhibit?

(A) The court should sustain the defendant's objections on both counts.

(B) The court should sustain the defendant's objection as to the witness's reading the diary entry, but should overrule the defendant's objection as to its entry as an exhibit.

(C) The court should overrule the defendant's objection as to the witness's reading it to the jury, but should sustain the defendant's objection as to the diary's entry as an exhibit.

(D) The court should overrule the defendant's objections on both counts.

180. A state amended its constitution to provide that "English is the state's official language and applies to all state employees during the performance of government business." A state employee sued the state's governor to enjoin application of this provision to her. She alleged that she worked in the state's Department of Motor Vehicles and often communicated with customers in Spanish, thereby facing possible adverse employment action in violation of her First and Fourteenth Amendment rights. The governor defends against this action by invoking the political question doctrine. Will the governor probably be successful?

(A) Yes, because the case presents a hotly contested question involving sensitive political issues.

(B) Yes, because a judicial decision would unnecessarily embarrass the governor.

(C) No, because the law does not require the judge to make any discretionary policy determinations.

(D) No, because the state constitutional provision has been properly challenged as violating individual constitutional rights.

181. Two friends, a chef and an electrician, together purchased a beachfront residence. They took title to the residence as joint owners, with the chef owning a 75% interest, and the electrician, a 25% interest.

The chef, during the time he used the residence, prepared elaborate meals. He advertized those meals, attracted a paying clientele, and made a net profit from them.

The electrician pointed out to the chef that the electrical system in the house was in dangerous condition. The chef, agreeing with the electrician that repair of the system was necessary, stated that he had neither the time nor the expertise to fix it himself and couldn't afford the cost of doing so. The electrician repaired it and demanded that the chef contribute to the cost of the repair. The chef refused.

The electrician brought an action for partition. The court ordered the sale of the residence. It was purchased by a third party for its appraised value.

In allocating the sale proceeds, should the court take into account either the chef's net profit from the meals or the electrician's repair of the electrical system?

(A) Only the electrician's repair of the electrical system.

(B) Only the chef's net profit from the meals.

(C) Both must the taken into account.

(D) Neither should be taken into account

182. An oral surgeon, who practiced in a rural area, determined that his patient required extensive surgery on his upper jaw. The oral surgeon was quite experienced, and had successfully performed many similar procedures in the past. The oral surgeon performed the surgery, having obtained the patient's informed consent. However, the procedure did not correct the patient's problem; indeed, the patient suffered severe side effects and lost feeling on one side of his mouth. After the patient's condition did not improve, he sued the oral surgeon for malpractice.

At trial, the patient offered testimony from a national expert that recent safety innovations have greatly reduced the risk of the particular side effect suffered by the patient, and that the oral surgeon's failure to apply the recent innovations constituted a breach of the national standard of care. The oral surgeon countered this testimony with his own expert testimony, which tended to show that no oral surgeons within the immediate jurisdiction applied the new safety innovations. Consequently, the oral surgeon's expert concluded that the required standard of care was not breached.

Later, the oral surgeon moved for summary judgment. How should the court rule on the motion?

(A) Deny the motion, because medical professionals are held to a national standard of care.

(B) Deny the motion, because a reasonable fact finder may determine that the local oral surgery standards are negligent.

(C) Grant the motion, because the oral surgeon's proffered expert testimony established that his surgical practices fell within the standard of care observed within the community.

(D) Grant the motion, because medical professionals are normally held to a local standard of care.

183. The defendant was convicted of armed robbery by a unanimous vote of a six-person jury. The applicable statute provides for a sentence of not more than 20 years imprisonment. However, if the defendant was previously convicted of specified crimes, including felony theft, the sentence could be increased to not more than 30 years imprisonment. Upon the introduction of evidence by the prosecution, the judge determined that defendant had been previously convicted of a felony theft and sentenced the defendant to 25 years imprisonment. On appeal, the defendant has challenged both his conviction and his sentence.

Should the appellate court uphold the conviction and the sentence?

(A) Yes as to the conviction because a six-person jury is permissible in a criminal trial and yes as to the sentence because it was validly imposed by the judge.

(B) Yes as to the conviction because a six-person jury is permissible in a criminal trial and no as to the sentence because it was not imposed by a jury.

(C) No as to the conviction because a six-person jury is not permissible in a criminal trial and yes as to the sentence because it was validly imposed by the judge.

(D) No as to the conviction because a six-person jury is not permissible in a criminal trial and no as to the sentence because it was not imposed by a jury.

184. A homeowner entered into an oral agreement with a landscaper to landscape the grounds surrounding her home for $75,000 while she was away for the summer. While the homeowner had described the overall effect that she wanted the landscaper to create as "stately," she left the choice of plants and other materials and their placement up to the landscaper. In order to secure the homeowner's assent, the landscaper promised her that she would be satisfied with the job or she would not have to pay him. Upon the homeowner's return in the fall, the landscaper sought payment from the homeowner. The homeowner refused to pay because, in her honest opinion, the landscaper had failed to create the effect she desired.

The landscaper filed a breach of contract action to recover $75,000 from the homeowner. At trial, the landscaper offers evidence that the landscaping was done in conformity with standards set forth by a national organization of landscapers and testimony from several witnesses that the homeowner was being unreasonable because the grounds were stately. Will the landscaper likely prevail?

(A) No, because the homeowner was not satisfied with the landscaping.

(B) No, because the contract was not in writing.

(C) Yes, because the landscaper performed in accordance with recognized standards.

(D) Yes, because the homeowner was being unreasonable in refusing to acknowledge that the landscaping had made the grounds stately.

185. An expert witness was called by the defendant to testify in a murder trial. The expert was to testify that the defendant was not responsible for his actions due to a specific mental defect. On cross-examination, the prosecutor brought to the expert witness's attention an authoritative book on psychological conditions, judicially noted to be a reliable authority in the field. The book described the symptoms of the mental defect at issue differently than the expert witness described them, and the prosecutor read the book's description into evidence. The prosecutor wanted the jury to be able to consider the book's description as substantive evidence, but the defendant objected that the description could be used for impeachment purposes only, and not as substantive evidence. The prosecutor further wanted to introduce the book itself into evidence; the defendant objected to this, as well.

Should the court allow the jury to consider the description in the book as substantive evidence, and should the book itself be introduced as evidence?

(A) The description should be considered for impeachment purposes only, and the book should not be introduced into evidence.

(B) The description should be considered as substantive evidence, and the book should not be introduced into evidence.

(C) The description should be considered as substantive evidence, and the book should be introduced into evidence.

(D) The book should be introduced into evidence, though its contents can only be used for impeachment purposes.

186. A city passed an ordinance prohibiting all "adult entertainment establishments," defined as "enterprises that sell, trade, or depict materials that are obscene or pornographic." The city justified its law on the basis of reputable studies that (i) obscene and pornographic materials degrade females and increase the tendency towards anti-social behavior of people who view it; and (ii) adult entertainment establishments are linked with criminal activity such as prostitution and drug dealing. The city also emphasized that the three cities bordering it all allow adult entertainment establishments.

An entrepreneur who wishes to open up an adult bookstore in the city sues the city in an appropriate federal court and claims that the ordinance is unconstitutional. Will she likely prevail?

(A) Yes, because the city's ordinance deprives her of her right to earn a living in violation of the Due Process Clause of the Fourteenth Amendment.

(B) Yes, because the First Amendment prohibits the city from banning all adult entertainment establishments.

(C) No, because the plaintiff has not been deprived of her constitutional right to earn a living, as she can open up his adult bookstore in one of the three nearby cities.

(D) No, because the city has legitimate reasons for banning adult entertainment establishments that are not based on the content of the material they are selling, trading, or depicting.

187. An individual rented an apartment in a multi-family dwelling on a month-to-month basis. Under the terms of the lease, the tenant had an absolute duty to repair the premises. At the time that the individual rented the apartment, the landlord made the tenant aware of several housing code violations that constitute a substantial threat to the individual's health and safety. After waiting a reasonable time for the landlord to correct the violations, the individual, in accord with a statutory provision, placed the monthly rent payment in an escrow account, rather than submitting it to the apartment owner.

After failing to receive the rent for two months, the apartment owner filed an action against the individual seeking eviction of the individual.

If the tenant raised the landlord's failure to correct the housing code violations as a defense, will the tenant be successful?

(A) No, because the tenant had a contractual duty to repair the premises.

(B) No, because the tenant was aware of the violations when the tenant assumed control of the premises.

(C) Yes, because of the implied warranty of habitability.

(D) Yes, because the landlord's actions constituted a constructive eviction.

188. Arriving home from work, a husband found his wife engaged in sex with his best friend. The husband flew into a rage and verbally threatened to shoot both of them, although he did not own a gun. The best friend quickly left and the husband eventually calmed down and regained his self-control after his wife promised not to see the best friend again. Nevertheless, the husband left the house to purchase a handgun. After making his purchase, he stopped by a local bar and became inebriated.

In the meantime, the best friend returned to drop off the husband's favorite hat, which the husband had left at the best friend's house the day before. Only the wife was home, but as the wife was giving the best friend a goodbye hug, the husband returned home, still inebriated. As both the wife and the best friend attempted to explain the innocent nature of their being together, the husband, his shock over their relationship returning, pulled the trigger. His shot missed the best friend and instead killed the wife.

The husband was charged with common law murder of his wife. Which of the following would be his best argument against the charge?

(A) He didn't intend to kill his wife.

(B) His intoxicated state prevented him from forming the intent necessary to commit the crime.

(C) The sight of his best friend and his wife together again reignited his feelings regarding his wife's adultery.

(D) A reasonable person would not have cooled off from the initial discovery of the adultery.

189. A wealthy businessman contracted with an animal trainer to perform a show with live animals, including specifically a lion, at the businessman's New Year's Eve party for $100,000. On the day of the party, the trainer called the businessman and informed him that she could not perform a show with a lion that evening, but could do a show with a white tiger instead. However, she refused to perform unless the businessman agreed to pay her $125,000. The businessman agreed. The show was a spectacular success with the guests.

After the show, the businessman paid the trainer $100,000. The trainer filed a breach of contract action against the businessman for $25,000. Is the trainer likely to prevail?

(A) Yes, because there was consideration for the contract modification.

(B) Yes, because, since the show was a success, the trainer substantially performed the contract.

(C) No. because the trainer had a pre-existing duty to perform the contract for $100,000.

(D) No, because a threat to breach a contract unless an additional amount is paid constitutes duress.

190. The Occupational Safety and Health Act of 1970 (OSHA) required all private employers in America to meet certain minimum federal standards to ensure safe and healthful work environments. Recently, Congress amended OSHA, extending its coverage requirements to state and local government employers.

A state sued in an appropriate federal court, challenging the constitutionality of this amendment. Will the court likely uphold the amendment as constitutional?

(A) No, because the amendment violates the Tenth Amendment.

(B) No, because the amendment violates fundamental principles of federalism, because Congress has directly impaired the states' ability to carry out their integral governmental functions.

(C) Yes, because the amendment merely affects the activities of states acting in their proprietary capacity.

(D) Yes, because the amendment is a valid exercise of Congress's Commerce Clause power.

191. A credit union loaned money to a married couple to enable them to purchase a mansion as their primary residence. The couple gave the credit union a mortgage on the mansion. The credit union promptly and properly filed the mortgage with the local land records office.

A little more than a year later, the homeowners financed the purchase of an expensive chandelier from a lighting supply store on credit. The couple gave the store a note and a security interest in the chandelier. Due to an employee oversight, the store failed to file the security interest with the local land records office until 15 days after the chandelier was installed in the mansion.

About two years after the purchase of the chandelier, the husband's business suffered a severe downturn, and the homeowners defaulted on their mortgage and their note to the store. The credit union initiated foreclosure proceedings and, upon learning that the store planned to remove the chandelier from the mansion, filed an action to prevent the store from doing so.

Whose rights to the chandelier are superior?

(A) The credit union, because it holds a purchase money mortgage on the mansion.

(B) The credit union, because it recorded its mortgage before the store recorded its security interest.

(C) The store, because the chandelier was a fixture.

(D) The store, because it timely and properly recorded its security interest.

192. A pedestrian was walking next to a building under construction. Suddenly, he was hit in the head by a falling brick. As a consequence, the pedestrian suffered a skull fracture and a severe brain injury.

The pedestrian sued the construction company. At trial, the pedestrian did not introduce any direct evidence of the construction company's negligence, but proved that the construction company's employees were in control of its bricks at all relevant times, and that a brick does not ordinarily fall from a building under construction without negligence. The construction company offers uncontroverted proof that the pedestrian was negligent by walking so close to an active construction site. The jurisdiction in which the lawsuit is proceeding applies pure comparative negligence rules.

At the close of all evidence, the construction company moved for a directed verdict. Should the court deny this motion?

(A) Yes, because the pedestrian's negligence does not reduce the likelihood of the construction company being negligent.

(B) Yes, because *res ipsa loquitur* requires a finding of negligence.

(C) No, because a party who is negligent may not prevail under a *res ipsa loquitur* theory.

(D) No, because the pedestrian has not produced any direct evidence of the company's culpability.

193. A plaintiff sued a defendant for injuries she sustained when she slipped on a wet floor in the defendant's restaurant. The plaintiff saw a physician, and underwent physical therapy sessions with him to treat her injuries. During one physical therapy session, the plaintiff said to her physician, "You know, I saw the 'Caution, Floor is Wet' sign before I fell, but I was in such a hurry to get back to my table that I ignored it." Another patient undergoing physical therapy with another physician overheard the statement, and informed the defendant, who happened to be his friend. The defendant wants to introduce the testimony of his friend, as whether the plaintiff had notice of the wet floor is at issue in the case. The plaintiff objects to the testimony.

Should the court allow the friend to testify as to the plaintiff's statement?

(A) No, because the statement is inadmissible hearsay.

(B) No, because the statement is privileged.

(C) Yes, because the statement is not hearsay.

(D) Yes, because the statement was made for the purposes of medical diagnosis or treatment.

194. A gas station entered into a contract with an oil distributor to purchase a specified quantity of gasoline for resale. The contract specified, per the gas station's request, that the gasoline was to be 99.5% free of impurities, as determined by industry-standard measurements. Another contract provision specified that the gasoline was to be delivered by July 31 at the latest.

The oil distributor delivered the gasoline to the gas station on July 30. Before accepting the delivery, the gas station manager checked the purity of the gasoline. The gasoline was only 99.3% free of impurities, and the manager rejected it. The oil distributor immediately informed the gas station manager that it intended to cure the defect by delivering a new shipment as soon as possible. The oil distributor delivered a new shipment of gasoline to the gas station on August 1, but the gas station manager rejected the new shipment. Both parties agree that the gasoline in the second shipment was 99.7% free of impurities.

Later, the oil distributor sued the gas station for breach of contract. Is it likely to prevail?

(A) No, because the oil distributor had no right to cure its defective tender.

(B) No, because an acceptable shipment needed to be delivered by July 31.

(C) Yes, because the second shipment was a conforming tender, and the gas station was required to accept it.

(D) Yes, because it properly cured its defective tender within a reasonable time.

195. A chef and her friend were cooking dinner. As the friend handed a knife to the chef, the knife slipped and fell, slicing into the chef's foot. While the chef's foot was being treated at the hospital, the chef contracted a severe infection, which eventually necessitated the amputation of her foot.

The chef sued the hospital and her friend in a jurisdiction that applies traditional joint and several liability rules, allows contribution, and uses a pure comparative negligence system. The jury determined that the chef suffered $1 million in damages, and apportioned the fault as follows: 30% to the chef, 55% to the friend, and 15% to the hospital.

How much, if anything, may the chef collect from the hospital, and how much, if anything, may the hospital seek in contribution from the friend?

(A) The chef may collect $150,000 from the hospital, and the hospital may not seek contribution from the friend.

(B) The chef may collect $150,000 from the hospital, and the hospital may seek $150,000 in contribution from the friend.

(C) The chef may collect $700,000 from the hospital, and the hospital may seek $550,000 in contribution from the friend.

(D) The chef may collect $700,000 from the hospital, and the hospital may not seek contribution from the friend.

196. A homeowner held title to her residence in fee simple absolute. During her ownership, the homeowner converted a first floor room into a library. She designed floor-to-ceiling bookcases with elaborate decorative items. She contracted with a carpenter to build and install the bookcases in the room. The bookcases were affixed to the walls of the rooms with screws rather than nails so that they could be more easily removed. She intended to take the bookcases with her if she ever moved.

In the sales brochure that was prepared by the homeowner's real estate broker and approved of by the homeowner, the room was described as a library, but no specific mention was made of the bookcases.

The contract of sale did not contain a reference to the bookcases. After the contract of sale was entered into, the homeowner had the bookcases removed from the house and repaired the damage to the walls caused by their removal.

On a walk-through of the premises prior to closing, the buyer discovered that the bookcases had been removed. The buyer, after balking at the transfer of the property without the bookcases, agreed to accept the deed but reserved the right to pursue an action regarding the removal of the bookcases.

In the action based on the removal of the bookcases brought by the buyer for money damages, which of the following would not be a strong argument that the specified party could make in support of its position?

(A) The seller argues that the damage done to the room from the removal of the bookcases was repaired.

(B) The seller argues that the seller's subjective intent, at the time of installation, was to remove the bookcases if the house was ever sold.

(C) The buyer argues that the bookcases were specially designed for use in the library.

(D) The buyer argues that the bookcases were important to the function of the room as a library.

197. A woman met a man at a party at the home of a third person. The woman noticed that the man was wearing an expensive gold watch. As the party was winding down and the woman and man were alone, the woman slipped a sedative into the man's drink. Waiting until the man passed out, the woman then removed the watch from the man's wrist and left the party. Later, the party's host discovered the man asleep, and revived him. When the man discovered that his watch was missing, the man called the police. The man, who lived at home with his parents, had taken the watch from his father's dresser for the evening, without his father's permission.

The woman was arrested and charged with robbery. Can she be convicted of the crime?

(A) Yes, because the woman used force to permanently deprive the man of the watch he was wearing.

(B) Yes, because the taking took place at a dwelling.

(C) No, because the watch belonged to the man's father and the man did not have permission to use it.

(D) No, because the man was unconscious when his watch was taken.

198. Over the course of one night, an attorney went to three different bars: Bar A, Bar B, and Bar C. The attorney stayed at each bar for roughly equal amounts of time, and each bar served him enough liquor to make him legally intoxicated. At the end of the night, the attorney left Bar C and was driving home erratically. A block away from his home, the attorney lost control of his car, careened into oncoming traffic, and collided with his neighbor's car. The attorney died in the collision, and his neighbor was permanently disfigured.

The neighbor sued Bar A in a jurisdiction that has adopted standard dram shop laws. Bar A filed a motion to dismiss the suit for failing to state a claim upon which relief can be granted. How should the court rule on the motion?

(A) Deny the motion, and order Bar B, Bar C, and the attorney's estate joined as defendants.

(B) Deny the motion, because a reasonable fact finder could determine that the neighbor's injuries were a continuing consequence of Bar A's actions.

(C) Grant the motion, because the attorney's criminal act of driving drunk was a superseding cause which cut off Bar A's liability.

(D) Grant the motion, because Bar A's negligence was not the "but-for" cause of the neighbor's injuries.

199. Congress enacted a law making it a federal crime "to transport, or cause to be transported, one's spouse across state lines for the purpose of murder." A wife paid a third party $10,000 to take her husband on a hunting trip to another state and kill him there. The third party did so. The wife was indicted for violating this criminal provision. Her defense is that this criminal provision exceeds Congress's constitutional powers. Will her defense likely succeed?

(A) Yes, because federalism prohibits Congress from interfering in an area of traditional state concern, the crime of murder.

(B) Yes, because the activity in question, murder, does not substantially affect interstate commerce.

(C) No, because Congress can protect the instrumentalities of interstate commerce.

(D) No, because Congress can keep the channels of interstate commerce free of immoral and injurious uses.

200. In a criminal trial for attempted murder, the prosecutor seeks to introduce a statement made by the victim immediately after he was attacked by the defendant. The victim, very seriously injured, shouted the defendant's name and said, "I can't believe you shot me! I'm dying!" At the time of the trial, the victim has mostly recovered from his injuries, but suffered permanent memory loss, has no recollection of the incident at all, and has no recollection of making the statement. The prosecutor seeks to introduce the statement as a dying declaration, but the defendant objects.

Should this statement be admissible under the "dying declaration" exception to the hearsay rules?

(A) No, the statement is not admissible as a dying declaration.

(B) No, because the victim did not die.

(C) Yes, because the victim is unavailable due to his inability to remember.

(D) Yes, because the proceeding in which the statement will be introduced is a criminal trial.

STOP.

IF YOU FINISH BEFORE TIME IS CALLED, CHECK YOUR WORK ON THIS TEST.

Themis®
BAR REVIEW

ANSWER KEY

Item	Answer	Subject
1	A	CONTRACTS
2	B	EVIDENCE
3	A	TORTS
4	C	TORTS
5	D	REAL PROP.
6	B	EVIDENCE
7	C	CRIM. LAW
8	A	CONST. LAW
9	B	CONTRACTS
10	C	REAL PROP.
11	C	CONTRACTS
12	B	CONST. LAW
13	D	EVIDENCE
14	D	CRIM. LAW
15	C	CRIM. LAW
16	A	REAL PROP.
17	C	TORTS
18	A	CONST. LAW
19	D	REAL PROP.
20	D	CONTRACTS
21	B	TORTS
22	C	CONST. LAW
23	A	CRIM. LAW
24	B	EVIDENCE
25	D	REAL PROP.
26	C	EVIDENCE
27	B	TORTS
28	A	CONTRACTS
29	D	CRIM. LAW
30	C	CONST. LAW
31	B	REAL PROP.
32	B	TORTS
33	A	REAL PROP.

Item	Answer	Subject
34	C	CONST. LAW
35	D	CRIM. LAW
36	C	TORTS
37	B	EVIDENCE
38	D	TORTS
39	A	CRIM. LAW
40	D	CONTRACTS
41	C	EVIDENCE
42	D	REAL PROP.
43	B	CONST. LAW
44	B	CONTRACTS
45	A	EVIDENCE
46	C	CONST. LAW
47	A	CRIM. LAW
48	A	REAL PROP.
49	C	CONTRACTS
50	D	CONTRACTS
51	C	TORTS
52	D	EVIDENCE
53	C	CONST. LAW
54	A	TORTS
55	C	REAL PROP.
56	C	CONST. LAW
57	D	EVIDENCE
58	A	CONST. LAW
59	B	CRIM. LAW
60	D	CONTRACTS
61	B	CRIM. LAW
62	A	EVIDENCE
63	C	CONTRACTS
64	D	EVIDENCE
65	B	REAL PROP.
66	D	TORTS

Item	Answer	Subject
67	B	CRIM. LAW
68	A	CONTRACTS
69	B	REAL PROP.
70	A	CRIM. LAW
71	D	TORTS
72	B	TORTS
73	D	CONST. LAW
74	C	CONTRACTS
75	A	REAL PROP.
76	B	CRIM. LAW
77	C	EVIDENCE
78	B	CRIM. LAW
79	D	CONST. LAW
80	C	TORTS
81	A	EVIDENCE
82	C	CONTRACTS
83	B	CONTRACTS
84	B	CONST. LAW
85	D	REAL PROP.
86	A	TORTS
87	C	REAL PROP.
88	C	EVIDENCE
89	D	CONST. LAW
90	A	TORTS
91	D	CRIM. LAW
92	A	EVIDENCE
93	B	CONTRACTS
94	A	TORTS
95	D	EVIDENCE
96	C	CONST. LAW
97	A	REAL PROP.
98	D	CRIM. LAW
99	C	CONTRACTS

Item	Answer	Subject
100	B	REAL PROP.
101	C	EVIDENCE
102	C	CRIM. LAW
103	D	CONTRACTS
104	A	CONTRACTS
105	C	CONST. LAW
106	B	REAL PROP.
107	D	CRIM. LAW
108	D	TORTS
109	A	CONST. LAW
110	B	EVIDENCE
111	C	REAL PROP.
112	A	TORTS
113	C	CRIM. LAW
114	B	CONST. LAW
115	B	CRIM. LAW
116	C	CONTRACTS
117	D	EVIDENCE
118	B	TORTS
119	D	REAL PROP.
120	D	CONST. LAW
121	A	TORTS
122	B	EVIDENCE
123	A	REAL PROP.
124	A	CONTRACTS
125	D	CRIM. LAW
126	C	CRIM. LAW
127	C	CONST. LAW
128	A	EVIDENCE
129	B	CONTRACTS
130	A	CONTRACTS
131	C	REAL PROP.
132	C	CRIM. LAW
133	A	CRIM. LAW

Item	Answer	Subject
134	B	CONST. LAW
135	A	TORTS
136	D	EVIDENCE
137	C	REAL PROP.
138	A	CRIM. LAW
139	A	EVIDENCE
140	D	TORTS
141	B	CONST. LAW
142	B	CONTRACTS
143	A	CONTRACTS
144	B	REAL PROP.
145	D	CONTRACTS
146	C	TORTS
147	D	EVIDENCE
148	B	CONST. LAW
149	D	TORTS
150	C	REAL PROP.
151	A	CONST. LAW
152	C	CRIM. LAW
153	A	EVIDENCE
154	D	CRIM. LAW
155	A	REAL PROP.
156	C	CONTRACTS
157	B	CONTRACTS
158	D	TORTS
159	C	REAL PROP.
160	A	CONST. LAW
161	C	TORTS
162	D	CONST. LAW
163	D	TORTS
164	C	EVIDENCE
165	B	CRIM. LAW
166	C	CRIM. LAW
167	B	EVIDENCE

Item	Answer	Subject
168	B	REAL PROP.
169	D	CONTRACTS
170	D	CONST. LAW
171	B	TORTS
172	D	CONTRACTS
173	A	EVIDENCE
174	A	CONST. LAW
175	B	REAL PROP.
176	D	CONTRACTS
177	D	TORTS
178	C	CRIM. LAW
179	C	EVIDENCE
180	D	CONST. LAW
181	A	REAL PROP.
182	B	TORTS
183	A	CRIM. LAW
184	A	CONTRACTS
185	B	EVIDENCE
186	B	CONST. LAW
187	C	REAL PROP.
188	C	CRIM. LAW
189	A	CONTRACTS
190	D	CONST. LAW
191	D	REAL PROP.
192	A	TORTS
193	C	EVIDENCE
194	B	CONTRACTS
195	C	TORTS
196	B	REAL PROP.
197	A	CRIM. LAW
198	B	TORTS
199	D	CONST. LAW
200	A	EVIDENCE

ANSWER TO QUESTION 1

Answer choice A is correct. The restorer's reliance on the collector's revocation estops the collector from asserting the existence of a contract. Answer choice B is incorrect because, under the mailbox rule, an acceptance is effective upon mailing. It is not required to be received by the offeror. Answer choice C is incorrect because, although the collector's letter constituted a valid acceptance since he had mailed within the month that the restorer stated that her offer would remain open, because the restorer received the collector's subsequent rejection first and relied on that rejection, the collector is estopped from asserting the existence of a contract. Answer choice D is incorrect because, while it is true that the "mailbox rule" does not apply where an acceptance is sent after a revocation, it generally does apply where the acceptance is sent prior to the revocation.

ANSWER TO QUESTION 2

Answer choice B is correct. An arrest for a bad act is not a bad act itself. Therefore, a witness may not be cross examined about an arrest. In this case, there was no evidence that the witness actually wrote any bad checks; as such, the subject may not be brought up on cross-examination. Answer choice A is incorrect because a witness may sometimes be asked on cross-examination about a prior bad act. There are some limitations, however: the judge must determine that the prior bad act is probative of untruthfulness, and the attorney must have a good faith basis for asking about the conduct. Answer choice C is incorrect because, even though actually writing bad checks would be probative of the witness's truthfulness, simply being arrested is not probative of truthfulness. Answer choice D is incorrect because, as mentioned above, being arrested is not probative of truthfulness. Further, time limits are relevant when a witness is being impeached with evidence that he has been convicted of a crime, not with evidence of prior bad acts.

ANSWER TO QUESTION 3

Answer choice A is correct. In order for a member of the public to successfully maintain a public nuisance action, that person must suffer a special injury that is different in kind to that suffered by the general public. The plaintiff's physical injury here constitutes a special injury. In addition, with respect to the use of a public passageway, the plaintiff's injury must arise from the use of that passageway and defendant's conduct must interfere with, obstruct, or render the passageway dangerous for passage. Answer choice B is incorrect because the attractive nuisance doctrine applies to a child-plaintiff who trespasses on the defendant's property and is injured by an artificial condition on that property. Here, the child was injured while legally on navigable water, not while trespassing on the defendant's property. Answer choice C is incorrect because, unlike a private nuisance, a public nuisance does not require that the plaintiff have an ownership interest in land. Answer choice D is incorrect because the plaintiff's suit is against the company that operated the golf course not the golfer personally. In addition, nuisance actions, whether public or private, may be based on the defendant's negligent conduct; the defendant's conduct need not be intentional.

ANSWER TO QUESTION 4

Answer choice C is correct. A misrepresentation can arise from nondisclosure where a person is under a duty to disclose. A misrepresentation can also arise from conduct and from the concealment of a fact. A person may generally rely on a misstatement unless the falsity of the misstatement is obvious. Answer choice D is incorrect because intentional misrepresentation is not confined to real property transactions, but can arise in any type of transaction in which the plaintiff suffers a pecuniary loss due to the defendant's misrepresentation. Answer choice A is incorrect because, as noted with respect to answer choice C, a misrepresentation need not be in written form. Answer choice B is incorrect because a person is not under a duty to investigate the truthfulness of a misrepresentation.

ANSWER TO QUESTION 5

Answer choice D is correct. Under the common law, a devise to a beneficiary who predeceases the testator lapses. An anti-lapse statute can operate to prevent the devise from lapse. In this instance, the anti-lapse statute applies because the brother is a descendant of the testator's parents. Consequently, the farm passes to the brother's children. Answer choice A is incorrect because, as noted with regard to answer choice D, the common law rule of lapse, which requires the beneficiary under a will to survive the testator in order to be entitled to a devise, is superseded by the anti-lapse statute with respect to the devise of the farm. Answer choice B is incorrect because the residuary clause only applies to property that otherwise does not pass under the terms of the will. In this instance, the devise of the farm to the brother is effective under the anti-lapse statute to pass the farm to the brother's children. In addition, a residuary clause does not create an alternative taker who is entitled to take the property because of the death of the primary beneficiary. Answer choice C is incorrect because the lapse rule is the default rule unless the anti-lapse statute applies. In order to overcome the presumption of lapse, the will must contain language that clearly indicates the testator's intent that the devise survive the beneficiary's death.

ANSWER TO QUESTION 6

Answer choice B is correct. The question at issue is a leading question, which is a question that suggests its answer. Leading questions are generally inadmissible on direct examination. However, the federal rules allow leading questions on direct examination in certain situations when it is necessary to develop testimony, such as when the witness is a child, when a witness has difficulty communicating due to age or a physical or mental problem, when the witness is hostile, when the witness is an adverse party, or when the witness is associated with an adverse party. In this case, the witness was hostile, so leading questions were an appropriate way to elicit testimony. Answer choice C is incorrect because a party's own witness may become hostile, and a party may call a witness who he knows is hostile. Answer choice D is incorrect because, as discussed above, leading questions were appropriate in this case, even though the witness was not a child or associated with the adverse party. Answer choice A is incorrect because it is too broad; a party may generally not ask leading questions of his witnesses unless the testimony is purely related to uncontested or incidental matters or when, as have been discussed above, it is necessary to develop the witness's testimony because she is a child, has some difficulty communicating, is hostile, is an adverse party, or is associated with an adverse party.

ANSWER TO QUESTION 7

Answer choice C is correct because the overt act need not be performed by the defendant, but may be performed by any party to the conspiracy. The girlfriend's act of searching through the wealthy man's bag suffices. Answer choice A is incorrect because, even though the jurisdiction has adopted a unilateral approach to conspiracy, the defendant must agree to commit an unlawful act in order to be convicted of conspiracy. Here, the man's mere recounting of his observations would likely be insufficient to establish such agreement. Answer choice B is incorrect. Under the Model Penal Code, a member of a conspiracy is not liable for a crime unless he aids and abets in its commission. This differs from the majority rule, in which a conspirator can be convicted of both the offense of conspiracy and all substantive crimes committed by any other co-conspirators acting in furtherance of the conspiracy. Here, because the Model Penal Code is in effect, the man could argue that he did not aid or abet in stealing the wealthy man's ring. Answer choice D is incorrect. Conspiracy is a specific intent crime for which voluntary intoxication may be a defense.

ANSWER TO QUESTION 8

Answer choice A is correct because the procedural aspect of the Due Process Clause requires that a state grant notice and a hearing to welfare recipients *before* terminating their welfare benefits. For this reason, answer choice C is incorrect. Answer choice D is incorrect because the Due Process Clause applies to a property interest created by the state as well as to private property interests. Consequently, while the state can establish procedures for the termination of welfare benefits, such procedures must comport with the constitutional due process requirement. Answer choice B is incorrect. While the department's action did terminate the individual's welfare payments, the action did not modify existing laws or regulations regarding the individual's entitlement to such payment, but instead was taken based on the department's determination that the individual did not have the right to welfare payments under the existing laws and regulations.

ANSWER TO QUESTION 9

Answer choice B is correct. Even if the manufacturer included an additional term in its acceptance and the retailer objected to that term, a contract was still formed on the terms of the original offer. Answer choice A is incorrect because, regardless of whether both parties are merchants, the retailer did not have a right to refuse to perform the contract; a contract was still formed based on the original terms. The fact that the retailer objected to the term means that it would not be part of the contract regardless of the parties' status as merchants. Answer choice C is incorrect because the knock-out rule, which applies to conflicting terms proposed by merchant parties, does not itself serve as a basis to void a contract. Under the knock-out rule, different terms in the offer and acceptance nullify each other and are knocked out of the contract. Answer choice D is incorrect because, even though the security interest term materially affected the bargain because it altered remedies available to the manufacturer if the store failed to pay, the retailer was still required to perform the contract per the original terms.

ANSWER TO QUESTION 10

Answer choice C is correct. Each of the speculator's lots is subject to an implied reciprocal servitude. Although normally an equitable servitude must be in writing, the existence of a common scheme is evidenced by the developer's advertizing and the insertion of the character and size provision into the deeds for the other 75% of lots. In addition, although the speculator had neither actual nor record notice of the size restrictions, the speculator had inquiry notice based on the uniformity in size of each of the other lots that had been sold. Answer choice A is incorrect because, as the name suggests, an implied reciprocal servitude does not require record notice, but is implied from the existence of a common scheme. Answer choice B is incorrect because obtaining governmental approval by complying with the applicable zoning ordinance does not protect an owner from also having to adhere to a private land use restriction. Answer choice D is incorrect because, although the speculator did not purchase the lots for the purpose of constructing a residence on each lot, the speculator did not use the property for nonresidential purposes.

ANSWER TO QUESTION 11

Answer choice C is correct because this was a unilateral mistake of the buyers, and there is no evidence that the risk of that mistake was assumed by the owner. Answer choice A is incorrect because the duty of good faith generally does not impose an affirmative duty to act, but instead simply requires honesty in fact. Here, the owner did not create the couple's erroneous belief and did nothing to lead credence to it. Answer choice B is incorrect because frustration of purpose involves something that happens in the future. This question involves a mistake about a present state of the property. Answer choice D is incorrect because, although the association of the historical figure with the house did not affect the condition of the house or its habitability, the couple "in large part" wanted the house because of its association with the historical figure. Thus, it was material to their bargain.

ANSWER TO QUESTION 12

Answer choice B is correct. EEA Section 1 unconstitutionally "commandeers" state legislatures by forcing them to enact laws against their will. By contrast, EEA Section 2 is constitutional because Congress, through the Spending Power, can "encourage" state action that it could not directly compel. For these reasons, answer choice A, C, and D are incorrect. Also, with respect to answer choice D, state officials cannot consent to an unconstitutional exercise of power by the federal government.

ANSWER TO QUESTION 13

Answer choice D is correct. While a prior, out-of-court statement of identification is often considered non-hearsay and can be admissible as substantive evidence, the witness who made the prior statement of identification must have testified at the present trial and have been subject to cross-examination concerning the identification for it to be admissible. Answer choice A is incorrect because, as stated, the witness must testify at the present trial for the statement to be considered nonhearsay. Answer choice B is incorrect because it misstates the law; while some hearsay exceptions do depend on the unavailability of the witness, prior statements of identification are considered nonhearsay, and are not exceptions to the hearsay rule. Further, as discussed above, for the statement to be considered nonhearsay and admissible, the witness must testify at the present trial. Answer choice C is incorrect because there is no requirement that the suspect or defendant be represented by counsel at a lineup for the statement to be considered nonhearsay; all that is required is that the witness testify at the present trial and be subject to cross-examination at trial as to the identification.

ANSWER TO QUESTION 14

Answer choice D is correct because derivative-use immunity protects the witness from the use of the witness's own testimony, or any evidence derived from that testimony, against the witness in a subsequent prosecution, but does not protect him from its use in a civil suit. Answer choice A is incorrect. While it is true that a witness need not be a defendant in order to be given immunity, such immunity does not extend to use of the witness's testimony at a subsequent civil trial. Answer choice B is incorrect because immunity, whether transactional or derivative-use immunity, does not apply to subsequent civil actions. Answer choice C is incorrect because immunity is not limited to federal prosecution despite the "separate sovereignty" doctrine. However, it is limited to criminal prosecutions.

ANSWER TO QUESTION 15

Answer choice C is correct. If a statute does not state the culpable mind applicable to all material elements of the crime, then the *mens rea* applicable to one material element is applicable to all material elements. Consequently, the "knowingly" state of mind is applied to both the "sell, distribute, or barter a sexually explicit film" element *and* the "featuring actors younger than the age of majority" element. Here, the woman subjectively did not know that the videos she was selling featured performers below the age of majority; thus, she cannot be convicted under the statute. For the foregoing reasons, answer choice B is incorrect. Answer choice A is incorrect because an honest mistake of law can be a valid defense when the mistake negates the required intent. Answer choice D is incorrect because it applies the "purposely" mental state, when "knowingly," a lesser mental state, is the *mens rea* required by the statute.

ANSWER TO QUESTION 16

Answer choice A is correct. An option contract, as a contract to transfer property, is subject to the Statute of Frauds. Answer choice B is incorrect because an option contract, unlike an offer, does not terminate upon the incapacity of the grantor of the option. Answer choice C is incorrect because, although an offeree rejects an offer by making a counteroffer, an option holder may propose to alter the terms for purchasing the property subject to the option without sacrificing the right to exercise the option. Answer choice D is incorrect because, although the option contract did constitute a restraint on alienation, it was reasonable in that it only prevented the sale of the ranch for 90 days.

ANSWER TO QUESTION 17

Answer choice C is correct. Under the learned intermediary rule, the manufacturer of a prescription drug typically satisfies its duty to warn by informing the prescribing physician of problems with the drug rather than the patient taking the drug. Answer choice A is incorrect because, for drugs which cannot be legally obtained without a prescription, the drug maker is generally not required to provide a warning directly to the patient, but may instead rely on the learned intermediary rule. Answer choice B is incorrect because in a strict products liability action, although the drug maker may be liable to a patient harmed by the drug as a commercial supplier, the product at issue must be defective. Since in this instance the patient sought to base the defective nature of the product on the maker's failure to warn, the drug maker is not liable because it satisfied its duty to warn by warning the prescribing physician. Answer choice D is incorrect because the manufacturer can be liable for a failure to warn where a small number of persons are at risk if the severity of the potential harm is great.

ANSWER TO QUESTION 18

Answer choice A is correct because the plaintiff does not have standing merely because she is a citizen or a taxpayer. In addition, she can't show that she has suffered a particularized "injury in fact" different than that suffered by all other citizens. Answer choice B is incorrect because the injury of which the plaintiff is complaining, service as president by a person who is not eligible to do so is presently occurring. Answer choice C is incorrect. The political question doctrine does not apply because neither has the Constitution assigned decision-making on this subject to a different branch of the government nor is the matter inherently one that the judiciary cannot decide. Answer choice D is incorrect because the abstention doctrine inapplicable; there is no strong state interests at stake.

ANSWER TO QUESTION 19

Answer choice D is correct. A mortgagor has a duty to not commit waste with respect to the mortgaged property when such waste impairs the mortgagee's security interest in that property. Answer choice A is incorrect because, even if the mortgagor is not bound by the terms of the mortgage to maintain or repair the mortgaged property, the mortgagor has a duty not to commit waste, at least to the extent that it impairs the mortgagee's security interest in the property. Answer choice B is incorrect because the mortgagor's duty not to commit waste is independent of the mortgagor's specific contractual obligations. Answer choice C is incorrect because the mortgagor's duty not to commit waste is not confined to commercial mortgages.

ANSWER TO QUESTION 20

Answer choice D is correct. The doctrine of frustration of purpose applies when an unexpected event arises that destroys one party's purpose in entering into the contract, even if performance of the contract is not rendered impossible. The event that arises must not be the fault of the frustrated party, and its non-occurrence must have been a basic assumption of the contract. The frustrated party is entitled to rescind the contract without paying damages. Here, relocation of the sporting event was not a foreseeable prospect, and only occurred because of an improbable event—an earthquake that damaged the stadium. Consequently, the contract should be rescinded and the $2,000 returned to the retailer. Answer choice A is incorrect because impracticability applies where the specific subject matter of the contract is destroyed or performance becomes impracticable. Here, the shirts have not been destroyed and could be printed in the manner called for in the contract. Answer choice B is incorrect because in order for the doctrine of unconscionability to be applied, all or part of the contract must have been unconscionable at the time of contract formation. Here, that was not the case. Answer choice C is incorrect because relocation of the game was not a mutual mistake among the parties; rather, it was unforeseen event that was not reasonably foreseeable by the parties.

ANSWER TO QUESTION 21

Answer choice B is correct. When a person using force in self-defense unintentionally harms an innocent third party, the person is not liable unless the use of force is negligent with respect to the third party. Answer choice C is incorrect because, even though the youth was an invitee, the owner's duty towards the youth was to act with reasonable care. Since the owner's shooting of the youth was accidental and also not negligent in light of the circumstances, the owner did not breach his duty towards the youth. Answer choice D is incorrect because the doctrine that a felon is not criminally responsible for the death of a co-felon directly caused by another person (e.g., victim of the felony, police officer) is irrelevant in determining civil liability. It applies only with respect to criminal liability and then only to protect the felon from such liability. Answer choice A is incorrect because self-defense is not a defense to harm caused to an innocent third party unless the action was not negligent with the respect to the third party.

ANSWER TO QUESTION 22

Answer choice C is correct. Although, for the reasons discussed below, the First Amendment to the United State Constitution does not require the mall owner to permit leafleting in this instance, the state constitution as interpreted state's highest court does. A state may expand, but cannot contract individual rights, such as free speech, granted by the United States Constitution. Answer choice A is incorrect because, although leafleting is a form of speech that enjoys First Amendment protection, such protection does not extend to leafleting on private property, even private property that is open to the public such as a mall. Answer choice B is incorrect because the fact that the purpose for leafleting has a logical relationship to the location where the leafleting is to be conducted, does not trigger First Amendment protection of the leafleting, where that location is private property. Answer choice D is incorrect because, as noted with respect to answer choice A, the opening of private property to the public does not convert it into a public or limited public forum at which leafleting must be permitted despite the object of the owner of the property.

ANSWER TO QUESTION 23

Answer choice A is correct because in order to impose the death penalty, the aggravating circumstance involved cannot be unconstitutionally vague. A crime being "heinous or brutal" has been held to be unconstitutionally vague. Answer choice B is incorrect because, although many jurisdictions use this as the criteria for the death penalty, it is not the only permissible criteria. Answer choice C is incorrect because the standard is vague. It does not matter that it passes the first prong of the aggravated circumstances test, whether the circumstance sets the murder apart from others. Answer choice D is incorrect because the fact that a reasonable jury could conclude that the murder was heinous is not enough to render the requirement constitutional.

ANSWER TO QUESTION 24

Answer choice B is correct. Under Federal Rule of Evidence 801(d), a prior inconsistent statement, which otherwise would qualify as hearsay, is treated as non-hearsay. A prior inconsistent statement may be used to impeach a witness. Further, if a prior inconsistent statement made under oath at a trial, hearing, or deposition, it is admissible both to impeach the declarant's credibility and as substantive evidence, so long as the witness testifies at the present trial or hearing and is subject to cross-examination concerning the statement. The witness need not actually *be* cross-examined, so long as she is *subject to* cross-examination at the present trial. Here, even though the defendant's attorney did not cross-examine the witness, he had the opportunity to cross-examine her. Therefore, the testimony can be used both as substantive evidence and for impeachment purposes. Answer choice A is incorrect because, as explained above, because this prior inconsistent statement was made under oath, the declarant is available to testify, and the declarant was subject to cross-examination, the statement is admissible both for impeachment and substantive purposes. Answer choice C is incorrect because, unlike at common law, the Federal Rules do not require that the witness have the opportunity to explain or deny the evidence before introducing a prior inconsistent statement. Answer choice D is incorrect because, as explained above, under Federal Rule of Evidence 801(d), a prior inconsistent statement, which otherwise would qualify as hearsay, is treated as non-hearsay.

ANSWER TO QUESTION 25

Answer choice D is correct. When a person who attempts to transfer real property that he does not own subsequently becomes owner of that property, the after-acquired title doctrine provides that title to the property automatically vests in the transferee. Answer choice A is incorrect because, while the nephew did record his deed, the friend did not. Consequently, the nephew, not the friend, was owner of record of the parcel. Answer choice B is incorrect because although the friend presumably did not have actual knowledge that the aunt owned the parcel, the friend was on constructive notice that the nephew did not own the property. Moreover, even assuming the friend's status was that of a good faith purchaser, this status is irrelevant in ascertaining the friend's rights in relationship to the subsequent buyer. Answer choice C is incorrect because the doctrine of equitable conversion, which treats a buyer as the equitable owner of property during the period between execution of the contract and delivery of the deed, is irrelevant.

ANSWER TO QUESTION 26

Answer choice C is correct. Prior inconsistent testimony is admissible as both impeachment evidence and as substantive evidence. A prior inconsistent statement made under oath at a trial, hearing, or deposition is considered nonhearsay, and is admissible to impeach the declarant's credibility and as substantive evidence. The witness's credibility may be called into question by showing that the witness has previously made a statement that is materially inconsistent with some part of her current testimony. Further, when that statement was made under oath, it may also be used to prove the truth of the matter asserted—in this case, that the defendant was in possession of the goods on the day after the robbery. Because answer choice C is the only choice that reflects that the testimony may be used for both purposes, answer choices A, B, and D are incorrect.

ANSWER TO QUESTION 27

Answer choice B is correct. To sustain a claim of intentional infliction of emotional distress, a plaintiff must prove that the defendant intended to cause severe emotional distress, or acted with recklessness as to the risk of causing such distress. The claimed conduct must be extreme and outrageous, and the plaintiff must suffer severe emotional distress. Here, there is no factual evidence that the bicyclist suffered severe emotional distress. A plaintiff can recover punitive damages in assault, battery, and trespass to chattels claims, if the defendant's behavior is willful and wanton. Here, the facts suggest such a situation, as the spectator was attempting to knock the cyclist out of the race. For these reasons, answers A, C, and D are incorrect.

ANSWER TO QUESTION 28

Answer choice A is correct. A warranty that the goods are fit for a particular purpose may be disclaimed by a conspicuous writing. Such a writing need not refer to this warranty by name. Answer choice B is incorrect because unlike the applicability of the Statute of Frauds to the sale of goods, there is no dollar threshold that a warranty related to goods must exceed in order to be effective. Answer choice C is incorrect because, although a warranty of fitness for a particular purpose was made under these facts, the merchant effectively disclaimed this warranty. Answer choice D is incorrect because any seller may provide a warranty of fitness for a particular purpose and any seller may disclaim such a warranty.

ANSWER TO QUESTION 29

Answer choice D is correct. A prosecutor is free to exercise his peremptory challenges in any manner he sees fit unless such exercise violates the Equal Protection Clause. The Equal Protection Clause prevents the exercise of peremptory challenges for racially or gender motivated reasons. Since the prosecutor's reason for the exercise of his peremptory challenges was for neither of these reasons, the judge should reject the defendant's challenge to the prosecutor's use of his peremptory challenges. Answer choice A is incorrect because a defendant's right to an impartial jury does not require that the defendant's petit jury be a fair cross-section of the community and therefore does not protect the defendant from the prosecutor's use of his peremptory challenges to exclude a distinctive group in the community. Answer choice B is incorrect because a defendant may raise the issue of the prosecution's violation of the Equal Protection Clause without being a member of the protected class. Answer choice C is incorrect because the prosecution, as well as the defense, is constrained by the Equal Protection Clause in its use of peremptory challenges.

ANSWER TO QUESTION 30

Answer choice C is correct because Congress may enact legislation that is necessary and proper to its spending power. Here the criminalization of the taking of bribes by an official of an entity that receives substantial federal funds is necessary and proper to ensure that such funds are properly spent. Answer choice A is incorrect. The Constitution does not require the bribe directly relate to the federal funds. The preferential treatment given the prisoner was a threat to the integrity and proper operation of the federal program, and hence justified imposition of criminal sanctions on the guard. Answer choice B is incorrect because the congressional authority for this criminal statute was based on the Spending Clause, not the Commerce Clause. While the Commerce Clause requires a link to interstate commerce, the Spending Clause permits Congress to act for the general welfare. Answer choice D is incorrect because Congress, unlike state legislatures, does not possess a general police power.

ANSWER TO QUESTION 31

Answer choice B is correct. The document, although valid as a deed, did not operate to transfer the farm to the son because there was no delivery. By keeping the deed in his possession until his death, the farmer retained the right to revoke it. Answer choice A is incorrect because, unlike a will, a deed need not be witnessed in order to be valid. Answer choice C is incorrect because, as noted with regard to answer choice B, the document did not operate as a deed to transfer title to the farm to the son because of the lack of delivery. Answer choice D is incorrect because the fact that the deed was executed after the will does not give it priority over the will. In addition, as noted with regard to answer choice B, mere execution of a deed is not sufficient to transfer title; delivery and acceptance are also required.

ANSWER TO QUESTION 32

Answer choice B is correct. Under a modified comparative negligence regime, a plaintiff's damages are reduced by the percentage that the plaintiff is at fault. Here, since the pedestrian was found to be 20% at fault, the pedestrian's damages ($200,000) are reduced by $40,000 ($200,000 x 20%). Answer choice A is incorrect because under a comparative negligence regime, unlike a contributory negligence regime, a plaintiff who is negligent is not automatically barred from recovering damages. Answer choice C is incorrect because the last clear chance doctrine has generally been abolished in jurisdictions that have adopted a comparative negligence regime. Answer choice D is incorrect because, while a minor defendant who engages in an adult activity is held to the adult standard in determining whether the minor has acted negligently, this does not foreclose application of the comparative negligence rules in determining the extent to which the minor is liable for damages.

ANSWER TO QUESTION 33

Answer choice A is correct. The concept of abatement permits the reduction or elimination of a devise when the assets of the estate are insufficient to pay all debts and satisfy all devises. Under abatement, a general devise (e.g., a bequest of money) is sacrificed in order to honor a specific devise. Answer choice B is incorrect because the concept of ademption applies only to a specific devise, not a general one, such as the son's monetary bequest. Answer choice C is incorrect because the concept of exoneration applies when a specific device is subject an encumbrance. The testator's residence was not subject to an encumbrance. Answer choice D is incorrect because the concept of lapse applies when a beneficiary dies before the testator. Both beneficiaries survived the testator.

ANSWER TO QUESTION 34

Answer choice C is correct because police officers are not members of a suspect classification and so the ordinance's discrimination against them is judged under the rational basis standard. Since this ordinance is rationally related to the legitimate state interest of public safety because it seeks to ensure the availability of police officers, the officer's challenge is likely to fail. For this reason, answer choice B is incorrect. Answer choice A is incorrect because the ordinance is not directed towards the suppression of the officer's expressive conduct (i.e., engaging in exotic dancing). However, even had the ordinance been so directed, similar ordinances (e.g., an ordinance that prohibits nude dancing in adult clubs) have withstood constitutional challenges based on the First Amendment's Free Speech Clause due to the important governmental interest in preventing the harmful secondary effects of such conduct on the neighborhood. Answer choice D is incorrect. Even though the Takings Clause of the Fifth Amendment, which has typically been applied to real property, has on occasion been applied to intangible property interests, such as contract rights, patent rights, and trade secrets, the plaintiff, as an at-will employee, does not have a property interest that has been taken by the ordinance.

ANSWER TO QUESTION 35

Answer choice D is correct. The man may be convicted of depraved heart murder. Depraved heart murder is a killing that results when the defendant recklessly acts with extreme indifference to human life. For this type of murder, the man need not have had the intent to cause either death or serious bodily injury. The woman's consent to the act that led to her death is not a defense. Nor is the fact that the woman's death would not have happened but for her rare medical condition, or the man's lack of awareness of that condition. For these reasons, answer choices A, B, and C are incorrect.

ANSWER TO QUESTION 36

Answer choice C is correct. To sustain a claim of intentional infliction of emotional distress, a plaintiff must prove that she suffered severe emotional distress as a result of the defendant's conduct, that the defendant intended to cause severe emotional distress, or acted with recklessness as to the risk of causing such distress, and that the defendant's conduct was extreme and outrageous. Here, a reasonable fact finder could determine that the coach acted recklessly as to the risk of causing the mother severe emotional distress, and that his conduct was extreme and outrageous. Consequently, the court should deny the motion for summary judgment. Answer choice A is incorrect, because recklessness is sufficient to satisfy the intent requirement. Answer choice B is incorrect because the physical manifestation requirement only applies to bystanders, and is not implicated in this fact pattern. Answer choice D is incorrect because the transferred intent doctrine does not apply to intentional infliction of emotional distress.

ANSWER TO QUESTION 37

Answer choice B is correct. Hearsay is an out-of-court statement, whether written or oral, offered to prove the truth of the matter asserted. Heresay is not admissible unless it falls within an exception. The record meets the hearsay definition and should not be admitted unless a specific exception applies. One possible applicable exception to the hearsay rule would be the business record exception. A record or other writing made in the course of regularly conducted business is admissible. However, records prepared in anticipation of litigation are not admissible as business records. In this case, it does not appear that this report was prepared as part of a regular practice of record-making. The owner only told the employee to make the record so there was a description of what happened in the event that the plaintiff sued. As such, the document is not a business record. Answer choice A is incorrect in part because nothing in the fact pattern indicates that the record is anything other than the original. In any event, assuming the best evidence rule was satisfied, the hearsay issue would still remain. Answer choice C is incorrect because the document is not a business record. In order for a record to qualify as a business record, the custodian of the record or some other qualified witness must establish that the record was made (i) at or near the time of the event, (ii) by a person with knowledge of the event and under a duty to report it, or from information transmitted by such a person, and (iii) as part of a regular practice of making the kind of entry in question during the regular course of business. The record in this case does not qualify as a business record because it was made not in the regular course of business, but in anticipation of litigation. Records prepared in anticipation of litigation are not admissible as business records. Answer choice D is incorrect first because the record is not a business record. If it was, however, the person who made the record is not necessarily required to authenticate it; business records are self-authenticating if they are certified to meet the requirements of the business records exception.

ANSWER TO QUESTION 38

Answer choice D is correct. While the possessor of a wild animal is generally strictly liable for the injuries caused by the animal, strict liability does not apply to injuries that do not result from the dangerous propensities of the animal. The student's injury was caused by tripping over the porcupine, and not from a dangerous propensity of the porcupine. Answer choice A is incorrect because, as noted with regard to answer choice D, the possessor of a wild animal is not strictly liable where the injury does not result from the dangerous propensity of the animal. Answer choice B is incorrect because the action brought by the student was based on strict liability, not negligence. Consequently, the professor's failure to act with reasonable care is irrelevant. Answer choice C is incorrect because the exception to strict liability for a possessor of a wild animal applies only to a trespasser who is injured by the wild animal on the possessor's property. It does not extend to a licensee, such as social guest, or an invitee.

ANSWER TO QUESTION 39

Answer choice A is correct. Under the Model Penal Code test, a defendant is not guilty when, at the time of the conduct, as a result of a mental disease or defect, he did not have substantial capacity to appreciate the wrongfulness of the act, or to conform his conduct to the law. Here, although the man appreciated the wrongfulness of the killing, he was unable to resist the urging of the gold fish. Answer choice B is incorrect because the fact that the defendant suffered from a mental illness is not sufficient to establish an insanity defense. Answer choice C is incorrect because, as noted with respect to answer choice A, the Model Penal Code test contains not only a cognitive prong but also a volitional prong; satisfying either is sufficient to establish an insanity defense. Answer choice D is incorrect because the volitional prong does not require that the defendant act impulsively, merely that he lack the will to conform his conduct to the law.

ANSWER TO QUESTION 40

Answer choice D is correct. The claim for $100,000 is a claim for reliance damages, which may be recovered if the non-breaching party incurs expenses in reasonable reliance upon the promise that the other would perform. Here, however, there is no breach, because the 200,000 subscriber requirement was a condition precedent, and not a promise. The failure of a promise is a breach, and gives rise to damages, while the failure of a *condition* merely relieves a party of the obligation to perform. Consequently, the publishing company need not perform by meeting its obligation to pay, but it is not entitled to damages. Answer choice A is incorrect because, while it correctly describes the condition and the failure of the newspaper company, it reaches the wrong conclusion. Answer choice B is incorrect because, as a failure to satisfy a condition does not generally give rise to damages, the mitigation of damages is irrelevant. Answer choice C is incorrect because, since the condition precedent was express, it must be complied with fully; substantial compliance is not sufficient.

ANSWER TO QUESTION 41

Answer choice C is correct. In a federal proceeding, the disclosure of a protected communication does not operate as a waiver if (i) the disclosure was inadvertent, (ii) the holder of the privilege took reasonable steps to prevent disclosure, and (iii) the holder promptly took reasonable steps to rectify the error, including contacting the party to whom the communication was disclosed and requesting that they return, sequester, or destroy the information. In this case, the facts indicate that the disclosure was inadvertent and that the attorney had acted diligently during discovery. Further, the facts indicate that the attorney immediately notified opposing counsel of her error. As such, the privilege is not waived by her inadvertent disclosure. Answer choice A is incorrect for the above reasons. Answer choice B is incorrect because the memo is privileged. A confidential communication between a client and an attorney is privileged, whether the communication is oral or written. Although the corporation itself is the attorney's client, communication through a representative of the client or attorney—in this case, through the corporation's chief executive officer—does not destroy the attorney-client privilege. Further, this communication was for the purpose of seeking legal advice; the communication directly relates to the attorney's representation of the corporation in the present litigation. Answer choice D is incorrect because, in order to be protected by the attorney-client privilege, the communication must be for the purpose of seeking legal representation or advice. Communications concerning the fact of employment, the identity of the client, fee arrangements, or communications made when the attorney is acting as a tax preparer, business partner, or witness to a will are generally not privileged.

ANSWER TO QUESTION 42

Answer choice D is correct. A builder or other commercial seller of a newly constructed residence gives a warranty of fitness or suitability to the buyer. When this warranty is not mandated by statute, the courts have implied such a warranty. The warranty covers material defects that could not have been uncovered by the buyer through a reasonable inspection prior to purchase. Here, the cracks are material in that they are the cause of the buyer's wet basement and, since they formed after the house was constructed, could not have been uncovered by the buyer prior to purchase. Answer choice A is incorrect because, as noted with respect to answer choice D, the warranty is implied; the builder need not specifically grant such a warranty. Answer choice B is incorrect because, while a buyer is under a duty to conduct a reasonable inspection of the premises prior to purchase, the buyer is thereby responsible only for those defects that such an inspection would have uncovered. As noted with respect to answer choice D, since the cracks formed after the house was constructed, an inspection by the buyer would not have uncovered them. Answer choice C is incorrect because a builder is not responsible for any material defect in the house, but only those that could not have been uncovered by the buyer during a reasonable inspection.

ANSWER TO QUESTION 43

Answer choice B is correct because, although the Supreme Court has recognized a Due Process liberty interest in adult males engaging in private, consensual sex and found that the Equal Protection Clause prevents discrimination against gays and lesbians in their efforts to seek governmental protection, the court has not recognized same-sex marriage as a constitutionally protected right. Consequently, the state merely needs a rational basis for its law, which may arguably include a desire to encourage traditional marriage as a basic social institution. Answer choice A is incorrect because the state code does not merely prevent gays and lesbians from enjoying special rights but instead imposes a special disability upon them in violation of the Equal Protection Clause. Answer choice C is incorrect because, while the statement justifies the state's protection of the right of association of heterosexual couples, it doesn't directly explain why the state can deny this right to homosexual couples. Also, the statement, serving as rational basis for the state's action, is not as complete an answer as answer choice B in justifying the state's denial of the right to marry to homosexual couples. Answer choice D is incorrect because the political question doctrine applies to forestall a court from deciding an issue that is better resolved by one of the other branches of the federal government. Here the actor is a state, not another branch of the federal government.

ANSWER TO QUESTION 44

Answer choice B is correct. Courts recognize the existence of an implied-in-law contract ("quasi-contract") when one party confers a benefit on another and has a reasonable expectation of compensation. Otherwise, the benefited party would be unjustly enriched. Such situations occur when: (i) the plaintiff has conferred a "measurable benefit" on the defendant; (ii) the plaintiff acted without gratuitous intent; and (iii) it would be unfair to let the defendant retain the benefit because either the defendant had an opportunity to decline the benefit but knowingly accepted it, or the plaintiff had a reasonable excuse for not giving the defendant such opportunity, usually because of an emergency. This is such a situation. Answer choice A is incorrect because an implied-in-fact contract is created only when conduct indicates assent or agreement (note the difference between implied-in-law and implied-in-fact contracts). Answer choice C is incorrect because when an emergent situation occurs, an actual contract is not always required for a plaintiff to recover. Answer choice D is incorrect because it describes why an implied-in-fact contract was not created. Conduct signifying assent is not required for the formation of a quasi-contract, as was the situation here.

ANSWER TO QUESTION 45

Answer choice A is correct. All relevant evidence is admissible unless excluded by a specific rule or law. Relevant evidence is evidence which has any tendency to make a material fact more or less probable than it would be without the evidence. To be relevant, evidence must be both material and probative. In this case, a set of photographs depicting a car running a red light, when the question of whether the driver of the car ran the red light is in dispute, is certainly relevant. Relevant evidence may be excluded if its probative value is outweighed by the danger of unfair prejudice, confusion of the issues, or misleading the jury, or if it is needlessly repetitive or prohibited by some specific rule. Since none of those seem to be an issue here, the set of photographs should be admitted. Answer choice B is incorrect because all tangible evidence, including photographs, must be authenticated before admitted into evidence. Real evidence may be authenticated by testimony, by distinctive markings, or by chain of custody; documentary evidence may be authenticated in several ways, including by proof. Further, all evidence, including photographs, must be considered relevant to be admitted. As such, the statement in answer choice B is too broad, and is therefore incorrect. Answer choice C is incorrect because the photograph is an original. The best evidence rule requires that the original document (including photographs) be used to prove the contents of that document when the contents are at issue. An "original" of a photograph includes the negative and any print made from it. The plaintiff's set of prints were made directly from the camera. As such, the prints possessed by the plaintiff are the "best evidence." Answer choice D is incorrect because the identity of the photographer is irrelevant, so long as the photograph can otherwise be properly authenticated. The facts here indicate that the plaintiff did lay a proper foundation for the photographs, so the fact that the "photographer" cannot testify should not be an issue.

ANSWER TO QUESTION 46

Answer choice C is correct because, under Section 5 of the Fourteenth Amendment, Congress can only enforce constitutional rights as declared by the Supreme Court—not create new rights. In this case, Congress is attempting to create a constitutional right to an abortion in the face of the denial of this right by the Supreme Court. Answer choice A is incorrect because, where Congress seeks to regulate intrastate non-economic activity, Congress must adduce facts establishing an actual substantial economic effect on interstate commerce. Answer choice B is incorrect because, under principles of separation of powers, Congress cannot expand as well as contract constitutional rights as defined by the Supreme Court. Answer choice D is incorrect because, acting pursuant to Section 5 of the Fourteenth Amendment, Congress has the power to enforce rights created by the Fourteenth Amendment against the states.

ANSWER TO QUESTION 47

Answer choice A is correct because the police officers could not compel the suspect to come to the stationhouse for fingerprinting in the absence of probable cause. Reasonable suspicions alone are insufficient. A seizure takes place when, in view of all the circumstances, a reasonable person concludes that he is not free to leave. Here, an illegal seizure took place because the police officers lacked probable cause. Consequently, the evidence seized was the poisonous fruit of the suspect's illegal seizure. Answer choice B is incorrect because the Fifth Amendment privilege applies only to testimonial evidence, and an individual's fingerprint is not testimonial evidence. Answer choice C is incorrect because, although fingerprint evidence presented by a properly qualified expert is not excludable under the evidentiary rules, here the fingerprint evidence was seized in violation of the suspect's Fourth Amendment rights.

Answer choice D is incorrect because a reasonable suspicion that a defendant committed a crime is not sufficient grounds for compelling the defendant to come to a stationhouse for fingerprinting.

ANSWER TO QUESTION 48

Answer choice A is correct. The requirements for an equitable servitude are met. The deed contains a clear intent that the promise be enforceable against successor-in-interest, the promise touches and concerns the land (i.e., refrain from building a fence on it), and party against whom it is enforced has notice of it. Although the husband has neither record nor actual notice of the promise, since the community association has rigorously enforced the height restriction, the husband is on inquiry notice because other fences in the community do not exceed six feet. Answer choice B is incorrect because waste is a doctrine that applies when the legal interest in the property is split among two or more parties, such as a landlord and tenant or a life estate owner and the holder of the remainder interest, and the nonpossessory party has the right to prevent the possessory party from altering the condition of the property. This right arises automatically by virtue of the nature of the property interests, unlike an equitable servitude, which must be intended by the property owner. Answer choice C is incorrect because there is not a vertical privity requirement for the enforcement of an equitable servitude. Answer choice D is incorrect because there is not a horizontal privity requirement for the enforcement of an equitable servitude.

ANSWER TO QUESTION 49

Answer choice C is correct. Since the contract cannot be performed within one year *from the time of the contract's making*, it is subject to the Statute of Frauds. The writings are not sufficient under the Statute of Frauds because, although together they state the essential terms of the bargain and each is signed by the promisor, neither writing references the other. In order to satisfy the Statute of Frauds, at least one of the writings must reference the others. Because the farmer's letter does not indicate the subject matter of the contract (i.e., why the farmer is paying the nurse $10,000 a month), the nurse will be unable to enforce the agreement against the farmer. Answer choice A is incorrect because, although this agreement can be performed within one year of the beginning of performance, it is subject to the Statute of Frauds because it cannot be performed within one year of the date of its making. Answer choice B is incorrect because, although together the writings contain the essential terms of the agreement, neither writing references the other. Answer choice D is incorrect because the writings do not have to establish the existence of a valid offer and acceptance, but instead must state the essential terms of the agreement and be signed by the party against whom enforcement is sought.

ANSWER TO QUESTION 50

Answer choice D is correct. A delegation of contractual duties is not permitted when the other party to the contract has a substantial interest in having the delegor perform the contract. This exception is normally invoked in contracts involving personal services. While this is not such a contract, the restaurant may argue that it repeatedly spurned more lucrative offers because it strongly preferred the service provided by the original supplier. Answer choice A is incorrect because delegation of duties is permitted in most circumstances. Answer choice B is incorrect because no consideration is necessary for an assignment or delegation to be valid. However, the presence or absence of consideration is relevant to the revocability of the assignment (an assignment supported by consideration is irrevocable, while one without consideration is not). Answer choice C is incorrect because parties to an assignment/delegation are not required to obtain the consent of a party to the original contract unless the contract specifically requires such consent.

ANSWER TO QUESTION 51

Answer choice C is correct. The store owner is not vicariously liable for an assault committed by one customer upon another. Any liability that the owner may have from the incident would arise from her employee's negligence for failure to prevent the assault. Answer choice D is incorrect because, while an employer is generally not liable for an employee's intentional torts, an employer may be liable for such a tort where the employer authorizes the employee's use of force or force is inherent in the nature of the employment. Moreover, it was the mother, not the employee, who committed an assault against the grandfather. Answer choice A is incorrect because, while the grandfather was reasonably apprehensive of an imminent battery by the mother, neither the employee, nor vicariously the owner committed an assault with respect to the grandfather. Answer choice B is incorrect because neither the employee nor the owner are liable for the grandfather's injuries on the basis of assault.

ANSWER TO QUESTION 52

Answer choice D is correct. All relevant evidence is admissible, unless excluded by a rule or law. Relevant evidence is that which has any tendency to make any fact of consequence more or less probable than it would be without the evidence. In this case, the witness's testimony may make the wife's claim—that her husband is dead—less true. Further, it does not seem to be subject to any exclusionary rules. Answer choice A is incorrect because the statute contains a rebuttable presumption. Under the "bursting bubble" approach followed by the federal rules and a majority of common-law jurisdictions, a presumption is not evidence in a civil case, but a preliminary assumption of fact that "bursts" after the introduction of evidence to sustain a contrary finding. Here, even though the witness's testimony is speculative, it may be sufficient to rebut the presumption that the husband is actually dead. Therefore, the presumption no longer controls, and the testimony is admissible. Answer choice B is incorrect because a witness's testimony does not have to be conclusive; as mentioned above, any evidence that is relevant and not excluded is admissible. As the witness's testimony is relevant to a material fact and may have a tendency to make that material fact more or less true, the witness's uncertainty alone is not sufficient to preclude the testimony. Answer choice C is incorrect because the Dead Man's Statute is irrelevant to this question. A Dead Man's Statute is a common-law statute that generally states that a party with a financial interest in the outcome in a civil case can not testify about a communication or transaction with a deceased person whose estate was a party to the suit and whose testimony was adverse to the decedent's estate, unless there was a waiver. The Dead Man's Statute, should this jurisdiction have one, is not relevant to this case. Note that the federal rules do not contain a restriction such as Dead Man's Statutes.

ANSWER TO QUESTION 53

Answer choice C is correct. The Due Process Clause of the Fourteenth Amendment incorporates the Takings Clause of the Fifth Amendment, thereby making it applicable to the states. State and municipal zoning laws survive challenges under the Takings Clause as long as the government has a legitimate interest, which includes aesthetic and environmental concerns, and does not deny the property owner the economically viable use of his property. For this reason, answer choice A is incorrect. Answer choice B is incorrect because a governmental regulation of property need only be rationally related to a legitimate public interest. Answer choice D is incorrect because a property owner is entitled to compensation only where governmental action results in a taking. Here, a three percent reduction in the value of the company's property due to the conditions placed on it by the city does not constitute a taking.

ANSWER TO QUESTION 54

Answer choice A is correct. As a commercial supplier of a defective product, the restaurant is strictly liable for personal or property injury cause by the product. Since the product was defectively manufactured (i.e., the dessert contained slivers of glass), the restaurant is strictly liable for the harm suffered by its customer in eating the dessert. Answer choice B is incorrect because, while a commercial supplier may be liable for its failure to warn, its duty to warn is limited to risks that are known or should have been known. Since the restaurant neither was aware of the presence of glass in the dessert nor had a reason to be aware, the restaurant was not required to warn the customer of the risk of glass in the dessert. Answer choice C is incorrect because, as a commercial supplier, the restaurant is liable for defects in the product produced by the manufacturer, even though the restaurant does not own or control the manufacturer of the product. Answer choice D is incorrect because, although a defendant in a products liability action must generally be a seller of the product, there is no requirement that the sale of the product produce a profit for the seller.

ANSWER TO QUESTION 55

Answer choice C is correct. The recording statute is a notice statute. Since the second mortgage was given by the mortgagee without notice as to the first mortgage, it has priority over the first mortgage. A purchase money mortgagee is treated as having paid value for purposes of the recording act. In addition, since the second mortgage was given by the couple before their deaths, the children's claims to the property as heirs of their parents are junior to the second mortgage. The recording act would not be helpful to the children's claim because the second mortgage was recorded before their interests arose and because as heirs they are not purchasers for value protected by the act. With regard to the first mortgage, while the children as heirs are not protected by the act, they are protected under the shelter rule because their parents were entitled to priority over the first mortgage by virtue of acquiring the property without notice of that mortgage. Answer choices A, B, and D are incorrect for the reasons articulated for answer choice C.

ANSWER TO QUESTION 56

Answer choice C is correct. The Fifth Amendment's Due Process Clause includes the rights guaranteed by the Equal Protection Clause, thereby making discrimination by the federal government subject to review under the same standards as discrimination by the states. The federal statute in question discriminates based on gender, and hence "intermediate scrutiny" is the appropriate standard of review. Here, the federal government has an important interest in remedying past discrimination against women in college athletics, and the law is substantially related to this interest. Both answer choices A and D are incorrect because they fail to apply the correct standard of review to the law's gender discrimination. Answer choice B is incorrect because, even though Congress lacks the power to directly compel a state to take a specific action (i.e., allocate the budget of a state institution in a manner that favors women), Congress may use its spending power to encourage a state to take such action (here, by reducing the state institution's federal funding if it fails to comply).

ANSWER TO QUESTION 57

Answer choice D is correct. The credibility of a witness may be attacked by reputation or opinion evidence only as to the witness's character for truthfulness or untruthfulness. Evidence that the witness was previously in a violent altercation has no bearing on the witness's credibility (unless the witness had previously denied being in such an altercation, which the facts here do not indicate). Answer choice A is incorrect because, while it contains a true statement, reputation or opinion evidence may only be used to attack the witness's character for truthfulness. Answer choice B is incorrect because, while it is true that a witness puts his own credibility at issue by testifying, the prosecutor did not attack his credibility in the appropriate way. Answer choice C is incorrect because a party may impeach or attack the credibility of any witness, even a witness the impeaching party called.

ANSWER TO QUESTION 58

Answer choice A is correct because the state's law protects local economic interests at the expense of out-of-state competitors and therefore discriminates against the out-of-state corporation in violation of the Dormant Commerce Clause. Answer choice B is incorrect because the Article IV Privileges and Immunities Clause has been interpreted as not applying to corporations. Answer choice C is incorrect because the Fourteenth Amendment Privileges and Immunities Clause has similarly been restricted; it does not apply to corporations. Answer choice D is incorrect because the Contracts Clause, although it does apply to state legislative actions, only prohibits laws that retroactively impair contractual rights. Here, the corporation is only prohibited from entering into new business deals within the state.

ANSWER TO QUESTION 59

Answer choice B is correct. At common law, burglary is defined as the breaking and entering of the dwelling of another at nighttime with the specific intent to commit a felony therein. When the man opened the door to the bedroom, he was merely curious to see the room, and did not intend to steal anything. Thus, a required element of burglary is lacking and he cannot be convicted of the crime. Answer choice A is incorrect because while the man originally entered the home with permission, he broke and entered a specific room in the house without permission, and that is sufficient to satisfy the breaking and entering requirement. Answer choice C is incorrect because it is an untrue statement: "force" does not necessarily require a feat of strength; twisting a door handle is sufficient force to satisfy the criteria for burglary. Answer choice D is incorrect because successfully absconding with the property of another is not a required element for burglary.

ANSWER TO QUESTION 60

Answer choice D is correct. Although normally expectancy damages are awarded in a breach-of-contract action, restitutionary damages are permitted in cases where the nonbreaching party has partially performed a below-market-price contract. Otherwise, the breaching party would profit from its breach. Consequently, the paving company may recover the benefit conferred upon the developer as measured by the amount the developer would have had to pay to secure the same performance as that rendered by the paving company. Answer choice A is incorrect because, although the increase in the defendant's property value due to the plaintiff's performance is one measure of restitutionary damages, that amount is less than the paving company's restitutionary damages as measured by the cost to the developer of obtaining the same performance rendered by the paving company. Answer choice B is incorrect because the paving company's reliance damages are exceeded by both its expectancy and restitutionary damages. Answer choice C is incorrect because the paving company's expectancy damages, based on the cost incurred by the company plus its profit on the contract, are less than the company's restitutionary damages.

ANSWER TO QUESTION 61

Answer choice B is correct. Only testimonial evidence is covered by the Fifth Amendment privilege; physical or real evidence is not. While defendant's handwriting in itself is not testimonial, the defendant's answer to the question would be, because he would be identifying himself as the person who wrote the note. Answer choice A is incorrect. Requiring a defendant to give a sample of his handwriting (i.e., a handwriting exemplar), for example, does not violate the privilege against self-incrimination because it is not testimonial. The answer is testimonial. Answer choice C is incorrect because the Fifth Amendment privilege can be invoked in civil proceedings if the witness's testimony can in the future be used against him in a criminal proceeding. Answer choice D is incorrect because the Fourteenth Amendment applies the Fifth Amendment to the states.

ANSWER TO QUESTION 62

Answer choice A is correct. The statement appears to be a hearsay statement, but it is actually an admission by a party-opponent (non-hearsay). A prior out-of-court statement by a party to the current litigation that is used against that party is not hearsay. The statement must be contrary to the declarant's present interest. Here, the statement was clearly against the declarant's interest; he implied that he was planning to do something "wrong" the following day. As such, it is admissible against him. The statement is also admissible against his co-defendant. Admissions made by one party may be imputed to another party based on certain relationships between the two, for example, when the parties are co-conspirators. Although a statement by one co-party may not be imputed to another co-party solely because they are co-parties, statements made by a conspirator during and in furtherance of the conspiracy are admissible as an admission against his other co-conspirators. In this case, the statement was made during and in furtherance of the conspiracy, as the declarant was "scoping out" the site of the planned robbery. As such, the declarant's statement is imputed to the non-declarant. Accordingly, answer choices B, C, and D are incorrect because they do not state that the statement is admissible against both defendants.

ANSWER TO QUESTION 63

Answer choice C is correct. A buyer who does not obtain good title can nevertheless transfer good title to a subsequent purchaser who buys the goods in good faith and for value. Here, the buyer did not obtain good title to the ring because the buyer did not pay for the ring. A payment by check is conditional on the check being honored. However, since the third party purchased the ring from the buyer in good faith and for value, the third party has good title to the ring. Answer choice A is incorrect because, although the buyer did not give value for the ring since the check was dishonored by the bank and therefore did not have good title to ring, the buyer nevertheless could transfer good title to the third party. Answer choice B is incorrect because, even though the buyer was not a merchant to whom the owner had entrusted the ring, the buyer could transfer good title to the ring by selling it to a good faith purchaser for value. Answer choice D is incorrect because the third party's status as a non-merchant is irrelevant in determining whether the third party has good title to the ring.

ANSWER TO QUESTION 64

Answer choice D is correct. A witness whose memory is incomplete is allowed to examine any item or thing in order to "refresh" his present recollection. The witness may not use the item to testify; he testifies only from his refreshed memory. The opposing party is entitled to examine the item, cross-examine the witness about it, and admit relevant portions of it into evidence, if she chooses. The pictures in this case simply reminded the child of what he already knew, and their use was permissible. Answer choice A is incorrect because the pictures are not being introduced into evidence. It is possible that either party would have to overcome a claim of privilege if the party wanted to introduce the pictures into evidence; however, these pictures are only being used to refresh the witness's recollection. Answer choice B is incorrect because, as mentioned above, the prosecution is not seeking to admit them. As stated above, a witness is allowed to use anything to refresh his recollection, even if that thing would be inadmissible as evidence. Answer choice C is incorrect because any witness's recollection may be refreshed; the ability to refresh one's recollection is not a special privilege extended to child witnesses.

ANSWER TO QUESTION 65

Answer choice B is correct. Although the landowner created an express easement, the easement was lost when both the servient and the dominant estates came under the ownership of the daughter. Subsequent actions did not revive the easement or create a new one. Answer choice A is incorrect because mere nonuse of an easement does not terminate an easement. Such nonuse must be accompanied by some manifestation of an intent to abandon the easement. Answer choice C is incorrect because, as noted with regard to answer choice B, despite being an express easement, it was terminated by merger of the two estates. Answer choice D is incorrect because, in order for an easement by implication from prior use to arise, the use must continue after the division of the property. Although the path to the river was likely apparent at the time the daughter sold the parcel to the third party sale since the landowner had used it about a year before, the path was not used for four years after the sale. The third party's prompt objection to the son's renewed use of the path refutes the argument that there was an implied agreement between the third party and the daughter that she could continue to use the path.

ANSWER TO QUESTION 66

Answer choice D is correct. The supplier of a component that is integrated into a product during its manufacture is not liable unless the component itself is defective or the supplier substantially participates in the integration process and the integration of the component causes the product to be defective. Here, the plastic resin provided by the supplier was not itself defective, and, although the supplier participated in the integration process, the supplier's participation did not lead to the defective hot water heater. Answer choice A is incorrect because although a supplier who is a commercial seller of a defective product can be liable in a strict products liability action, the supplier in question, as the maker of a component of the defective hot water heater, was not liable for the reasons discussed in answer choice D. Answer choice B is incorrect because, even though the melting of the plastic tank caused the homeowner's harm, the supplier of the plastic resin is not liable because the supplier of this component bore no responsibility for the defective product. Answer choice C is incorrect because a plaintiff can recover in a strict products liability action for damage to the plaintiff's property caused by a defective product, even though the plaintiff does not suffer a physical injury.

ANSWER TO QUESTION 67

Answer choice B is correct. When a police officer executing a valid search warrant fails to adhere to a "knock and announce" statute, the evidence seized is not subject to the exclusionary rule despite that failure. Answer choice A is incorrect because the police officer's good faith reliance on a valid warrant is irrelevant. The fact that the warrant itself is valid is sufficient to constitutionally justify the search or arrest authorized by the warrant. Answer choice C is incorrect because items that are in plain view, such as the illegal drugs, may be seized by an officer who is executing a valid warrant. Answer choice D is incorrect because, although the officer violated the "knock and announce" statute, this violation does not require the exclusion of evidence seized pursuant to a valid search warrant.

ANSWER TO QUESTION 68

Answer choice A is correct. The supplier failed to perform its contractual obligation to deliver the forklifts to the manufacturer. Upon the supplier's breach, the manufacturer sought cover by purchasing the forklifts from another source at a higher price. The manufacturer can recover the difference between the cover price and the contract price from the supplier. Under the UCC, either party can demand assurance of performance if there are reasonable grounds for insecurity about the other party's ability or willingness to perform. Once such assurances are requested, performance may be suspended until they are provided. Failure to give adequate assurances within a reasonable time, not exceeding 30 days, can be treated as repudiation. Here, the manufacturer failed to provide assurances within 30 days, so the supplier was within its rights to reject the assurances and repudiate the contract. However, the supplier did not cancel the contract or take any action in reliance on the failure to timely provide assurances. Consequently, when the manufacturer provided the supplier with such assurances and retracted its implied repudiation of the contract by requesting delivery of the forklifts, the supplier was contractually obligated to the deliver the forklifts. Answer choice B is incorrect because, even though the supplier's information regarding the manufacturer's financial position was in error, the supplier was entitled to seek assurances from the manufacturer because the supplier had reasonable grounds for believing that the manufacturer was unable to pay for the forklifts. The forklift distributor was within its rights to repudiate the contract, and its personal guarantee demand was essentially an offer to form a new contract. Answer choice C is incorrect because, as mentioned above, although the manufacturer's failure to provide adequate assurances of its ability to pay within a reasonable time (which by statute cannot exceed 30 days) constituted an anticipatory repudiation of the contract, the supplier did not cancel the contract or take any action in reliance on the repudiation. Consequently, the supplier was contractually obligated to the deliver the forklifts. Answer choice D is incorrect because the supplier, having received adequate assurances from the manufacturer, lacked reasonable grounds upon which to demand that the manufacturer's CEO guarantee payment of the forklifts.

ANSWER TO QUESTION 69

Answer choice B is correct. Under the doctrine of equitable conversion, the couple became equitable owners of the property upon the execution of the contract of sale. As such they bear the risk of loss. Answer choice A is incorrect because the determination of the party who bears the risk of loss does not turn on whether the contract is recorded. Answer choice C is incorrect because, unless the contract specifies otherwise, neither party has a duty to insure the property. Answer choice D is incorrect because, under the majority rule, the risk of loss is not determined by possession of the property.

ANSWER TO QUESTION 70

Answer choice A is correct. Since the girl was 14 years old, sexual intercourse with her is rape only if it is against her will. Fraudulent conduct does not negate consent in most situations. Here, the boyfriend induced the girl to consent to sexual intercourse through false promises but that, standing alone, does not negate consent. The boyfriend did not conceal the actual nature of the act. Consequently, the fraud was in the inducement, not in the factum. For that reason, answer choice C is incorrect. Answer choice B is incorrect. The statute provides for increasing the crime from second degree rape to first degree rape if the victim is 14 or 15 years old and the perpetrator is at least four years older, but does not define consensual sex between such persons as rape. Answer choice D is incorrect. Although a defendant cannot defeat a rape charge by pleading lack of knowledge as to the true age of the person with whom the defendant had sex, consensual sex with a 14-year-old, the girl's true age, is not rape under the wording of the statute.

ANSWER TO QUESTION 71

Answer choice D is correct. A defendant is liable for trespass to chattels if he intentionally commits an act that interferes with a plaintiff's right of possession of the chattel, or intermeddles with the chattel, and causes damage. Here, the neighbor intermeddled with the man's chattel (i.e., his car) by firing shots that caused damage to the car. Furthermore, punitive damages may be available, as the neighbor's conduct was willful and wanton. Answer choice A is incorrect because the facts do not indicate that the man suffered severe emotional distress as a result of the incident. Answer choice B is incorrect because the man was able to repair the car, and thus he wasn't totally deprived of the benefit of the property. Answer choice C is incorrect because an assault requires the plaintiff to experience reasonable apprehension of an immediate battery. Here, the man did not see the neighbor until after the shooting occurred.

ANSWER TO QUESTION 72

Answer choice B is correct. Here, the man is the victim of a battery; the only question is whether his implied consent serves as a defense. Consent is implied where rough contact is common; a hockey game certainly qualifies, particularly given the league's reputation. However, the battery in question was not routine contact; the goal had already been scored and play was stopped. Consequently, the contact fell outside the implied scope of consent. Answer choice C is incorrect because, while the man may have consented to rough play, the opposing player's action occurred after play had stopped. Answer choice A is incorrect, because willful and wanton conduct is a requirement for obtaining punitive damages, and not for establishing a battery claim. Answer choice D is incorrect because the intent required for a battery is the intent to perform the act that causes injury; intent to injure is not necessary.

ANSWER TO QUESTION 73

Answer choice D is correct because the Eleventh Amendment prevents an action by a citizen of one state against another state where the basis for the action is the violation of state law. Answer choice A is incorrect because, although the plaintiff seeks an injunction rather than damages, the Eleventh Amendment prohibits the action because it is based on state law. Similarly, answer choice B is incorrect because, although the action is brought against the state official rather than the state, the Eleventh Amendment prohibits the action because it is based on state law. Answer choice C is incorrect. Although a plaintiff can pursue an action despite the Eleventh Amendment in order to prevent the enforcement of an unconstitutional state statute, the plaintiff is not advancing such an argument here. Since the plaintiff is not challenging the constitutionality of the state statute under the Due Process Clause of the Fourteenth Amendment, the issue of whether the plaintiff is asserting a fundamental right is irrelevant.

ANSWER TO QUESTION 74

Answer choice C is correct. Generally, the parol evidence rule prevents a party to a written contract from presenting other evidence that contradicts the terms of the contract as written. If a document is determined not to be "integrated," the parol evidence rule may not apply. When documents are only partially integrated, the parties are permitted to present extrinsic evidence only as long as the evidence is consistent with the writing. In this case, the note is inadmissible, regardless of whether the written agreement is a partial or complete integration, because the note contradicts the agreement with regard to the restoration work to be performed on the engine. Answer choice A is incorrect because, even in a partially integrated agreement, the parol evidence may not contradict the writing. Answer choice B is incorrect because the parol evidence rule applies to any previous or contemporaneous evidence prior to integration, and not just oral evidence. Answer choice D is incorrect because, although the contract is not governed by the Uniform Commercial Code, the parol evidence rule nevertheless applies to the transaction.

ANSWER TO QUESTION 75

Answer choice A is correct. Since the friend paid the buyer's loan obligation in full in order to protect his own interest, the friend became subrogated to the lender's rights based not only on the personal obligation of the buyer, but also on the mortgage on the land itself. Answer choice B is incorrect because the way in which the friend acquired his interest in his own parcel is irrelevant to the issue of subrogation. Answer choice C is incorrect because, while the friend does not have an ownership interest in the buyer's parcel, the friend may nevertheless seek to foreclose on the mortgage on that parcel, which it holds through its right of subrogation. Answer choice D is incorrect because, although payment of another person's obligation that is secured by a mortgage by a person who is under a legal duty to do so, can give rise to the right of subrogation, payment of such an obligation by a person in order to protect his property interest is also entitled to subrogation.

ANSWER TO QUESTION 76

Answer choice B is correct. The man's mistake was connected with the ownership status of the car, and not the law of larceny in the jurisdiction. Thus, his mistake was one of fact and not of law. Larceny is a specific intent crime, and an honest mistake of fact, whether reasonable or not, serves as a defense to a specific intent crime because such an honest mistake negates the required *mens rea*. Consequently, he should not be convicted of larceny. Answer choice C is incorrect because the mistake was of fact, not of law. Answer choice D is incorrect because an honest but unreasonable mistake of fact serves as a defense to a specific intent crime. Answer choice A is incorrect because, although taking abandoned property is not a crime, the car had not been abandoned.

ANSWER TO QUESTION 77

Answer choice C is correct. A witness can be impeached with prior bad acts that bear upon truthfulness; failing to clear ice from a walkway has no bearing on truthfulness. Generally, a witness can also be impeached with evidence that contradicts a material part of his testimony, but nothing about the plaintiff's questions would contradict the defendant's testimony. Evidence of prior bad acts generally cannot be used as evidence that a witness/defendant acted in a particular way on the occasion in question. Answer choice A is incorrect because, while evidence of a person's habit is admissible to prove conduct in conformity with the habit on a particular occasion, there is no evidence here that the defendant has a habit of not clearing ice from his walkway. The fact that there have been two claims over three winters that the defendant failed to sufficiently clear ice is not enough to establish a habit. Answer choice B is incorrect because, as explained above, a witness can be impeached with prior bad acts that bear upon truthfulness by demonstrating dishonesty; failing to clear ice does not constitute an act bearing on honesty. Answer choice D is incorrect because the outcome in the prior claims is irrelevant to the claims' admissibility. A witness can be impeached with prior bad acts that do not result in convictions or judgments (if they relate to truthfulness, as explained above). However, even if the customers in the other cases had brought successful claims against the defendant in the past, those claims have no bearing on the defendant's veracity in this instance.

ANSWER TO QUESTION 78

Answer choice B is correct. In order to reverse a conviction on the grounds of ineffective assistance of counsel, the defendant must prove both that the lawyer's conduct was not objectively reasonable, and that the ineffective counsel actually prejudiced the defendant. Here, the lawyer's conduct was objectively reasonable. Answer choice A is incorrect because, while strategic decisions at trial usually rest with the lawyer, those decisions must be objectively reasonable. Answer choice C is incorrect because the standard for ineffective assistance of counsel is objective, not subjective. Answer choice D is incorrect because prejudice from a strategic decision is not enough to reverse a conviction. The lawyer's conduct must be objectively unreasonable.

ANSWER TO QUESTION 79

Answer choice D is correct. Although the city's decision had an adverse impact on mentally retarded children, they are not a suspect classification under the Equal Protection Clause. Therefore, the city needed only a rational basis for its action. Although a city that acts to prevent the mentally retarded from living in an area due to fear while permitting other groups, such as fraternities or private clubs, to maintain facilities in the same area has acted irrationally, a city that consistently acts to preserve the quality of life and the environment by denying non-residential occupation has acted rationally. Answer choices A, B, and C are incorrect because each applies a more strict standard or review than the rational basis standard.

ANSWER TO QUESTION 80

Answer choice C is correct. In order for a person who is not within the zone of danger to recover under a theory of negligent infliction of emotional distress, she must be a bystander, that is a witness to the harm negligently inflicted on another person. In the instant case, the mother is not present at the scene of the accident. Thus, the mother's claim cannot succeed. Answer choice A is incorrect because although a bystander must be closely related to the person directly harmed in order to recover, the existence of this relationship is not the sole requirement for recovery. Similarly, answer choice B is incorrect because, although the mother's fainting, shock, and sleeping problems are sufficient indicia of severe emotional distress, the existence of such distress is not the sole requirement for recovery. Answer choice D is incorrect because "extreme and outrageous conduct" is an element of *intentional* infliction of emotional distress, not *negligent* infliction of emotional distress.

ANSWER TO QUESTION 81

Answer choice A is correct. Evidence of juvenile adjudications is not admissible in civil cases. The court may occasionally permit evidence of a juvenile adjudication of a witness other than the accused under certain circumstances, but only in a criminal trial. Because the witness was a juvenile when she was convicted and because she is a witness in a civil trial, the conviction is not admissible. Answer choice B is incorrect for several reasons. First, prior bad acts are not necessarily inadmissible; a witness may be asked about prior bad acts on cross-examination if the judge determines that the acts are probative of untruthfulness, and the lawyer has a good-faith basis for asking about the conduct. Additionally, a conviction of a crime does not constitute a "prior bad act." Subject to certain rules, a witness may always be impeached with evidence that he has been convicted of a crime. Answer choices C and D are incorrect because, as mentioned above, the general rules regarding impeachment with convictions do not apply to juvenile convictions. If this was not a juvenile conviction, it would be true that this conviction would be admissible, as a witness may be impeached with evidence that she has been convicted of any crime involving dishonesty or false statements within 10 years of the conviction. Further, even if the crime did not involve dishonesty or a false statement, convictions of felonies that are less than 10 years old may be admissible, if the probative value outweighs the prejudicial effect.

ANSWER TO QUESTION 82

Answer choice C is correct. Under the common law, which applies to a construction contract, a contract generally cannot be modified without consideration. Here, the contractor proposed modifying the contract to increase the contractor's compensation in exchange for the removal of the mold from the basement. Since the homeowner agreed to the modification and the contractor finished the basement in accord with the modified contract, the homeowner is liable to the contractor for the additional $2,000. Answer choice A is incorrect because, although it is true that the modification of a construction contract generally requires consideration, consideration exists in this case. Answer choice B is incorrect because, since there was consideration for the modification, it is irrelevant whether the circumstances that gave rise to the modification were unforeseen. Answer choice D is incorrect because the fact that the modification arose because neither party was aware of the presence of the mold is irrelevant to the enforcement of the contract as modified. While it is unlikely that this mistake would have been judged to have a material effect on the parties' contractual obligations and thereby given the homeowner grounds for avoiding the contract, the homeowner is not seeking to void the contract but merely to avoid the consequences of the modification to the contract, which occurred after the parties became aware of the presence of the mold.

ANSWER TO QUESTION 83

Answer choice B is correct. A promise to make a gift generally does not create an enforceable contract because there is no consideration for the promise. While the promise of a charitable donation is enforceable under the doctrine of promissory estoppel (i.e., detrimental reliance), and some courts recognize the application of this doctrine without explicit proof that the charity relied on the promise, in order to enforce such a promise, the Second Restatement requires that the promise be in writing. Answer choice A is incorrect because, in order to be enforceable, a promise to make a charitable contribution need not be supported by consideration, but can be enforceable under the doctrine of promissory estoppel. Answer choice C is incorrect because, since the philanthropist's promise was not in writing, it did not qualify as a charitable subscription. Answer choice D is incorrect because, while some courts do not require that a charity establish that it has relied on a donor's promise in order to enforce that promise, the Second Restatement does require that such a promise be in writing in order to be enforceable.

ANSWER TO QUESTION 84

Answer choice B is correct. By outlawing the deed absolute, the state violated the Contracts Clause by substantially and unreasonably impairing the obligations of contract owed to mortgagees as to loan contracts that had already been made at the time the statute was enacted. Answer choice A is incorrect because, as to future loans, no contract obligations had been incurred, and thus a state law could not impair them. Answer choice C is incorrect because, since the mortgagees' interest in the freedom to contract is not a fundamental right, the law must merely pass the rational basis test. Under this test, which the government is almost always able to meet, the law must be rationally related to a legitimate state interest. Answer choice D is incorrect because, since the class of mortgagees is not a suspect classification, the constitutionality of the law is also judged under the rational basis test.

ANSWER TO QUESTION 85

Answer choice D is correct. While the contract is subject to an implied warranty of marketable title, the objections to marketability, as noted in answer choices A and B, are not valid. Answer choice A is incorrect because, while an outstanding mortgage does constitute an encumbrance, if the amount of the mortgage is less than the selling price, at closing the seller can apply the proceeds from the sale of the property to pay off the balance of the mortgage and remove the encumbrance. Answer choice B is incorrect because, since the nephews had only an expectancy rather than a property interest in the lot that vanished when the widow sold the lot during her lifetime, their failure to join in the widow's transfer of the lot does not create a cloud on the title. Answer choice C is incorrect because a covenant of marketable title is implied in every land sale contract, commercial as well as residential, unless specifically waived by the buyer.

ANSWER TO QUESTION 86

Answer choice A is correct. In a contributory negligence jurisdiction, the plaintiff's contributory negligence is a complete bar to the plaintiff's recovery. Here, the runner was negligent in running against her doctor's advice. Consequently, despite the driver's negligence in failing to properly maintain his car, which led directly to the accident, the runner cannot recover from the driver. Answer choice B is incorrect because, although the driver was aware of the runner's predicament before the accident, the driver could not avoid hitting the runner by acting reasonably. The driver's negligence (i.e., his failure to repair the car's brakes) occurred prior to his awareness of the runner's predicament and could not be corrected after gaining such awareness before the accident. Answer choice C is incorrect because, although the runner was unable to extricate herself from the situation since she was unconscious, the driver may be liable if he had the last clear chance to avoid the accident. However, as explained with regard to answer choice B, the driver did not have the last clear chance to avoid the accident and is not liable. Answer choice D is incorrect because, in a contributory negligence jurisdiction, the negligence of the defendant is not sufficient to permit the plaintiff to recover where the plaintiff is also negligent.

ANSWER TO QUESTION 87

Answer choice C is correct. Regardless of the type of recording act that governs, the grantee of real property is protected from a subsequent purchaser's claims of ownership to the property by recording his deed prior to the subsequent conveyance. Answer choice A is incorrect because, although the recording act does not protect a subsequent grantee who is a donee from an unrecorded deed, it does protect any grantee, including a donee, who records his deed prior to the subsequent conveyance. Answer choice B is incorrect because there is no requirement that the owner of real property make productive use of the property. Answer choice D is incorrect because the son's payment of the real estate taxes on the property is irrelevant to a priority dispute between the son and a subsequent purchaser.

ANSWER TO QUESTION 88

Answer choice C is correct. While settlement offers and negotiations are generally not admissible for public policy reasons, they are admissible in order to prove the bias or prejudice of a witness. Because the former defendant was offered a reduced sentence in exchange for his testimony, the jury should be able to weigh that fact when considering the former defendant's credibility. Answer choice A is incorrect because the statement is not hearsay; it is not being introduced to show the truth of the matter asserted, it is being introduced to impeach the witness's credibility. Note, though, that a statement made for the purposes of settlement cannot be admitted as a prior inconsistent statement to impeach a party. Answer choice B is incorrect because, as explained above, even though a settlement offer is not admissible to prove liability, it can be introduced for other reasons, such as to prove the bias or prejudice of a witness (as here), to negate a claim of undue delay, or to prove obstruction of a criminal investigation or prosecution. Answer choice D is incorrect because, as mentioned above, it can be relevant to prove—among other things—bias, which could affect how much weight the trier of fact gives the witness's statement.

ANSWER TO QUESTION 89

Answer choice D is correct. Article IV's Privileges and Immunities Clause protects citizens of one state from discrimination by another state in their exercise of fundamental rights. Here, the state can charge higher licensing fees for out-of-state residents because recreational deer hunting is not a fundamental right, and the differential treatment is fair because state residents' taxes help to fund the state's fish and game department. For this reason, answer choice B is incorrect. Answer choice A is incorrect because, since out-of-state deer hunters are not a suspect classification, the Equal Protection Clause merely requires that the state action satisfy the rational basis standard, which it does. Answer choice C is incorrect because the Dormant Commerce Clause generally prohibits a state from giving its own residents a preferred right of access to natural resources, such as by charging nonresidents additional fees to access such resources. In addition, since the state is not directly buying or selling goods, it is not acting as a market participant.

ANSWER TO QUESTION 90

Answer choice A is correct. In order for the attractive nuisance doctrine to apply, the landowner must know or have reason to know that the artificial condition is located in a place that children are likely to trespass. Since the owner lives in a retirement community that greatly restricts access by nonresidents, this requirement is not satisfied. Answer choice B is incorrect because, despite its name, the attractive nuisance doctrine does not require that the child be enticed onto the property by the presence of the condition. Answer choice C is incorrect because the purpose of the attractive nuisance doctrine is to permit a child trespasser to recover for a landowner's negligence. Answer choice D is incorrect. In order for the attractive nuisance doctrine to apply, the child, because of his youth, must not appreciate the danger presented by the condition. A warning will often protect a landowner from the liability by bringing the condition to the attention to the child. In this case, despite the warning, the child, while deciding that he should go on the dock, did not realize that the reason he should not do so was its dangerous condition.

ANSWER TO QUESTION 91

Answer choice D is correct. Although a defendant who is not the aggressor is justified in using reasonable force in self-defense against another person to prevent immediate unlawful harm to himself, the defendant's belief that the other person's actions represent an immediate threat must be reasonable. When such belief is unreasonable but honest, the defendant is entitled to assert "imperfect self-defense," which reduces his crime from murder to voluntary manslaughter. Consequently, the homeowner cannot be convicted of murder, since he acted in self-defense on his honest but unreasonable belief that the officer threatened him with death or serious bodily harm. Answer choice A incorrect because, although the homeowner did kill the officer, his imperfect self-defense reduces the charge from murder to voluntary manslaughter. Answer choice B is incorrect because, while the homeowner's unreasonable belief of the need to use deadly force prevents him from successfully asserting self-defense, his honest belief of the need to use deadly force permits him to successfully lay claim to the imperfect self-defense. Answer choice C is incorrect because, although an accurate statement of the law, the absence of a duty to retreat protects the homeowner from criminal liability for the use of deadly force only when the homeowner's belief as to the need to use deadly force was reasonable.

ANSWER TO QUESTION 92

Answer choice A is correct. A witness may be impeached by showing that the witness has made statements that are inconsistent with some material part of the witness's testimony. Note that because these statements are being used to impeach the witness and not to prove the truth of the matter asserted, they are not hearsay. Note, too, that because the statements were not made under oath in a prior proceeding, they may not be considered as substantive evidence. Answer choice B is incorrect because both the testimony and the email are admissible for impeachment purposes. Impeachment with a prior inconsistent statement may occur by cross-examination or by use of extrinsic evidence, such as the testimony of another witness or documentary evidence. Answer choice C is incorrect because, unlike the common law, the Federal Rules do not require that the witness have the opportunity to explain or deny the evidence before introducing a prior inconsistent statement. Answer choice D is incorrect because the facts indicate that whether the defendant possessed the knowledge in question is a central issue in the case; that is, it is a material matter. It is true that extrinsic evidence of a prior inconsistent statement cannot be used to impeach a witness regarding a collateral, or immaterial, matter; when a witness testifies as to an immaterial matter, the questioning party is bound by the answer the witness gives.

ANSWER TO QUESTION 93

Answer choice B is correct. The UCC generally provides that the seller retains the risk of loss until some event occurs. Generally, a merchant seller retains the risk of loss in the absence of a contract term to the contrary until the buyer receives the goods. However, where the buyer is in breach of the contract, the risk of loss passes to the buyer to the extent of any deficiency in seller's insurance coverage. Here, the store, as buyer, is in breach of the contract by failing to pick up the ornaments by 2:00 pm. Although the UCC only requires that the delivery time be "reasonable" in the absence of a specific contract term, the parties here modified the contract in that regard by agreeing that the seller should pick up the ornaments by 2:00 pm. Consequently, answer choice B is correct and answer choice C is incorrect. Answer choice A is incorrect because, although the risk of loss passes to the buyer upon tender of delivery of the goods where the seller is not a merchant, the artisan is a merchant (he has specialized knowledge or skill peculiar to glass ornaments). Consequently, the risk of loss does not pass until the buyer receives the goods unless the buyer is in breach of the contract (as is the case here). Answer choice D is incorrect because, although the store, as buyer, was a merchant with respect to the ornaments, this status is irrelevant to issue of risk of loss. It is the seller's status a merchant that can delay the shift in the risk of loss from the tender of delivery by the seller to the buyer's actual receipt of the goods.

ANSWER TO QUESTION 94

Answer choice A is correct. For negligence *per se* to apply, a plaintiff must prove that he was in the class of people intended to be protected by the statute; his interest was of the type intended to be protected; the harm suffered was of the type intended to be protected against; and the harm materialized in the manner that was of legislative concern. Here, the fourth factor fails, as the statute is clearly designed to prevent the consequences of a driver suffering a seizure while behind the wheel. Here, the man was not suffering a seizure, so the statute is inapplicable to the issue of his negligence. Answer choice B is incorrect because the pedestrian was hit by a vehicle; this harm is clearly within the type contemplated by the statute. Answer choices C and D are incorrect because they ignore the "manner of harm" requirement for negligence *per se*.

ANSWER TO QUESTION 95

Answer choice D is correct. Although the witness is "unavailable" for the purposes of the hearsay rules (as will be discussed below), and there is a "former testimony" exception to the hearsay rule, the former testimony exception does not apply. Grand jury testimony does not fall within the former testimony exception. While grand jury testimony could be admissible as a prior inconsistent statement, since the witness is not testifying here, there is no statement that is "inconsistent" with a prior statement. To be admissible, the former testimony of an unavailable witness must be given under oath in a hearing or deposition, and the party against whom the testimony is being offered must have had an opportunity and similar motive to develop the testimony by direct or cross-examination; grand jury testimony does not meet this standard because the defendant does not have the opportunity to cross-examine grand jury witnesses. Answer choice A is incorrect because, as discussed above, even though the witness is unavailable to testify, grand jury testimony does not fall within the former testimony exception. Answer choice B is incorrect because items used to refresh the witness's recollection are not admitted into evidence and because the witness has no recollection that can be refreshed. Answer choice C is incorrect because the witness meets the standard for "unavailability." A witness is considered unavailable if that person is exempt on the grounds of privilege, refuses to testify, lacks memory of the subject matter of the statement, is unable to testify due to death or physical or mental disability, or is absent and cannot be subpoenaed or otherwise made to appear. The witness's lack of ability to remember the subject of his testimony due to a brain injury qualifies the witness as unavailable.

ANSWER TO QUESTION 96

Answer choice C is correct because presidential power under Article II with respect to domestic matters is greatest when the president acts pursuant to Congressional authorization. Here, Congress expressly authorized the President to seize plants to prevent a shutdown that would threaten national security. Answer choice A is incorrect because, although the delegation of legislative power to the executive is subject to the requirement that the exercise of such power must be subject to a specific, intelligible standard, the Supreme Court has so loosely interpreted this requirement that almost any standard has satisfied this requirement. Answer choice B is incorrect because, although the President's power as Commander-in-Chief may not extend to this specific domestic action, it is unconstitutional because it has been authorized by Congress. Answer choice D is incorrect because action by the President in domestic affairs that has been authorized by Congress need not be subsequently approved by Congress in order to be valid.

ANSWER TO QUESTION 97

Answer choice A is correct. An easement by necessity can arise even though there has not been a prior use of the servient estate that corresponds with the easement so long as the easement is strictly necessary. Answer choice B is incorrect because the creation of an easement by necessity stems from the existence of a necessity. There is no requirement that owner of the dominant estate first request the owner of the servient estate to acknowledge the existence of the easement before seeking court recognition of the easement or that the existence of the easement depends on the assent of the owner of the servient estate. Answer choice C is incorrect because, although the son did not own both the servient and dominant estates, both were under common ownership at one time and the necessity arose at the time of the severance of the property into the parcels of land. Moreover, with respect to the daughter's property, the existence of a private road that accessed the public road at the time of severance evidences an intent by the father that her property has access to the public road. Answer choice D is incorrect because, unlike an easement by implication, an easement by necessity does not require the easement to be based on a prior use of the servient estate by the common owner of both estates.

ANSWER TO QUESTION 98

Answer choice D is correct because the Eighth Amendment prohibition does not prohibit life sentences for three-time repeat felony offenders, even if they are non-violent. Answer choice A is incorrect because the Eighth Amendment prohibition does not apply in this situation. Answer choice B is incorrect because this type of recidivism statute has been judged not to violate the Double Jeopardy Clause. Answer choice C is incorrect because the Eighth Amendment applies to all cruel and unusual punishment, not just that which involves the use of force. Some sentences that are not proportional to the crime have been held to violate the Eighth Amendment even if the sentences do not involve the use of force.

ANSWER TO QUESTION 99

Answer choice C is correct. Generally, the parol evidence rule prevents a party to a written contract from presenting other evidence that contradicts the terms of the contract as written. Specifically, when a writing is the complete integration of the parties' agreement, evidence of a prior or contemporaneous agreement between the parties is generally not admissible. Answer choice A is incorrect because terms that supplement a written agreement are only admissible if the writing is a partial integration of the parties' agreement. Answer choice B is incorrect because, while the Statute of Frauds does require that a contract for the sale of goods for $500 or more be in writing, the Statute of Frauds does not generally prevent enforcement of an oral agreement for the provision of services valued above $500. Answer choice D is incorrect because the parol evidence rule does not bar all evidence of an oral agreement between parties who have entered into a written contract. For example, the parol evidence rule does not apply when a party is raising an excuse, establishing a defense, evidencing a separate deal, proving a condition precedent, clarifying an ambiguity, proving subsequent agreements, or making certain clarifications under the UCC.

ANSWER TO QUESTION 100

Answer choice B is correct. Upon the owner's death, the institution had a fee simple subject to an executory interest in the land and the daughter had an executory interest. Under the common law Rule Against Perpetuities the daughter's interest could, and if fact would, vest more than 21 years after her death. In such case, her interest would be stricken, and the son, having been devised the owner's other real property interest, (and not the owner's heirs) would hold a possibility of reverter in the land. However, the jurisdiction has adopted the "wait and see" approach to the Rule. Since the daughter's interest did vest within 90 years of its creation, it does not violate the jurisdiction's Rule. An executory interest may be devised; the daughter devised her executory interest to her child. Since the condition imposed on the institution (i.e., use of the property for educational purpose) would be violated by the developer, the property would then automatically pass to the daughter's child. Consequently, the institution must secure her approval for the transfer in order to convey marketable title. For the reasons discussed above, answer choices A, C, and D are incorrect.

ANSWER TO QUESTION 101

Answer choice C is correct. A statement offered as circumstantial evidence of the declarant's mental state is admissible as nonhearsay. Answer choice A is incorrect because this statement is not offered to prove the truth of the matter asserted (i.e., that the defendant is the president) but to support the defense attorney's assertion that the defendant has a mental defect. Answer choice B is incorrect because, as the statement is not hearsay, it does not need to fall under a hearsay exception; there is a distinction between the "state of mind" exception to the hearsay rule and using a statement as circumstantial evidence for a declarant's state of mind. Answer choice D is incorrect because while defendants in a criminal trial are occasionally subject to different evidentiary standards than the prosecution, they are almost always subject to the same hearsay rules.

ANSWER TO QUESTION 102

Answer choice C is correct. A defendant has the right to the assistance of counsel at any trial that results in incarceration, even when that sentence is suspended. Answer choice A is incorrect because a misdemeanor that results in a sentence involving incarceration requires the assistance of counsel. Answer choice B is incorrect because the fact that the sentence was suspended does not waive the requirement that defense counsel be provided. Answer choice D is incorrect because assistance of counsel is not required for a crime that is punishable by imprisonment as long as that punishment is not imposed.

ANSWER TO QUESTION 103

Answer choice D is correct. A provision for liquidated damages is enforceable and not construed as a penalty if the amount of damages stipulated in the contract is reasonable in relation to either the actual damages suffered or the damages that might be anticipated at the time the contract was made. While the deposit was twice as large as the dealership could have estimated its damages would be in the event of a breach by the buyer, the deposit ended up being exactly equal to the dealership's actual damages. Consequently, the woman will not prevail. For the foregoing reasons, answer choice A is incorrect. Answer choice B is incorrect because, although the uniqueness of a good is a factor in an action for specific performance, it is irrelevant with regard to the enforceability of a liquidated damages clause. Answer choice C is incorrect because, although a court may consider language in the contract stating that the liquidated damages provision is not a penalty, such an exculpatory term is not controlling.

ANSWER TO QUESTION 104

Answer choice A is correct. The parol evidence rule does not apply because the second agreement was entered into after the writing was executed; the rule only applies to agreements reached before or contemporaneous with the writing. Answer choice B is incorrect because, although consideration is generally necessary for the modification of a contract to be enforceable, the issue is the admissibility of the evaluation agreement, not its validity. Answer choice C is incorrect because evidence of a subsequent agreement is not subject to the parol evidence rule, even if a written agreement is fully integrated. Answer choice D is incorrect because this agreement happened subsequent to the execution of the writing. Therefore, it is irrelevant that it dealt with the same subject matter.

ANSWER TO QUESTION 105

Answer choice C is correct. Although governmental regulation of speech based on its content is generally prohibited, among the limited exceptions permitting such regulation is speech that represents a clear and present danger of imminent lawless action. Moreover, while a prior restraint on speech or the press is typically presumed to be unconstitutional, and has been rejected even where national security was at issue, it is possible that in the face of an immediate threat of grave and irreparable harm, such as a terrorist attack that would be triggered by messages in the newspapers, a prior restraint on their publication would be upheld. Answer choice A is factually incorrect. The president's order would prevent the four newspapers from publishing for two week, and thus constitutes a prior restraint on speech and the press. Answer choice B is incorrect because suppression of subversion speech is generally not permit unless it presents a clear and present danger, but, if suppression is allowed, there is no requirement, unlike the taking of property under the Takings Clause of the Fifth Amendment, that the government compensate the person whose speech has been suppressed. Answer choice D is incorrect because where a prior restraint, even one based on national security, is imposed on Freedom of Speech, the burden is on the government to justify the restraint.

ANSWER TO QUESTION 106

Answer choice B is correct. The escrow arrangement seeks to circumvent the buyer-mortgagor's equitable right to redeem the mortgaged property. The court will strike down the escrow arrangement and permit the buyer to redeem the mortgaged property. Answer choice A is incorrect because the lender's knowledge and the applicability of the recording statute are irrelevant. Although the lender obviously had notice of the prior mortgage since the lender was the mortgagee, the lender did not challenge the priority of the mortgage, but merely refused to foreclose on the property based on the mortgage. Answer choice C is incorrect because the lender has obtained title to the property by means of an arrangement that seeks to prevent the buyer-mortgagor from exercising the equitable right of redemption. As a consequence, the court will void the lender's title. Answer choice D is incorrect because a mortgagor's equitable right of redemption does not depend on the amount of the original mortgage loan that the mortgagor has paid.

ANSWER TO QUESTION 107

Answer choice D is correct. The crime of false pretenses occurs when an individual (i) obtains title to property (ii) of another person (iii) through the reliance of that person (iv) on a known false representation of a material past or present fact (v) and the representation is made with the intent to defraud. All elements of the crime are implicated in the man's conduct of paying the discounted price for the suit—he obtained legal title to the suit through fraudulent means. Answer choice A is incorrect because forgery requires the making of a false writing with apparent legal significance such as a check or a contract. Here, the red label lacked legal significance. Answer choice B is incorrect because embezzlement occurs when a defendant originally held the property pursuant to a formal or informal trust agreement. No such agreement took place here. Answer choice C is incorrect because larceny by trick involves obtaining the mere *possession* of another's property. Here, the man obtained not only possession of the suit, but full title as well.

ANSWER TO QUESTION 108

Answer choice D is correct. Claims for pure economic loss generally cannot be brought under a negligence theory. A plaintiff must show physical injury or damage to persons or property to recover for negligence. Here, the electronics manufacturer's $750,000 loss is purely economic, so any negligence claim is improper. For this reason, answer choices A, B, and C are all incorrect.

ANSWER TO QUESTION 109

Answer choice A is correct. Unlike the Fourteenth Amendment and the Contracts Clause, the Thirteenth Amendment does not require state action. Rather, it abolishes slavery and its "badges and incidents," including racial discrimination in private transactions like contracts. Moreover, Section 2 of the Thirteenth Amendment authorizes Congress to enact legislation to implement its guarantees. For this reason, answer choices B and D are incorrect. Answer choice C is incorrect because the General Welfare

Clause has been interpreted as permitting Congress to exercise its spending and taxing powers for any public purpose, but not as creating a specific general power to legislate for the public welfare.

ANSWER TO QUESTION 110

Answer choice B is correct. This case is in federal court. In federal court (and in a minority of jurisdictions), one spouse may choose to testify against the other. The general rule of spousal immunity, one of the two "spousal privileges," is that the spouse of a criminal defendant may not be called as a witness by the prosecution, and one spouse cannot be compelled to testify against the other in a criminal trial. However, in federal court, the witness spouse holds this privilege, and may choose to testify; the other spouse cannot prevent her from doing so by claiming the privilege. Note that this is different for the "confidential marital communications" privilege, the other half of the "spousal privilege." The confidential marital communications privilege prevents either spouse from testifying as to communications made dependant on the sanctity of marriage, and one spouse can prevent the other from testifying. However, since in this case, the wife found incriminating paperwork, and her testimony is not about a marital communication, her husband cannot prevent her from testifying. Answer choice A is incorrect because, for the purposes of spousal immunity, it is irrelevant that the wife is not being called to testify at her husband's trial. A married person may not be compelled to testify against her spouse in any criminal proceeding, including a grand jury proceeding, regardless of who is the defendant. Therefore, the fact that the trial in question is not the husband's would not prevent spousal immunity from applying in this case. Answer choice C is incorrect because, as discussed above, in federal court, the witness spouse holds the privilege, and may choose to testify; unlike in many jurisdictions, the other spouse cannot prevent a willing spouse from becoming a witness against him. Answer choice D is incorrect for the reasons listed above; a witness spouse can choose to testify against her spouse, even during the marriage. Note though that the end of a marriage does end spousal immunity; the spousal immunity privilege can only be asserted during a valid marriage.

ANSWER TO QUESTION 111

Answer choice C is correct. The actions by the buyer in paying a portion of the purchase price to the owner and constructing of a garage on the lot, which constitutes a substantial improvement of the lot, is persuasive evidence that a contract between the parties exists. The doctrine of part performance may be asserted by either party to a land sale contract in order compel specific performance of the contract. Answer choice A is incorrect because, although the buyer did not sign the written agreement and otherwise would enjoy the protection of the Statute of Frauds, the buyer's actions with respect to the lot are sufficient to establish the existence of the contract through part performance. Answer choice B is incorrect because, although the owner's remedy at law of damage is adequate, the owner is permitted to seek specific performance under the theory of mutualities of remedies. Answer choice D is incorrect because the facts do not support an argument that the seller detrimentally relied on the buyer's agreement to purchase the property in a manner that would create a hardship.

ANSWER TO QUESTION 112

Answer choice A is correct. Consent is effective if a plaintiff, by words or actions, manifests the willingness to submit to a defendant's conduct. Here, the fisherman clearly consented to his neighbor's use of the vehicle to tow her boat. However, a defendant's conduct may not exceed the scope of the consent. By using the vehicle a second time, the neighbor exceeded the scope of the fisherman's consent. Thus, she is liable for conversion. Answer choice B is incorrect because, while the concept of frolic and detour may be applicable to determine an employer's vicarious liability for an employee's action, it is not applicable to determine liability for conversion in a non-employment situation. Answer choice C is incorrect because once the scope of consent has been exceeded, the purpose of defendant's conduct is irrelevant. Answer choice D is incorrect because the neighbor exceeded the scope of the fisherman's consent.

ANSWER TO QUESTION 113

Answer choice C is correct. A defendant can be convicted of involuntary manslaughter when he acts with criminal negligence: reckless action that puts another person at a significant risk of injury or death. It requires more than the ordinary negligence required for tort liability and something less than the extremely negligent conduct required for depraved heart murder. Here, the defendant's act of securing his handgun in an ill-fitting holster certainly put others at risk of injury or death. For these reasons, answer choice D is incorrect. Answer choice A is incorrect because a defendant is guilty of first degree felony murder when he commits an unlawful killing during the commission of a statutorily enumerated felony. Typically enumerated are the following five inherently dangerous felonies: burglary, arson, rape, robbery, and kidnapping. While the man's failure to register the gun may have been a felony in that particular jurisdiction, it is not one of the five enumerated felonies. In addition, the shopper's death was not a natural and probable consequence of the man's commission of the "failure-to-register" felony. Consequently, he cannot be convicted under a typical felony murder statute. Answer choice B is incorrect because voluntary manslaughter occurs only when a defendant acts in the heat of passion.

ANSWER TO QUESTION 114

Answer choice B is correct because Congress cannot authorize a legislative committee to "veto" agency regulations. The constitution requires that legislative power be excised in accord with bicameralism (i.e., passed by both Houses of Congress) and the Presentment Clauses of Article I (i.e., requirement that, in order for bill to become law in must be presented to the president for his approval or return). Answer choice A is incorrect because Congress is not prohibited from delegating legislative power to an executive agency so long as Congress specifies intelligible standards for the agency to follow. Answer choice C is incorrect because, although Congress is reasonably trying to vindicate its Article I legislative power by ensuring the accountability of executive agencies that make law, the chosen means constitute an unconstitutional legislative veto. Answer choice D is incorrect because, although the joint committee action would constitute the exercise of legislative rather than executive power, the action would not comply with the constitutional requirements.

ANSWER TO QUESTION 115

Answer choice B is correct. Voluntary intoxication is a defense to specific intent crimes if it prevents the formation of the required intent. Here, the man's intoxication negated his intent to commit the crime of rape. While rape is a general intent crime, *attempted rape* is a specific intent crime, and thus the man's voluntary intoxication is a sufficient defense to the crime. For that reason, answer choice C is incorrect. Answer choice D is incorrect because, while intoxication is indeed not a defense to malice crimes, rape is not a malice crime. Answer choice A is incorrect because it wrongly applies part of the M'Naghten insanity test to a case of voluntary intoxication.

ANSWER TO QUESTION 116

Answer choice C is correct. The nightclub owner is seeking to enforce only the non-compete covenant in the contract. Courts rarely grant specific enforcement of contracts for personal services, but will restrain breaching parties from working for another when the contract contains a non-compete clause. Consequently, the court should grant the injunction. Answer choice A is incorrect because the nightclub owner is not seeking to force the pianist to play at his nightclub. Answer choice B is incorrect because a failure to mitigate damages does not bar a suit; rather, it limits the damages that may be recovered. Here, the nightclub owner is seeking an injunction, not damages. Answer choice D is incorrect because an injunction cannot generally be obtained where a party has breached a contract unless it is established that damages are an inadequate remedy.

ANSWER TO QUESTION 117

Answer choice D is correct. The former supervisor may not testify about the falsified records because it would be impeachment by extrinsic evidence of a prior bad act. A prior bad act, if used to impeach the credibility of a testifying witness, may not be proved by the introduction of extrinsic evidence. The adverse party may cross-examine the witness about the prior bad act, but must take his answer as he gives it. Since the evidence about the falsification of records is only admissible, if at all, to impeach the witness, extrinsic evidence—such as the supervisor's testimony—may not be used to refute the defendant's denial. Answer choice A is incorrect because when a person is charged with one crime, extrinsic evidence of a prior bad act is inadmissible to establish that the defendant had a propensity to commit that crime. Since the facts do not indicate that the prior bad act is being used as evidence for something circumstantial and relevant, such as motive, common plan or scheme, or identity, the supervisor's testimony is not admissible as substantive evidence. Answer choice B is incorrect because, for the reasons listed above, extrinsic evidence is not admissible to prove a witness's prior bad act. Answer choice C is incorrect because the alleged hearsay statement is an admission by a party-opponent, and therefore nonhearsay; further, it would constitute a prior inconsistent statement.

ANSWER TO QUESTION 118

Answer choice B is correct. The tort of negligent entrustment allows the owner of a vehicle to be held liable for the negligent acts of a driver to whom the car was entrusted if the owner knows or should know of the driver's negligent propensities. In the instant case, the neighbor had a clean driving record, and the enthusiast had no reason to believe that the neighbor had negligent propensities. Consequently, a negligent entrustment claim will not lie, and answer choice D is incorrect. Answer choice A is incorrect because specific instructions, no matter how clearly or sternly worded, do not insulate a vicariously liable party from being held accountable. Answer choice C is incorrect because an operative permissive use statute would have vested liability in the enthusiast. In jurisdictions with "permissive use" statutes, the owner of an automobile may be liable for the tortious acts of anyone driving the car with permission.

ANSWER TO QUESTION 119

Answer choice D is correct. The general rule is that the purchase of property at a foreclosure sale eliminates, not only the mortgage being foreclosed, but also all junior mortgages on the property. This rule applies even though the purchaser is one of the junior mortgagees. For this reason, answer choices A, B, and C are incorrect.

ANSWER TO QUESTION 120

Answer choice D is correct. Under the Equal Protection Clause of the Fourteenth Amendment, a discrimination claim requires proof that the government intentionally discriminated. Here, there is no evidence that the city intended to discriminate against Asian Americans. Rather, its fitness test had the neutral purpose of ensuring that all firefighters met certain standards of physical fitness so that they could perform their jobs. Answer choice A is incorrect because merely proving a negative disparate impact upon a group of persons, such as Asian American, that fall within a suspect classification is not sufficient to establish a discrimination claim. Answer choice B is incorrect because establishing past governmental discrimination as the cause of the negative disparate impact on a racial group is not sufficient to prove that the current governmental action has a discriminatory purpose or intent. (Note: Establishing such past discrimination may justify current governmental action to help such a racial group (i.e., affirmative action).) Answer choice C is incorrect because a constitutional claim of discrimination does not require the plaintiff to establish that a property interest that has been denied.

ANSWER TO QUESTION 121

Answer choice A is correct. Express assumption of the risk through a contractual limitation on liability is a bar to recovery for harms arising from the negligence of the party protected by the contract. This bar applies even where the state has adopted a comparative negligence statute. Here, the patron entered into a valid agreement to exculpate the ranch from liability for its negligence. Consequently, answer choices B, C, and D are incorrect.

ANSWER TO QUESTION 122

Answer choice B is correct. Lay witnesses may testify as to their own opinions when such opinions concern the witness's common sense impressions. The opinions must be rationally based on the witness's own perceptions and must be helpful to a clear understanding of the witness's testimony or the determination of a fact in issue. Here, the witness's opinion that the signature is not genuine is based on his own perceptions of it compared to a signature with which he is familiar. His familiarity with the doctor's signature and the differences between the doctor's signature and the allegedly forged signature are helpful to the jury in determining whether the signature is genuine, which is a material fact in issue. Answer choice A is incorrect because it is not necessary that the witness be an expert. Further, there is nothing in the fact pattern indicating that the witness is an expert on handwriting in general. Answer choice C is incorrect because, as explained above, a lay witness can testify as to his opinions based on his own perceptions. While it is true that lay witnesses are not permitted to testify as to any opinion based on scientific, technical, or specialized knowledge, a witness's own familiarity with someone's handwriting is permissible. Answer choice D is incorrect because jury verification is not the only way to verify handwriting. An expert witness or the jury may compare the writing in question with another writing that has been proven genuine in order to determine the authenticity of the writing in question. Additionally, a lay witness with personal knowledge of the claimed author's handwriting may testify as to whether the document is in that person's handwriting, as long as the lay witness has not become familiar with the handwriting for the purposes of litigation. Answer choice D excludes these alternate methods of verification.

ANSWER TO QUESTION 123

Answer choice A is correct. While the fact that the buyer entered into a contract would generally indicate that the buyer was both ready and willing to complete the purchase, the buyer's contractual duty was subject to a condition precedent, a satisfactory resolution of any defects uncovered by the home inspection. Since that condition was not satisfied, the buyer was not ready and willing to purchase the home. Answer choice B is incorrect because, although the buyer's demand that the seller upgrade the electrical wiring led to the termination of the contract, the buyer was within his contractual rights to make such a demand. The inability of the buyer and seller to agree constituted the failure of condition precedent. Answer choice C is incorrect because, although typically a buyer's entry into a purchase agreement with the seller indicates that the buyer is ready and willing, in this case, as noted with regard to answer choice A, the buyer conditioned his agreement on a satisfactory resolution of any issues uncovered during the home inspection. Since the parties could not agree on a resolution, the buyer was not ready and willing to purchase the home. Answer choice D is incorrect because, although the seller's refusal to upgrade the home's electrical wiring led to the termination of the contract, the seller was within his contractual rights to refuse. As noted with regard to answer choice B, the inability of the buyer and seller to agree constituted the failure of condition precedent.

ANSWER TO QUESTION 124

Answer choice A is correct. The "mailbox rule" does apply in this situation. Under this rule, an acceptance creates a contract when it is sent, not when it is received. Even if an offeree sends an acceptance and later a rejection, the acceptance will control even if the rejection was received first, unless the offeror detrimentally relies on the rejection. Answer choice B is incorrect because the phone call was a proper means of rejecting a written offer, but the offer was already accepted. The mirror image rule applies to acceptance on the same terms as the offer. Answer choice C is incorrect because personal service contracts can be enforced in certain situations. Problems with these contracts usually deal with unique talent and services and a specific performance remedy. Answer choice D is incorrect because, although the "mailbox rule" does not apply to a rejection, it does apply to the violinist's acceptance and results in the formation of contract.

ANSWER TO QUESTION 125

Answer choice D is correct. Under the "Dual Sovereignty" doctrine, prosecution of a defendant by the federal government for a crime arising out of an event does not prevent a state from prosecuting the defendant for a crime arising out of the same event. (Note: Under this doctrine, the reverse is also true.) Under *Blockburger*, robbery and conspiracy to commit robbery are separate offenses. Each contains an element that the other does not. Consequently, prosecution of the defendant for either robbery or conspiracy to commit robbery by the state is not prohibited by double jeopardy. For these reasons, answer choices A, B, and C are incorrect.

ANSWER TO QUESTION 126

Answer choice C is correct. A state (or the federal government) may place the burden of proving an affirmative defense, such as self-defense, on the defendant without violating the Due Process Clause. The preponderance of the evidence standard for judging whether the defendant has met this burden is also constitutional. The jury instructions, however, improperly prevent the jury from considering the defendant's self-defense evidence, not as an affirmative defense, but as a defense to the elements of the crime that the prosecution must prove. Used in such a manner, this evidence need not satisfy the preponderance standard before being considered by the jury. For these reasons, answer choices A, B, and D are incorrect.

ANSWER TO QUESTION 127

Answer choice C is correct because the Elections Clause of Art. I explicitly empowers Congress to override state laws concerning federal elections. This express provision makes irrelevant general principles of federalism embodied in the "commandeering" cases. For this reason, answer choices A and B are incorrect. Answer choice D is incorrect because, although conducting elections is a traditional function of state governments, the Elections Clause sanctions congressional interference with that function to the extent that it involves the election of United States senators and representatives.

ANSWER TO QUESTION 128

Answer choice A is correct. The victim's statement to the doctor is hearsay within hearsay, which means that both levels of hearsay must fall within a hearsay exception in order to be admissible. The medical record itself falls within the business records exception; medical records are considered business records to the extent that they relate to diagnosis or treatment. Statements related to fault associated with the injury are not admissible under this exception. The victim's statement would have to fall under its own hearsay exception, and none is applicable here. Answer choice B is incorrect for the reason given above—the statement within the record must fall under its own hearsay exception. Answer choice C is incorrect because the statement was not made for the purpose of medical treatment; while statements of fault can be admissible if reasonably pertinent to diagnosis or treatment, this statement was made during a check-up, after treatment, and therefore not likely necessary for diagnosis. Answer choice D is incorrect because the declarant's availability is immaterial to the business records exception. Further, the victim would not be the declarant of the record itself; some member of the emergency room's personnel would be.

ANSWER TO QUESTION 129

Answer choice B is correct. The UCC Statute of Frauds generally requires that a modified contract be in writing where the value of the goods is $500 or more. There is an exception for specially manufactured goods, but for this exception to apply, the goods cannot be suitable for sale to others in the ordinary course of the seller's business. Because the dealer sold the car to another customer, this exception would not apply. Since the written evidence of the parties' agreement fixed the price of the car at $35,000 and the dealer received this amount from another customer, the dealer would not be entitled to damages. Answer choice A is incorrect because the preexisting duty rule does not apply to a sale of goods governed by the UCC. Answer choice C is incorrect because, although the Uniform Commercial Code (UCC) permits a good faith modification of a contract without consideration, the Statute of Frauds prevents the enforcement of an oral modification. Answer choice D is incorrect because, as noted with respect to answer choice B, the exception to the Statute of Frauds for specially manufactured goods does not apply where the seller can sell the goods in the ordinary course of business.

ANSWER TO QUESTION 130

Answer choice A is correct. Nondisclosure of a known fact is tantamount to a misrepresentation that the fact does not exist if the party not disclosing the fact knows that disclosure would correct a mistake of the other party as to a basic assumption, and the failure to disclose would constitute lack of good faith and fair dealing. An innocent or negligent misrepresentation will still render a contract voidable *by the adversely affected party* if the misrepresentation is *material*—that is, the misrepresentation would cause a reasonable person to agree or that the person making the misrepresentation knows would cause this particular person to agree. Here, the seller's nondisclosure was material, because the buyer would not have consummated the transaction had he known of the condition. Thus, the contract is voidable by the buyer. Therefore, answer choice C is incorrect. Answer choice B is incorrect because the seller has no right to void the contract. Answer choice D is incorrect because a contract is void only in instances of fraud in the factum—where a fraudulent misrepresentation prevents a party from knowing the character or essential terms of the transaction.

ANSWER TO QUESTION 131

Answer choice C is correct. The holder of a future interest, such as a remainder interest, has a license to inspect the property for waste. This license is not subject to revocation by the holder of the current possessory interest in the property. Answer choice A is incorrect because, although the mother does have the right to possess the residence, that right is subject to the son's privilege, as holder of the remainder interest, to inspect the premises for waste. Answer choice B is incorrect because, although the mother as holder of the right to possess the residence may generally refuse to permit anyone to enter the premises, the son has an irrevocable license to do so. Answer choice D is incorrect because the owner of a property interest is generally free to grant or deny entry to anyone.

ANSWER TO QUESTION 132

Answer choice C is correct. For a larceny, the initial taking and aspiration of another's property must be trespassory: that is, the defendant must not be legally entrusted with the property. Here, the woman entrusted the mechanic with her vehicle (and the tires on the vehicle). Thus, the initial taking of the tires was not trespassory, and the mechanic's crime was embezzlement, not larceny. Answer choices A and B are incorrect because, while both correctly apply elements of larceny, they incorrectly state that the mechanic should be convicted. Because the mechanic had the intention of permanently depriving the woman of the tires at the time of the taking, answer choice D is incorrect. That he later returned them to the woman is of no matter.

ANSWER TO QUESTION 133

Answer choice A is correct. The man owed no duty to the woman, since he had no special relationship with her. Consequently, his failure to act to prevent his friend from raping her does not constitute an *actus reus* on which criminal liability can be predicated. Answer choice B is incorrect because accomplice liability, unlike conspiracy, does not require an agreement between the parties. Answer choice C is incorrect. Although the man failed to take any action to stop his friend from raping the woman or even to report the crime, he did nothing to encourage or to assist the friend in committing the rape. Answer choice D is incorrect because mere awareness that a crime is occurring is not sufficient to trigger accomplice liability.

ANSWER TO QUESTION 134

Answer choice B is correct because the language of the federal statute indicates a specific intent by Congress to preempt the field of airline regulations with regard to rates, routes and services. Under the Supremacy Clause, the federal law trumps conflicting state law. Answer choice A is incorrect because commercial speech is subject content regulation. The Freedom of Press Clause does not granted the press greater free speech rights than the public at large enjoys. Answer choice C is incorrect because, although there is a judicially recognized presumption against preemption with respect to a conflict between state and federal law, this presumption is rebuttable. Answer choice D is incorrect because, although the state law does not purport to deal specifically with interstate commerce in general or airline travel in specific, there is clear conflict between the federal statute and the state law with respect to the fee charged by the airline.

ANSWER TO QUESTION 135

Answer choice A is correct. Ordinarily, a plaintiff has the burden of proving by a preponderance of the evidence that each defendant's actions were an actual and proximate cause of the claimed injury. However, if the plaintiff is injured through the negligence of only one of several defendants, and it is not clear which defendant caused the injury, the burden shifts to each defendant to exonerate himself. This type of burden-shifting usually only occurs in cases with a small number of defendants—like in the instant case. For that reason, answer choice C is incorrect. Answer choice B is incorrect because res ipsa loquitur is not applied to cases where the defendant is not in control of the instrumentality or condition that caused the plaintiff's harm or at least responsible for those with such control. Answer choice D is incorrect because the motion must be denied unless the movant-defendant is able to produce evidence that he was not a substantial factor in the injury.

ANSWER TO QUESTION 136

Answer choice D is correct. While a criminal defendant is permitted to introduce evidence of his good character as being inconsistent with the crime charged, the evidence must be relevant to the character trait at issue. Here, the defendant's reputation as being "helpful and trustworthy" is not relevant to the crime charged, which is battery. If the defendant had a reputation in the church community as being nonviolent or peaceful, that would be admissible. However, since the character traits have nothing to do with getting in a barroom brawl, they are irrelevant. While the testimony as to the schoolyard incident does speak to the character trait of nonviolence, evidence of a specific act is an inappropriate way to introduce good character evidence. The defendant can offer reputation or opinion testimony by another witness to prove character, but not evidence of a specific act unless character is an essential element of a crime or defense, which is not the case here. Answer choice A is incorrect for the reasons listed above: while the defendant can introduce evidence of his own good character, it must be (i) a character trait relevant to the crime charged and (ii) presented as reputation or opinion testimony, unless character is an essential element of a crime or defense. Answer choices B and C are incorrect because they both admit one of the pieces of inadmissible evidence.

ANSWER TO QUESTION 137

Answer choice C is correct. By assuming the mortgage, the corporation became personally liable for the mortgage loan payments. In general, it is the lender-mortgagee's choice whether to proceed against the original mortgagor or a transferor who has assumed the mortgage obligation. Answer choice A is incorrect because a transferee who assumes a mortgage obligation is not sheltered from personal liability by a prior transferee's refusal to assume the mortgage obligation. The shelter principle applies in the context of the recording statute to shelter a transferee who otherwise would not qualify for protection under the statute when a prior transferee did. Answer choice B is incorrect because the Statute of Frauds does not apply to an assumption agreement. Answer choice D is incorrect because, while the holder of a purchase money mortgage is entitled to priority when the proceeds of a foreclosure sale are distributed, the loan's status as a purchase money mortgage obligation does not affect the liability of a transferee of the mortgage.

ANSWER TO QUESTION 138

Answer choice A is correct. In order to qualify as a lawful search incident to arrest, a search of a car in which the defendant was an occupant must be made at the time that the defendant has access to the car or to uncover evidence of the crime for which the defendant was arrested. Here, neither of those circumstances is applicable. Consequently, answer choice D is incorrect. Answer choice C is incorrect because, although the automobile exception permits a police officer to search a car without a warrant, the exception only applies when the police officer has probable cause to conduct the search. Answer choice B is incorrect because a police officer's arrest of an individual for a misdemeanor that is punishable only by a fine is not unreasonable under the Fourth Amendment.

ANSWER TO QUESTION 139

Answer choice A is correct. When a hearsay statement is admitted into evidence, the credibility of the declarant may be attacked by any evidence that would be admissible if the declarant had testified as a witness. In this case, if the declarant co-conspirator had testified, the defendant's attorney would have been able to cross-examine him as to his bias against the defendant. Because a witness may be influenced by his relationship with a party or in the outcome of a case, evidence of the witness's bias is always material. Here, the co-conspirator had an incentive to testify against the defendant, in exchange for a better deal from the prosecutor. This is relevant and an appropriate way to impeach the witness. Answer choice B is incorrect because misdemeanor convictions are only admissible to impeach a witness if they are probative of untruthfulness. In this case, public intoxication, disorderly conduct, and vandalism have nothing to do with the witness's character for truthfulness. As such, the misdemeanors are inadmissible for impeachment. Answer choice C is incorrect because the credibility of a witness may only be attacked by reputation or opinion evidence as to the witness's character for truthfulness or untruthfulness. The fact that the witness has a reputation for being violent is not probative of truthfulness, and is therefore inadmissible. Answer choice D is incorrect because the conviction is more than 10 years old. A witness may be impeached with evidence that he has been convicted of a crime, subject to certain limitations. Any crime involving dishonesty or a false statement, whether a felony or a misdemeanor, may be used to impeach, if it is less than 10 years old. Any crime not involving dishonesty that is less than 10 years old may only be used for impeachment if the crime is a felony. If more than 10 years have elapsed since conviction, evidence of the crime is not admissible unless the court determines that the probative value substantially outweighs its prejudicial effect. In this case, nothing indicates that the felony's probative value would be substantial in any way. The conviction does not involve dishonesty, and it is over 10 years old. As such, it is inadmissible for impeachment purposes.

ANSWER TO QUESTION 140

Answer choice D is correct. In a comparative negligence jurisdiction, implied assumption of the risk is not recognized as a separate defense. Instead, the plaintiff's knowledge of the risk of her conduct is generally taken into account in determining the degree to which she is at fault. Answer choice A is incorrect because, even assuming that the woman did voluntarily assume that risk, such a defense is not recognized as a separate defense in a comparative negligence jurisdiction. Answer choice B is incorrect because assumption of the risk is only an absolute bar to recovery in a contributory negligence jurisdiction, not a comparative negligence jurisdiction. Answer choice C is incorrect because assumption of the risk requires the plaintiff, not the defendant, to be aware of the risks of the plaintiff's conduct.

ANSWER TO QUESTION 141

Answer choice B is correct because the statute violates the fundamental liberty and privacy interests of married couples under the substantive aspect of the Due Process Clause. Answer choice A is incorrect because there is a rational basis for the statute. By criminalizing the parenting of more than two children, the statute would discourage some people from having children and thereby address the problem of overpopulation and help to preserve the state's natural resources. In addition, since the statute affects fundamental rights, the appropriate standard for judging its constitutionality is strict scrutiny rather than rational basis. Answer choice C is incorrect because the statute does not grant to a prosecutor the right to decide who can have children. The statute clearly subjects a man who fathers or a woman who gives birth to more than two children to criminal penalties. Answer choice D is incorrect because individuals who have more than two children are not members of a suspect classification. Consequently, the statute needs only satisfy the rational basis standard under an Equal Protection analysis.

ANSWER TO QUESTION 142

Answer choice B is correct. When, prior to acceptance, the offeree detrimentally relies on the offeror's promise, the doctrine of promissory estoppel implies an option contract where it was reasonably foreseeable that such detrimental reliance would occur. Here, the farmer incurred costs to produce the seedlings requested by the garden center. Answer choice A is incorrect because, when a contract is unilateral, as this contract was since the garden center sought the delivery of seedlings by the farmer, not a promise from the farmer to do so, the beginning of performance by the offeree creates an option contract that prevents the offeror from revoking the offer. However, at the time that the garden center revoked its offer, the farmer had not begun performance of the contract, but merely had engaged in preparations to perform the contract. Answer choice C is incorrect because, although the garden center did revoke its offer before the farmer accepted it by the delivery of seedlings to the garden center, the farmer is entitled to recover under the doctrine of promissory estoppel. Answer choice D is incorrect because an output contract is not invalid for lack of consideration. The promise to deliver one's output is not illusory.

ANSWER TO QUESTION 143

Answer choice A is correct. Even though the misrepresentation was not fraudulent, it nevertheless renders the contract voidable. Here, the buyer justifiably relied on a certified inspection, and it was a material misrepresentation because the presence of termites is a major factor in buying a house. Answer choice B is incorrect because the misrepresentation did not rise to the level of unconscionability. The contract was not unfair or one-sided. Answer choice C is incorrect because, although there was not a mutual mistake present because the misinformation did not go to the heart of the bargain, there was still a material misrepresentation that was justifiably relied upon. Answer choice D is incorrect because, while it is possible that the inspector's negligence would be imputed to the seller who employed the inspector, whether the seller's misrepresentation was innocent or negligent, it would still provide grounds for avoiding the contract.

ANSWER TO QUESTION 144

Answer choice B is correct. The acquaintance has adversely possessed the condominium unit for more than the requisite 10-year period. The acquaintance's possession is adverse, however, only as to any property owner with the current right to possess the unit at the time that the adverse possession begins. Since only the wife's life estate was a current possessory interest at the time that the acquaintance's adverse possession began, the acquaintance is only entitled to her life estate. Answer choices A and C are incorrect. Since the daughter's remainder interest is not currently a possessory interest, the limitations period on the daughter's ability to bring an action to eject the acquaintance has not yet begun to run. Answer choice D is incorrect because, although the acquaintance originally entered the unit with the permission of the owner (i.e., the wife), the acquaintance's possession unit became adverse when the acquaintance decided to remain in the unit without such permission. While incapacity of the property owner at the time that the adverse possession begins will toll the statutory period during the period of incapacity, the wife's incapacity arose after the acquaintance's possession became adverse.

ANSWER TO QUESTION 145

Answer choice D is correct. In a sale of goods transaction, such as the purchase of shirts, the Uniform Commercial Code (UCC) requires that the goods tendered by the seller conform in all respects to the contract. Although the shirts shipped to the school conformed to the specifications of original contract, this contract was modified by the subsequent emails between the principal and the seller. Answer choice A is incorrect because the fact that the shirts were specially manufactured goods is relevant only when the buyer is claiming the statute of frauds as a defense. The fact that the goods were specially manufactured is irrelevant to the validity of the written agreement to modify the original contract in this case. Answer choice B is incorrect because the UCC, rejecting the preexisting duty rule, does not require consideration in order for the good-faith modification of a contract to be valid. Answer choice C is incorrect because the school's status as a non-merchant is irrelevant to determining the terms of this contract or its breach.

ANSWER TO QUESTION 146

Answer choice C is correct. A failure by the plaintiff to mitigate his damages can be taken into account in determining the amount of the plaintiff's damages. Answer choices A and B are incorrect because the defendant's conduct, while contributing to the plaintiff's injuries, produced the condition that the defendant undertook to treat. Consequently, the surgeon is not liable for such injuries, but only for the harm caused by the surgeon's negligent treatment of those injuries. Answer choice D is incorrect because, since the jurisdiction continues to adhere to the collateral source rule, the defendant cannot reduce his damages by amounts received by the plaintiff from a third party.

ANSWER TO QUESTION 147

Answer choice D is correct. The Federal Rules establish a privilege that protects victims of sexual offenses. The rule states that evidence offered to prove that any alleged victim engaged in other sexual behavior and evidence offered to prove any alleged victim's sexual predisposition is not admissible, subject to certain exceptions. None of the exceptions, detailed below, apply in this instance. As such, the evidence is not admissible. Answer choice A is incorrect because, while reputation testimony can be an admissible form of character evidence, there are certain privileges allotted to victims of sexual assault. Evidence of a victim's past sexual behavior or sexual disposition is generally not admissible in any civil or criminal proceeding involving sexual misconduct. While there are exceptions, the victim's reputation for promiscuity is not one of them. Answer choice B is incorrect because it misstates the law. One of the exceptions to the general rule stated above is that in a criminal case, evidence of a victim's past sexual conduct is admissible to show the victim's past sexual behavior with the defendant in order to prove consent. The victim's past sexual behavior in general cannot be used to prove consent; only the victim's past behavior with the defendant is relevant. Answer choice C is incorrect because, as mentioned directly above, there are some instances in which a victim's past sexual behavior may be relevant and admissible. Other examples include (i) to prove an alternate source of semen or injury, (ii) when the constitutional rights of the defendant require admission of the evidence, (iii) in civil cases, when the probative value substantially outweighs danger of harm to the victim, and (iv) in civil cases, when the victim herself has placed her reputation in controversy.

ANSWER TO QUESTION 148

Answer choice B is correct. A state cannot place an "undue burden" on a woman's fundamental Fourteenth Amendment Due Process liberty interest in having an abortion before fetal viability. However, the state law here does not constitute such an undue burden, as states may try to persuade women not to choose abortion and may impose reasonable waiting periods, so long as states do not hinder a woman's right to choose abortion thereafter. For this reason, answer choices C and D are incorrect. Answer choice A is incorrect because, even though a state has a rational basis (or even a compelling justification) for the restrictions, the restrictions are unconstitutional where they place a substantial burden on a woman's right to seek an abortion.

ANSWER TO QUESTION 149

Answer choice D is correct. Although the pest control company, by engaging in an abnormally dangerous activity, is strictly liable for harm that results from the conduct of that activity, assumption of the risk is a defense to strict liability. The tenant's decision to remain in the apartment and thereby possibly expose himself to the gas was both knowing and voluntary. Answer choice A is incorrect because, as noted with respect to answer choice D, even though the company is strictly liable, assumption of the risk is a defense to strict liability. Answer choice B is incorrect because the company exercised reasonable care in fumigating the building. Answer choice C is incorrect because the company's strict liability to the tenant is not based on residency in the fumigated building.

ANSWER TO QUESTION 150

Answer choice C is correct. The basic rule of "first in time, first in right" would entitle the aunt to $100,000 (answer choice A). In addition, the status of the aunt's interest as a seller-financed security interest would give the aunt first priority to the net proceeds from the foreclosure sale (answer choice B). However because of the subordination agreement, the aunt's interest, which arises from the installment sale contract, takes a back seat to the bank's mortgage. While the jurisdiction has a race-notice recording act which protects subsequent purchasers from unrecorded installment sale contracts without notice, and the patient, as judgment lien holder obtained the lien without notice of the aunt's interest in the property, the holder of the judgment lien is not treated as a purchaser protected by the recording act. Consequently, the aunt's interest, by preceding the judgment lien, has priority over it, but not over the bank's interest. Therefore, answer choice C, not D, is correct.

ANSWER TO QUESTION 151

Answer choice A is correct because the Article IV Privileges and Immunities Clause prohibits a state from discriminating against nonresidents with respect to the exercise of a fundamental right, such as earning a living, unless there is substantial justification for the discrimination. Here, the state imposed a fee on nonresidents that was 10 times greater than the fee on residents. While nonresidents may contribute to problem that the state was seeking to address (i.e., overfishing), there are other means of addressing this problem, such as limiting the amount of fish that can be caught, that are less restrictive on the rights of nonresidents. Answer choice B is incorrect because, since nonresident fishing guides are not members of a suspect classification, the rational basis standard is applied to determine whether the statute violates the Equal Protection Clause. Under this standard, the statute is likely to be upheld since indirectly limiting the number of guides could reduce the number of individuals who go fishing and thereby the number of fish caught. Answer choice C is incorrect because, although engaging in fishing is not a fundamental right, the right to earn a livelihood is. Answer choice D is incorrect because, even if the state has traditionally regulated fishing, the state cannot do so in a manner that violates individual rights set forth in the Constitution. The conflict here is not between a state statute and a federal statute, but between the state statute and the Constitution.

ANSWER TO QUESTION 152

Answer choice C is correct because, in order for a witness to be prevented from identifying the defendant in court due to a previous impermissibly suggestive photo array, the witness's in-court identification must be unreliable. Answer choice A is incorrect because there is no right to counsel at a photo identification. Answer choice B is incorrect because, even though the identification procedure was impermissibly suggestive, the witness's in-court identification was reliable. Answer choice D is incorrect because neither the location of the photo array nor the identity of the person who conducted it is relevant to the issue of whether the witness's in-court identification of the defendant should be suppressed.

ANSWER TO QUESTION 153

Answer choice A is correct. A criminal defendant may introduce evidence of the victim's character when it is relevant to the defense asserted. If the defendant does so, the prosecution may offer rebuttal evidence of the victim's good character regarding that trait, and evidence of the defendant's bad character for the same trait. In this case, because the defendant did decide to introduce evidence of the victim's violent character, the prosecutor may rebut that evidence with evidence of the victim's peacefulness, and evidence of the defendant's violent nature. Answer choice B is incorrect because the victim's character is relevant to a defendant's actions, particularly if relevant to the defendant's asserted affirmative defense, and particularly if the defendant has already introduced evidence of the victim's character. Note, though, that if a defendant ever seeks to introduce evidence of the character of a victim of sexual assault, he will be subject to significant limitations. Answer choice C is incorrect because, even though it is true that a prosecutor cannot offer evidence of a defendant's bad character unless the defendant makes his own character an issue, the prosecutor may offer evidence about a defendant's bad character if the defendant calls into question the victim's character; the prosecutor may only offer evidence about that same character trait used against the victim. Answer choice D is incorrect for the reasons already discussed above.

ANSWER TO QUESTION 154

Answer choice D is correct. Felony murder does not require that the defendant act maliciously in bringing about the death of the victim. Answer choice A is incorrect because, in order for a death to be punishable as felony murder, it must be causally connected to the felony. While it is likely that the pilot's death, occurring as it did during an attempt to locate the carpenter, would be treated as natural and probable consequence of the carpenter's felony, if it were established that it was not causally connected, it would be a defense. Answer choice B is incorrect because, in order for a death to be punishable as felony murder, it must occur in the commission of the felony. Here, arguably, the carpenter had made good his escape and the death did not occur during the commission of the felony. In any case, if established, it would be a defense. Answer choice C is incorrect because felony murder requires the commission of an inherently dangerous felony, most commonly burglary, arson, robbery, rape, or kidnapping. The carpenter did not commit such a felony. While the carpenter clearly committed larceny, the facts do not suggest that the carpenter's actions constitute robbery or burglary. If it is established that the carpenter did not commit an inherently dangerous felony, it would be a defense.

ANSWER TO QUESTION 155

Answer choice A is correct. A tenant is free to sublet the leasehold unless the landlord and tenant agree otherwise. Any lease clause that purports to limit this right is narrowly construed. Although the lease prohibited the assignment of the leasehold without the prior written permission of the owner, it did not restrict the physician's right to sublet the leasehold. Since the arrangement between the psychiatrist and the general practice physician encompassed only one of the two years remaining on the physician's lease of the office space from the owner, the arrangement was a sublease rather than an assignment. Answer choice B is incorrect because, although the majority of jurisdictions prevent a landlord who has consented to assignment from objecting to a subsequent assignment, this rule is not applied to a sublet. Answer choice C is incorrect because, as noted with regard to answer choice A, the lease term that required the owner's prior written permission applied only to an assignment of the lease. Answer choice D is incorrect because, although the lease did permit the owner to reject an assignment for any reason, the physician's arrangement with the psychiatrist was a sublease not an assignment.

ANSWER TO QUESTION 156

Answer choice C is correct. Under the Restatement (Second) of Contracts, a third party must be a vested intended beneficiary of a contract in order to enforce its provisions. An intended beneficiary is one to whom the promisee wishes to make a gift of the promised performance or to satisfy an obligation to pay money owed by the promisee to the beneficiary. The promisee must have an intention (explicit or implicit) to benefit the third party, or the beneficiary is incidental. Here, while the metalworking company's performance is essential for the paint company to sell the full volume of paint to the toy company, there is no indication that the metalworking company had an implicit intention to benefit the paint company. Additionally, the contract lacks any explicit provision establishing the paint company as an intended beneficiary. Consequently, the paint company is an incidental beneficiary, and has no rights to enforce the contract. For that reason, answer choice A is incorrect. Answer choice B is incorrect because vesting of rights is only possible in an intended beneficiary. Answer choice D is incorrect because an explicit grant is not necessary; the intention for a third-party to benefit may also be implicit.

ANSWER TO QUESTION 157

Answer choice B is correct. The defense of impracticability may be raised if performance has become illegal after the formation of the contract. However, the defense is unavailable to a party who has assumed the risk of an event happening that makes performance impracticable. Here, the helicopter manufacturer entered into a contract with the subcontractor knowing that the helicopters were to be used in a "severely war-torn region." The subcontractor was not informed of this information, and consequently had no opportunity to assess the risk involved in the contract. Consequently, it can be fairly said that the helicopter manufacturer assumed the risk, and cannot advance the defense of impracticability. For that reason, answer choice C is incorrect. Answer choice A is incorrect because the subcontractor was not a third-party beneficiary of the contract between the manufacturer and the hospital. A party is a third-party beneficiary when two parties enter into a contract with the understanding and intent that the performance by one of the parties is to be rendered to that person. Answer choice D is incorrect because, for the defense of frustration of purpose to be invoked, the triggering event, if not completely unforeseeable, must be unexpected and not a realistic prospect. The hospital was in a "severely war-torn region" and consequently an embargo was a realistic prospect at the time of contract formation.

ANSWER TO QUESTION 158

Answer choice D is correct. The father is not liable because the father's actions were reasonable. The son was an experienced golfer and of an advanced age, and the activity of swinging the golf club is unlikely to be considered a particularly dangerous activity. Thus, a reasonable person under similar circumstances would be unlikely to take precautionary measures to restrict the son's access to the golf club or to supervise his use of it. Answer choice A is incorrect because, while the son's failure to maintain a proper grip on the golf club constituted a breach of the duty of care for a child of his age and experience, this failure is not imputed to his father. Answer choice B is an incorrect statement of the law. A parent is not vicariously liable for a child's torts. Answer choice C is incorrect because a parent continues to have a duty to supervise a child until the child reaches the age of majority. However, as noted with respect to answer D, the father did not breach that duty.

ANSWER TO QUESTION 159

Answer choice C is correct. By giving only a special warranty deed, the child warranted only that an encumbrance was not created on the property during her ownership. Since the encumbrance was created by her father, the child has not breached the warranty against encumbrances. Answer choice A is incorrect because the fact that the third party recorded the deed is irrelevant to the third party's right as buyer to enforce warranties given by the child as seller. Answer choice B is incorrect because the fact that the third party purchased the property is irrelevant to the third party's right as buyer to enforce warranties given by the child as seller. Answer choice D is incorrect because the fact that the child came into possession of the property through a donative transfer does not affect the warranties give by the child as seller of the property to the third party as buyer.

ANSWER TO QUESTION 160

Answer choice A is correct. Under the Free Exercise Clause of the First Amendment, a state may enact a neutral law of general applicability. Here, the state enacted its law for the neutral purpose of protecting public health and safety, and the law applies generally to everyone in the state. Answer choice B is incorrect because the absence of a primary effect of advancing religion and the avoidance of the excessive entanglement of government in religion are two of the three prongs of the *Lemon* test. The test has been used to determine whether governmental action violates the Establishment Clause of the First Amendment, not the Free Exercise Clause. Answer choice C is incorrect because neutral laws of general applicability that have an impact on religious conduct are subject only to the rational basis test. Answer choice D is incorrect because the focus in determining whether governmental action does not violate the Free Exercise Clause is on whether such action has an effect on the religious conduct that is incidental to the action's intended purpose, not on the degree to which the governmental action affects such conduct. Here, although the law may interfere with an integral part of the religious entity's worship service, such effect is incidental to the law purpose of saving lives by prohibiting contact with venomous snakes.

ANSWER TO QUESTION 161

Answer choice C is correct. A deceased person cannot legally be defamed. The estate of the deceased official **cannot** maintain an action for defamation since the defamatory statement was made after the official's death. Answer choice A is incorrect, because, even though presumed damages are permitted in a libel action, the defamatory statement was made after the official's death. Answer choice B is incorrect because, even though the newspaper acted with a reckless disregard for the truth of its statement about the official's involvement in illegal drug activity, which is sufficient to constitute malice, the statement was made about a deceased person. Answer choice D is incorrect because a statement that a person has engaged in conduct that is substantially different from the conduct in which the person did in fact engage, such as different kinds of crime, is not considered to be true.

ANSWER TO QUESTION 162

Answer choice D is correct because state may impair the obligations of contract, including a contract entered into by the state with a private citizen, where the impairment is not substantial, or if the impairment is substantial that it is not unreasonable. In case of a contract to which the state is a party, the state must show that its important interest cannot be served by a less restrictive alternative and that the impairment it seeks is necessary because of unforeseeable circumstances. Here, the impairment is arguably not substantial because the contractor is receiving the full contract amount plus interest to compensate the contractor for the delay in receiving the money. Assuming that the impairment is substantial, the state's actions are reasonable in light of the unforeseen budget crisis and arguably there is not less restrictive alternative. Answer choice A is incorrect because, while the state may have plenary power with regard to road repairs, the state's action runs afoul of the Contract Clause. Answer choice B is incorrect because the state's action does not violate the Dormant Commerce Clause because it neither discriminates against, nor places an undue burden on, interstate commerce. The fact that the state is acting as a market participant would only serve as an exception were its actions discriminatory. Answer choice C is incorrect because the contractor is alleging that he has suffered a direct injury-in-fact (i.e., a delay in payments that are contractually owed to him) and that his injury stems from the state's violation of the Contract Clause.

ANSWER TO QUESTION 163

Answer choice D is correct. To recover for assault, a plaintiff must prove that the defendant's intentional overt act caused him to experience reasonable apprehension of an immediate battery. Here, the lender threatened the borrower with harm two hours later in time; thus, the threatened battery was not immediate, and an assault claim cannot prevail. Answer choice A is incorrect because although the lender threatened the borrower with harmful or offensive bodily contact, the threat was not immediate, and thus the borrower will not prevail. Answer choice B is incorrect because the lender's subjective intent is irrelevant; he need only to have intended the act that made the borrower experience reasonable apprehension of an immediate battery. Answer choice C is incorrect because, while words alone generally do not qualify as an overt act for the purposes of an assault claim, they may be sufficient if coupled with conduct or other circumstances. The lender's words along with his conduct (i.e., carrying a baseball bat) are sufficient to constitute an overt act.

ANSWER TO QUESTION 164

Answer choice C is correct. The parol evidence rule operates to exclude evidence that, if introduced, would change the terms of a written agreement. However, only evidence of prior or contemporaneous negotiations is subject to the parol evidence rule; evidence of negotiations conducted after the execution of the written contract is not prohibited by the parol evidence rule and may be offered to prove subsequent modifications. Because the buyer sent the email after the contract was executed, it would not be prohibited by the parol evidence rule. Answer choice A is incorrect because, as mentioned above, the parol evidence rule only affects evidence of prior or contemporaneous negotiations, not evidence of communications that take place after the written contract is executed. Even if a writing is fully integrated, the parties are free to modify their contract after the fact, which is what the parties did here. Because the conversations here took place after the writing was executed, the parol evidence rule is inapplicable. Answer choice B is incorrect much for the same reason as answer choice A. It is true that the parol evidence rule prohibits evidence that directly contradicts the writing. However, because the negotiations here took place after the contract was executed, the parol evidence rule is inapplicable. Answer choice D is incorrect because attempting to prove fraud or duress is only one reason that the introduction of extrinsic evidence may be introduced, despite the parol evidence rule. There is no requirement that fraud or duress be present in order for the parol evidence rule to be applicable.

ANSWER TO QUESTION 165

Answer choice B is correct. The man can be convicted of solicitation because he asked his friend to commit the crime of arson with the intent that the friend do so. While solicitation to commit a crime is a completed crime in itself, it merges into the completed crime being solicited. However, the completed crime here was a different crime from the crime solicited because it involved the burning of a different structure. The man can be convicted of arson because he burned down his office building at a time when a person was inside. The fact that the person inside was not harmed is irrelevant. The man's unreasonable mistake as to the person's presence in the building is not a defense to a malice crime. For these reasons, answer choices A, C and D are incorrect.

ANSWER TO QUESTION 166

Answer choice C is correct because a third party's consent to a search is not invalid if he lacks the authority to do so, if the police reasonably believe that he does have such authority. Answer choice A is incorrect because an otherwise voluntary consent is not void merely because the police do not warn the person that he has the right to refuse to consent. Answer choice B is incorrect because, even though the friend lacks actual authority to consent to the search of the friend's bedroom, the police reasonably believed he did. Answer choice D is incorrect because, even though the police have probable cause to search a residence, they cannot do so without a warrant unless one of the warrant exceptions, such as consent, applies.

ANSWER TO QUESTION 167

Answer choice B is correct. A settlement offer made by any party is not admissible to prove liability for, invalidity of, or the amount of a disputed claim, nor can it be used as a prior inconsistent statement to impeach a party. Admitting communications made during settlement negotiations would be against public policy, as they would discourage parties from entering settlements. Communications made during settlement negotiations may be admitted for some very limited purposes, such as to prove the bias or prejudice of a witness, to negate a claim of undue delay, or to prove obstruction of a criminal proceeding, but none of these circumstances applies in this case. The statement was made to prove the invalidity of the plaintiff's claim and the amount in controversy; it is therefore inadmissible. Answer choice A is incorrect because, if there was not a blanket prohibition on statements made during settlement negotiations, the statement would constitute an admission by a party opponent, and would be nonhearsay. Answer choices C and D are incorrect because they would both allow for the admission of the statement, and the circumstances involved in this case are not of the type that would allow communications made during settlement negotiations into evidence. The federal rules specify that such statements may not be admitted as a prior inconsistent statement to impeach a party.

ANSWER TO QUESTION 168

Answer choice B is correct. While the oldest daughter has a fee simple interest in the parcel upon turning 21 since her grandmother's life estate has been terminated due to the grandmother's remarriage, her sister has a springing executory interest in the parcel that will vest, if and when, her sister turns 21. Although her sister was not alive at the time that the future interest in the son's children was created, the determination of the children who can enjoy that interest (i.e., who are member of the class) is not made until the first child reaches age 21 because the jurisdiction follows the rule of convenience when the language is not clear as to who is a class member. Since the oldest daughter is now 21 and her sister is alive, her sister is a member of the class. Answer choice A is incorrect because, while the Rule Against Perpetuities applies to a contingent remainder, the contingency remainder in the son's surviving children will vest within 21 years of either the death of the owner's son, who was a life in being at the time of the time of the devise. Answer choice C is incorrect because, since the jurisdiction has abolished the common law rule regarding the destructibility of contingent remainder, the failure of her remainder to vest upon the termination of the preceding life estates does not cause it to be destroyed. Answer choice D is incorrect because the grandmother's life estate terminated either upon her death or her remarriage. Since she remarried, her life estate terminated and the property passed to her son for his life. Since her son had died, the property reverted back to the grantor until the son's oldest daughter reached age 21.

ANSWER TO QUESTION 169

Answer choice D is correct. The widow was an intended beneficiary of the agreement between the children. In this case, she was the one to whom the promisee wished to make a gift of the promised performance. An intended beneficiary may sue a promisor to enforce the contract once her rights have vested. The rights of an intended beneficiary vest when the beneficiary a) detrimentally relies on the rights created; b) manifests assent to the contract at one of the parties' request; or c) files a lawsuit to enforce the contract. Here, none of these three vesting events occurred before the rescission of the contract. Consequently, the widow cannot enforce the contract. For that reason, answer choice A is incorrect. Answer choice B is incorrect because, although the contract did involve a wedding, each child was bargaining for the return promise of the other, and not making promises for which the consideration was marriage. Answer choice C is incorrect because, although a promise to make a gift is generally unenforceable for lack of consideration absent detrimental reliance on the promise by the promisee, here the exchange of such promises constituted valid consideration.

ANSWER TO QUESTION 170

Answer choice D is correct. The Dormant Commerce Clause requires that a state law not discriminate against out-of-state commerce and not constitute an undue burden on interest commerce. The law in question satisfies these two requirements. Answer choice A is incorrect. Although Congress has the power to regulate interstate commerce, where Congress has not acted with respect to a particular aspect of interstate commerce, a state may regulate that aspect of interstate commerce. Answer choice B is incorrect because law imposes a fine not a tax. Even if the fine were construed to constitute a tax, it is not assessed on the value of property, and therefore is not an ad valorem tax. Answer choice C is incorrect because, since the law does not discrimination against out-of-state commerce, the fact that the law satisfies the exception to the anti-discrimination rule that permits laws that are necessary to an important state interest to survive a challenge is irrelevant.

ANSWER TO QUESTION 171

Answer choice B is correct. The video pried into a matter over which the plaintiff retained a privacy interest (i.e., the existence or lack of underwear) and the manner in which the voyeur did so (i.e., by a hidden camera) was highly offensive to a reasonable person. Answer choice A is incorrect because, while a plaintiff's consent to the defendant's intrusion into a secluded area is a defense to this type of invasion of privacy action, the absence of such consent does not necessarily give rise to a cause of action. Answer choice C is incorrect because, while this type of invasion of privacy action generally does not protect a plaintiff in a public place, there are some matters, such as the existence or lack of underwear, about which a plaintiff retains an expectation of privacy even in a public place. Answer choice D is incorrect because, unlike other types of invasion of privacy actions, the intrusion upon seclusion does not require that the private information about the plaintiff be published to a third party.

ANSWER TO QUESTION 172

Answer choice D is correct because contracts with minors are voidable, but only by the minor. Answer choice A is incorrect because the contract is not one for necessities. Necessities include items that parents would but are not providing, such as food, shelter, and in some cases educational expenses, but not a car. Answer choice B is incorrect because part performance does not prevent a contract from being voidable. Answer choice C is incorrect because the fact that the contract is fair does not prevent it from being voidable.

ANSWER TO QUESTION 173

Answer choice A is correct. A prior out-of-court statement by a party to the current litigation that is used against that party is not hearsay; admissions by party opponents are specifically excluded from the definition of hearsay. The statement need not have been against the declarant's interest at the time it was made; it must only be contrary to his present interest. Here, the declarant, the other driver, is the defendant in the current litigation. Further, he made the statement that he ran a stop sign, which is against his interest. Because the statement is not hearsay, it can be used as substantive evidence that the man did run the stop sign, and to impeach his current testimony. Answer choice B is incorrect because the statement against interest exclusion allows the statement to be entered into evidence both substantively and for impeachment purposes. However, the answer choice states a correct rule of law; since the prior inconsistent statement was not made under oath, it would only be admissible for impeachment purposes (were it not for the statement against interest exclusion). Answer choice C is incorrect because the fact that the declarant is available has no bearing on this hearsay exclusion. Answer choice D is incorrect first because the statement is not hearsay, and second because it is admissible, for the reasons discussed above.

ANSWER TO QUESTION 174

Answer choice A is correct because a classification based on national origin is subject to strict scrutiny. Assuming that the state has a compelling interest in public safety that may include requiring police officers to speak English adequately, its law is not narrowly tailored to meet that interest. People born in the U.S. may speak and understand English poorly, whereas people born outside the U.S. may speak and understand English well. Rather, the state could achieve its goal simply by giving an English test. Answer choice B is incorrect because the substantive aspect of the Due Process Clause does not impose a strict scrutiny standard on governmental interference with non-fundamental rights, such as the right to earn a living. Such interference instead is judged under the rational basis standard which the ordinance in question satisfies. Answer choice C is incorrect. While a state law that restricts or prohibits an alien's participation in governmental functions, such as the denial of a job as police officer, need only meet the rational basis standard instead of the strict scrutiny standard usually applied to state discrimination against an alien, the law in question discriminates on the basis of ethnicity, not alienage. The plaintiff in this case is a United States citizen. Answer choice D is incorrect because neither did the law directly prohibit the plaintiff from speaking a language other than English, nor was its purpose to prohibit the plaintiff from speaking a language other than English. Instead, the purpose of the law was to ensure that the plaintiff could speak English well.

ANSWER TO QUESTION 175

Answer choice B is correct. The three children took the property as joint tenants because each had an equal interest in the property with the right of survivorship. Upon the daughter's sale of her interest to her cousin, the cousin held the property as a tenant in common with the two sons, who each held his interest with his brother as joint tenants. Upon the death of one of the sons, his interest passed automatically to his brother. The deceased son's attempt to devise his interest to a friend was a nullity. Consequently, the cousin and surviving son own the property as tenants in common, with the friend owning a one-third interest and the surviving son owning a two-thirds interest. Base on the above analysis, answer choices A, C and D are incorrect.

ANSWER TO QUESTION 176

Answer choice D is correct. Normally a shipment of goods by a seller made in response to an order placed by the buyer constitutes acceptance of the buyer's offer. Such a shipment does not constitute acceptance, however, where the seller indicates that the shipped goods are made as accommodation. Since the supply company so designated the blades that it sent, the shipment did not constitute acceptance by the supply company of the hospital's offer. Consequently, no contract was formed. Answer choice A is incorrect because, although the perfect tender rule does apply to a sale of goods, such as scalpel blades, it only applies where a contract exists between the buyer and seller. Answer choice B is incorrect because, although a seller may accept a buyer's offer by shipment of the goods, as well as by a promise to ship the goods, a shipment of goods as an accommodation does not constitute an acceptance of the buyer's offer. Answer choice C is incorrect because a seller's shipment of goods in response to a buyer's order can constitute acceptance even where the goods do not conform to the contract.

ANSWER TO QUESTION 177

Answer choice D is correct. A company's duty to ensure the safety of its workforce is a critical function, and therefore a non-delegable duty. Consequently, the manufacturer's decision to outsource its equipment supplying functions will not relieve it from liability associated from the negligent furnishing of faulty equipment. Answer choice A is incorrect for that reason. Answer choice B is incorrect, because inherently dangerous activities are only one subset of non-delegable duties. Answer choice C is incorrect because employers are not liable for the torts of true independent contractors, except where (i) an employer is negligent in selecting a contractor, (ii) where the function is inherently dangerous, or (iii) as in this case, where the function is non-delegable.

ANSWER TO QUESTION 178

Answer choice C is correct because drawing blood is not considered a major medical procedure. Little intrusion or pain is involved. Consequently, the procedure is reasonable in light of the Fourth Amendment. Answer choice A is incorrect because this type of procedure is routine and common, and therefore would not be the type of medical procedure that shocks the conscience, such as an operation to remove a bullet. Answer choice B is incorrect because the Fifth Amendment privilege applies only to testimonial evidence, and the blood sample is physical or real evidence, not testimonial evidence. Answer choice D is incorrect. The fact that the defendant had been charged with a felony is irrelevant to the determination of admissibility.

ANSWER TO QUESTION 179

Answer choice C is correct. If a witness is unable to testify about a matter for which a record exists, the substance of the record may be admitted into evidence if (i) the record contains a matter about which the witness once had knowledge, (ii) the record was prepared or adopted by the witness when the matter was fresh in her memory, (iii) the record accurately reflects the witness's knowledge, and (iv) the witness states that she has insufficient recollection of the event to testify fully and accurately, even after consulting the record while on the stand. In this case, the diary entry regarding the description satisfies all of these elements. However, even when all of these elements are satisfied, the record may be read to the jury, but may not be introduced as an exhibit unless it is offered by the opposing party. Here, the prosecutor is entitled to have the entry read to the jury, but cannot introduce it as evidence. Because this is the only answer choice that reflects that the diary entry may be read to the jury but may not be introduced as an exhibit, answer choices A, B, and D are incorrect.

ANSWER TO QUESTION 180

Answer choice D is correct because the political question doctrine applies only to acts of Congress and the Executive Branch, not the states. Here, the state employee has brought a plausible claim that her individual constitutional rights have been violated. Answer choice A is incorrect because the political question doctrine focuses on whether the Constitution has assigned decision-making on this subject to a different branch of government or the matter is inherently one that the judiciary cannot decide. The political question doctrine does not necessarily preclude a court from deciding a matter that involves sensitive political issues or presents a hotly contested question. Answer choice B is incorrect because the political question doctrine does not turn on the effect of a court's decision on a state office. Answer choice C is incorrect because it states the wrong standard for determining whether the political question doctrine applies.

ANSWER TO QUESTION 181

Answer choice A is correct. The friends have a tenancy in common interest in the residence. The electrician's repair of the electrical system must be taken into account because the repair was necessary. However, the chef's profit is not taken into account. Net income from a business operated by a co-tenant on the premises is not required to be shared with any other cotenants. Based on this analysis, answer choices B, C, and D are incorrect.

ANSWER TO QUESTION 182

Answer choice B is correct. Ordinarily, a professional person is expected to exhibit the same skill, knowledge, and care as another practitioner in the same professional community. However, while evidence of custom in a community or profession may be offered to establish the proper standard of care, such evidence is not conclusive. The fact finder may determine that the entire community or industry may be negligent. Thus, while the oral surgeon may have complied with widespread local practices, a reasonable fact finder may determine that those practices are negligent. For that reason, answer choices A, C, and D are incorrect. The fact finder may determine the applicable standard of care.

ANSWER TO QUESTION 183

Answer choice A is correct. With respect to the conviction, a six-person jury may render a verdict in a criminal trial without violating the defendant's right to a jury trial. With respect to the sentence, generally only a jury is permitted to find a fact that serves to increase the maximum penalty that can be imposed for a crime. However, an exception exists if that fact is a prior conviction of the defendant. In that case, the judge, rather than the jury, may find that such a fact exists. For these reasons, answer choices B, C, and D are incorrect.

ANSWER TO QUESTION 184

Answer choice A is correct. Where the satisfaction of a party with the other party's performance in a matter involving aesthetics is a condition of that party's contractual performance, the party's dissatisfaction need only be in good faith in order to excuse that party's contractual performance. Since the homeowner honestly believed that the landscaping was not stately, the homeowner's duty to pay the contract price of $75,000 was excused. Answer choice B is incorrect because the contract was not the type of contract that is required to be in writing under the Statute of Frauds. Answer choice C is incorrect because, while the landscaper's failure to adhere to landscaping standards could have provided the homeowner with grounds for treating the landscaper's performance as a breach of contract, compliance with those standards is not sufficient to prevent the performance from constituting a breach where the performance is subject to a condition of personal satisfaction. Answer choice D is incorrect because a condition of personal satisfaction as to a matter of aesthetics does not require the party's dissatisfaction be reasonable, only in good faith.

ANSWER TO QUESTION 185

Answer choice B is correct. Evidence such as this book, while technically hearsay, is admissible under the learned treatise exception to the hearsay rule. A statement contained in published treatises or periodicals on a subject of history, medicine, or other science or art is admissible if (i) the treatise is established as a reliable authority by the testimony of a witness, expert, or by judicial notice, and (ii) an expert relied on it during direct examination or it was brought to the expert's attention on cross-examination. If these requirements are met, the statement contained in the treatise may be read into evidence, and may be used as substantive evidence and for impeachment. The treatise itself, however, is not admitted into evidence. Answer choice A is incorrect because it states that the statement may be used for impeachment purposes only. Answer choices C and D are incorrect because they both indicate that the treatise may be introduced into evidence. Answer choice D is also incorrect because it states that the statement may be used for impeachment purposes only.

ANSWER TO QUESTION 186

Answer choice B is correct. Under the First Amendment, a city can regulate adult entertainment establishments (e.g., by localizing them in a particular area), but cannot impose a blanket ban on all pornography. It does not matter that (i) the city might have legitimate reasons for such a ban (e.g., decreasing crime), or (ii) other neighboring cities allow such establishments. For these reasons, answer choices C and D are incorrect. Answer choice A is incorrect because the substantive aspect of the Due Process Clause does not impose a strict scrutiny standard on governmental interference with non-fundamental rights, such as the right to earn a living. Such interference instead is judged under the rational basis standard, which the ordinance in question satisfies.

ANSWER TO QUESTION 187

Answer choice C is correct. For most residential leases, including a multi-family dwelling, an implied warranty of habitability is imposed on the landlord. A violation of the housing code that constitutes a substantial threat to the tenant's health or safety is a breach of this warranty. A breach of this warranty can provide a tenant with a defense to an eviction action. While generally the tenant is required to notify the landlord of conditions that constitute a breach of this warranty, the facts indicate that the owner in this case was already aware of them. Answer choice A is incorrect because a lease provision that imposes an absolute duty to repair the premises is void. Answer choice B is incorrect because a tenant's awareness of the housing code violations at the time of entry does not absolve the landlord from his duty to correct the conditions that cause the violations. Answer choice D is incorrect because, in order to assert constructive eviction, the tenant must vacate the rental premises. Here, the individual remained on the premises.

ANSWER TO QUESTION 188

Answer choice C is correct. Adequate provocation reduces common law murder to voluntary manslaughter. Although the discovery of his wife's adultery would likely have been adequate provocation, the husband cooled off long enough to regain his self-control before finding his wife and his best friend together a second time. Merely seeing his wife embrace his best friend would not constitute adequate provocation. However, assuming this second incident rekindled the passions that had been inflamed by the earlier incident, the husband could reclaim the partial defense of adequate provocation. Answer choice A is incorrect because, under the doctrine of transferred intent, the husband's intent to kill his best friend is treated as satisfying the *mens rea* requirement for his killing of his wife. Answer choice B is incorrect because voluntary intoxication is not a defense to common law murder, which is a malice crime. Answer choice D is incorrect because the husband himself had cooled down and gained his self-control. Consequently, regardless of whether a reasonable person would have done so, the husband cannot rely on his initial discovery of the adultery as an adequate act of provocation.

ANSWER TO QUESTION 189

Answer choice A is correct. Although the original contract called for the trainer to perform an animal show that included a lion in exchange for a payment of $100,000, the business agreed to compensate the trainer an additional $25,000 for a show that included a white tiger instead of a lion. Since the modification required a different performance by the trainer, there was consideration for the modification of the businessman's duties. Answer choice B is incorrect for several reasons. The facts do not indicate that the businessman's duty to pay the trainer was linked to the satisfaction of his guests. Moreover, a party's substantial performance of her contractual obligations does not entitle that party to a full recovery under the contract. Instead, the nonbreaching party is entitled to damages attributable to the other party's breach of the contract, even if the breach is a minor breach, rather than a material breach. Most importantly, the trainer's performance is not judged on the basis of the original contract, which called for a lion, but on the basis of the modified contract, which called for a white tiger. Consequently, the trainer does not have to rely on the doctrine of substantial performance. Answer choice C is incorrect because, although the trainer did have a duty to perform the show for $100,000. Answer choice D is an incorrect statement of the law. A threat to breach a contract can, but does not necessarily constitute duress. Such a threat constitutes duress where it breaches the duty of good faith and fair dealing.

ANSWER TO QUESTION 190

Answer choice D is correct because the amendment regulates an intrastate economic activity (i.e., the workplace itself) that has a substantial effect on interstate commerce. Answer choices A and B are incorrect because neither the Tenth Amendment nor the principle of federalism prevents the application of the federal standards to the state workers. Answer choice C is incorrect because the amendment does not limit its application to state proprietary activities, but applies to state workers involved in carrying out integral or traditional governmental functions. Such application to state workers in general is not unconstitutional, but instead is a valid exercise of the Commerce Clause.

ANSWER TO QUESTION 191

Answer choice D is correct. The security interest in the chandelier was a purchase money security interest in a fixture. As such, the store has priority over a previously filed mortgage on the real property in which the fixture was installed, if it is recorded in the local land records office before or within 20 days after the fixture is installed. Since the store's security interest was timely and properly filed, it has priority over the credit union's mortgage. Answer choice A is incorrect because, while a mortgagee who holds a purchase money mortgage is entitled to priority over other mortgagees, the secured party who holds a purchase money security interest in a fixture is entitled to priority over any previously recorded mortgage when the secured party timely and properly records its security interest. Answer choice B is incorrect because, as noted with respect to answer choice A, merely recording a mortgage before a security interest in a fixture is not sufficient, if the security interest is a purchase money security interest and that interest is timely and properly filed. Answer choice C is incorrect because, while the chandelier was a fixture, in order to have priority over a previously recorded mortgage, the store had to timely and properly record its security interest.

ANSWER TO QUESTION 192

Answer choice A is correct. To obtain a *res ipsa loquitur* jury instruction, a plaintiff must prove that i) his injury was caused by an instrumentality or condition which was under the defendant's exclusive control, ii) that the injury would not have occurred if the defendant had used ordinary care while the instrumentality was under his control; and iii) that he was not responsible for his own injury. The third requirement is not satisfied if a plaintiff's own negligence increases the likelihood of the defendant's negligence. In this case, the pedestrian's proximity to the construction site had nothing to do with the construction company's negligent control of the brick. Answer choice B is incorrect because a *res ipsa loquitur* instruction permits the jury to find negligence even in the absence of direct evidence, but does not require the jury to do so. Answer choice C is incorrect because it is an inaccurate statement of the law. Answer choice D is incorrect because *res ipsa loquitur* allows a finding of negligence even in the absence of direct evidence.

ANSWER TO QUESTION 193

Answer choice C is correct. The statement qualifies as an admission by a party-opponent. A prior out-of-court statement by a party to the current litigation used against that party is not hearsay. The statement need not have been against the party's interest at the time it was made, so long as it is against her present interest. This statement, that she saw but ignored a warning sign, is against her interest now that notice is an issue in the case. As such, the statement is not hearsay, and is admissible. For the reasons just stated, answer choice A is incorrect. Answer choice B is incorrect because, while communications between a physician and patient are often privileged, the privilege does not apply if the statement was made for a reason other than treatment. The plaintiff's statement that she ignored the wet floor sign is not necessary for her diagnosis or treatment, and therefore would not be privileged. In addition, the privilege only applies to confidential communications; there is no privilege when, as happened here, a third party overhears the conversation. Answer choice D is incorrect for two reasons. First, the statement is not hearsay. Second, there is an exception for statements made for the purposes of medical diagnosis or treatment, but only if those statements are made to a licensed physician or other medical personnel for the purposes of diagnosis or treatment. The plaintiff's statement that she ignored the wet floor sign does not appear to be necessary for her diagnosis or treatment, and therefore would not fall under this exception.

ANSWER TO QUESTION 194

Answer choice B is correct. A seller has the right to cure a defective tender if i) the time for performance under the contract has not yet lapsed, or ii) if the seller had reasonable grounds to believe the buyer would accept the goods despite the nonconformity. Here, neither condition is satisfied; the gas station insisted on the purity provision in the contract, and so there were no reasonable grounds to believe that the station would accept a lower-quality gasoline. Nonetheless, the oil distributor retained the right to cure the defective tender by July 31. It did not deliver conforming gasoline until August 1, and consequently, the gas station was justified in rejecting the second shipment. Answer choice A is incorrect because the oil distributor had the right to cure its defective tender by July 31. Answer choice C is incorrect because while a buyer must accept a proper cure, it must only do so if the cure was timely; the oil distributor's cure was one day too late. Answer choice D is incorrect because the cure needed to occur by the date specified in the contract, not within a reasonable time of the defective tender.

ANSWER TO QUESTION 195

Answer choice C is correct. In a jurisdiction that retains traditional joint and several liability rules and applies pure comparative negligence principles, a plaintiff may recover his total damages—reduced by the proportion of his own fault—from any defendant. Where the jurisdiction also permits contribution, the paying defendant may then seek contribution from the other defendant(s) in proportion to their own fault. Here, the chef's damages were calculated to be $1 million, and she was 30% at fault. Thus, she may collect $700,000 from either of the defendants. The hospital was 15% at fault, thus it may, in turn, seek $550,000 in contribution from the friend—who was 55% at fault. Answer choices A and B are incorrect because the chef may recover the full judgment from the hospital, and the paying defendant may seek contribution from the other defendants. Answer choice D is incorrect because this jurisdiction allows contribution among defendants.

ANSWER TO QUESTION 196

Answer choice B is correct. In determining whether an object is a fixture that can be removed by a seller of real property, the seller's subjective intent is not controlling. Instead, various factors are examined to ascertain the seller's objective intent. Answer choice A is incorrect because the fact that the removal of the bookcases occurred without significant damage to the library is an argument that supports the seller's position that the bookcase were removable fixtures. Answer choice C is incorrect because the fact that the bookcases were specially designed for use in the library is an argument that supports the buyer's position that the bookcases were not removable fixtures. Answer choice D is incorrect because the integral nature of the bookcases to the function of the room as a library is an argument that supports the buyer's position that the bookcases were not removable fixtures.

ANSWER TO QUESTION 197

Answer choice A is correct. Robbery is defined as (i) larceny, (ii) by force or intimidation, (iii) where the taking of the property is from the person or presence of the victim. The force used by a defendant must be more than the amount necessary to effectuate taking and carrying away the property. Force can include giving a victim drugs in order to induce unconsciousness and thereby permit the larceny to occur. Answer choice B is incorrect because, although common law arson and burglary both may require a link between an act and a dwelling, robbery may occur anywhere. Answer choice C is incorrect because a victim need not own the stolen item at the time of the robbery; the item need only be in the victim's possession and the victim's right to possess the item is superior to the thief's. Answer choice D is incorrect because, although the man was not intimidated during the theft of his watch since he was unconscious, the larceny did occur by force.

ANSWER TO QUESTION 198

Answer choice B is correct. The attorney's drunk driving was a foreseeable continuing consequence of Bar A's negligent activities. Thus, Bar A can be held liable for the accident, because its actions were a "substantial factor" in causing the neighbor's injuries. Bar A may not escape liability simply because other negligent actors exist. Answer choice A is incorrect because Bar A, as a substantial factor in causing the neighbor's injuries, can be held liable for all of his damages. Answer choice C is incorrect because the attorney's drunk driving was foreseeable, and thus is not a superseding cause. Answer choice D is incorrect because Bar A's actions were a substantial factor in causing the neighbor's injuries, and thus are considered a cause-in-fact.

ANSWER TO QUESTION 199

Answer choice D is correct because the Commerce Clause authorizes Congress to regulate the channels of interstate commerce for any purpose. Here, the law punishes the transportation of a spouse across state lines for the purpose of murder. Answer choice A is incorrect because, although federalism concerns do require that an intrastate, non-economic activity, such as the commission of a crime, have a substantial economic affect on interstate commerce in order to be subject to congressional regulation under the Commerce Clause, such a requirement does not apply to the indirect regulation of an non-economic activity that is facilitated by the use of interstate commerce. Answer choice B is incorrect because, although Congress may generally only regulate a non-economic activity that has a substantial economic affect on interstate commerce, indirect regulation of such an activity that is directly facilitated by use of interstate commerce is permitted under the Commerce Clause. Here, the law does not criminalize murder but the transportation of a spouse across state lines for the purpose of murder. Answer choice C is incorrect because the law in question does not seek to regulate an instrumentality of interstate commerce, such as a car, truck, or airplane.

ANSWER TO QUESTION 200

Answer choice A is correct. A dying declaration only qualifies as a hearsay exception if (i) the statement is made by an individual who believes she is dying, (ii) the individual believes that her death is imminent, and (iii) the statement pertains to the cause or circumstance of her death. The statement made by this victim likely would meet this standard. However, under the Federal Rules, a dying declaration is only admissible in homicide prosecutions and civil actions. Because this is a criminal trial for attempted murder, and not homicide or a civil case, the statement is not admissible as a dying declaration. Answer choice B is incorrect in part for the reasons explained above, but also because the Federal Rules do not require that the declarant actually die, nor do they require that the declarant be the victim in the case at hand. The declarant must simply be unavailable for some reason. Answer choice C is incorrect because, while unavailability is a requirement for the dying declaration exception, the statement is still inadmissible because the trial in question is not a homicide or civil trial. Answer choice D is incorrect because it misstates the law for the reasons discussed above.